The Start-up Entrepreneur

The Start-up

How You Can Succeed in Building Your
Own Company into a Major
Enterprise Starting
from Scratch

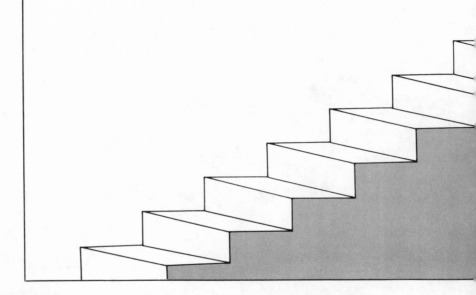

Entrepreneur

James R. Cook

T·T TRUMAN TALLEY BOOKS / E. P. DUTTON / NEW YORK

Grateful acknowledgment is made for permission
to reprint copyright material:

From *Be My Guest* by Conrad Hilton.
Copyright © 1957, renewing 1985.
Reprinted by permission of the publisher, Prentice-Hall, Inc.

From *Fast-Growth Management* by Mack Hanan.
Copyright © 1979 by AMACOM,
a division of American Management Associations.
Reprinted by permission of AMACOM. All rights reserved.

From *Grinding It Out* by Ray Kroc.
Copyright © 1977 by Ray A. Kroc.
Reprinted by permission of Contemporary Books, Inc.

From *Minding the Store* by Stanley Marcus.
Copyright © 1974 by Stanley Marcus.
Reprinted by permission of Little, Brown and Company.

From *My Years with General Motors* by Alfred P. Sloan, Jr.
Copyright © 1963 by Alfred P. Sloan, Jr.
Reprinted by permission of Harold Matson Company, Inc.

From *Quest for the Best* by Stanley Marcus.
Copyright © 1979 by Stanley Marcus.
Reprinted by permission of Viking Penguin Inc.

From *Statler* by Floyd Miller.
Copyright © 1968 by Floyd Miller.
Reprinted by permission of John Schaffner Associates, Inc.

Published in the United States
by Truman Talley Books · E. P. Dutton,
a division of New American Library,
2 Park Avenue, New York, N.Y. 10016

Library of Congress Cataloging-in-Publication Data

Cook, James R.
The start-up entrepreneur.
"A Truman Talley book."
Bibliography: p.
Includes index.
1. New business enterprises.   2. Entrepreneur.
I. Title.
HD62.5.C664 1985   658.4′2   85-16160

ISBN 0-525-24372-0

Published simultaneously in Canada
by Fitzhenry & Whiteside Limited, Toronto

W

DESIGNED BY MARK O'CONNOR

10 9 8 7 6 5 4 3 2 1

First Edition

To the late Bernard T. Daley (1934–1982), my dear friend and mentor. An entrepreneur, gentleman, and philosopher, Bernie was loved by many who miss him these days.

No great enterprise will ever begin if all obstacles must first be overcome.

—NAPOLEON HILL

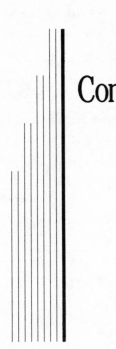

Contents

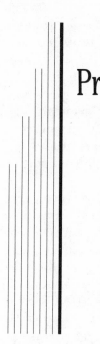

Preface

This book has five goals. Each of them should be mentioned briefly in order of importance. The foremost goal of the book is to get you started as an entrepreneur. Many people think they would like to begin their own enterprise, but never do. The obstacles often seem insurmountable. I hope to break down some of these impediments and show exactly how you can overcome them and get started. There is a lot in the way of "how to" throughout the book.

Much of this advice needs to be reread a number of times throughout the early months and years of a start-up. You simply cannot absorb it all in one reading.

Any lesson you might learn from this book could save you

the hardship of a nasty personal experience. You get enough pounding as it is when you begin your enterprise. Why not have a few lessons out of the way?

The second goal of this book is to keep you going once you have begun. Starting a new business can be a painful experience. The greater your goal, the more severe your suffering. It will take a lot more than this one book to keep you from quitting. I list additional volumes in the Appendix that are useful for keeping your mental state upbeat. I also show you the difficulties many others have waded through.

My personal experience and study of virtually every great entrepreneur over the past one hundred and fifty years have shown me a clear-cut formula to great wealth and success. I am hardly the originator of this system. Every entrepreneurial giant has voiced essentially the same credo. It is there for the taking. If you apply this formula diligently, you simply cannot fail.

I also want to teach you how to run a business. If you learn the basics of proper management from your first days, you will forgo many later problems. There is a popular business myth that entrepreneurs can start a business but cannot manage it. I don't place much credence in that theory. You can and should become exceedingly competent in running your own show. You don't learn management techniques through osmosis. You learn them from instructions.

The book is interspersed with commentary on the value of entrepreneurs, their role in the economic system, and the effects of political, legal, and tax matters on them. High taxes and too much government have diminished the fertility of the economic environment that gives rise to great entrepreneurs and their causes. We need to correct detriments to economic vigor and, especially, encourage incentives for new ventures.

Finally, any worthwhile book should hope to entertain, enthrall, and at times amuse the reader. For this, I have relied on certain anecdotes from my own experience and on the neglected lore of past entrepreneurial heroes. They are a crusty and fit lot to emulate.

American entrepreneurs have awed the world for well over a century. We need to continue to do so. If in some small way this book can contribute to the conception and growth of a single embryonic enterprise, my efforts will have been worthwhile.

The Start-up Entrepreneur

Introduction

Entrepreneurs are people who are richly rewarded by providing new products or services that are wanted or needed. Most often, entrepreneurs are thought to be involved in company start-ups. They create a new enterprise out of nothing. They pioneer ventures where risk is high.

However, some giant corporations are known to be entrepreneurial, and a gypsy cabdriver can be an entrepreneur.

The term *entrepreneur* implies success. It means new products and breakthroughs, quality, and service. Within a company, it means a special kind of spirit, vitality, and excellence. Business columnist E. A. Butler calls it, "the excitement of creation."

Above all, it means a specific kind of hard-charging individual whose will, creativity, persistence, and inevitable success make that person a leader and contemporary hero. This last accolade stems from a remarkable change in public attitudes toward entrepreneurs. The chills and fevers of a stop-and-go economy are teaching us the immense value of these men and women. To a great extent, our future economic well-being hinges on the quality of our entrepreneurs.

Today most new jobs are created by entrepreneurial companies. Improved goods and services, new technology and advancements frequently arise from entrepreneurial environments. Small firms and beleaguered entrepreneurs striving to put new ideas into action are the fount of our prosperity.

Edwin Land started Polaroid Corporation in a barn while still in college. Almost two decades later he put his first instant camera on the market. He built a company from scratch that not only led to thousands of new jobs and untold prosperity, but presented the world with a push-button camera that delighted consumers everywhere.

In 1971 Intel, then a tiny company of entrepreneurs, made an important breakthrough in microprocessors. Within five years the company created eight thousand new jobs and thousands more outside its direct employ.

Virtually all of America's largest and greatest corporations were founded by a single dedicated entrepreneur. Business editor Robert Fierro states, "There would have been no IBM, General Motors, Control Data, Polaroid, Xerox, CBS, Pan Am, or alas, Penn Central, if it were not for that one person who not only thought he had a better idea but also had the courage of his convictions to break away."

Somewhere, sometime, it all started with a lone entrepreneur. Over the decades the entrepreneurs have produced an uncomparable flow of goods and services that makes the poverty of today resemble the luxury of other centuries.

Entrepreneurs are formidable foes and competitors. They consistently mount attacks against entrenched corporations. Dozens of the top 100 companies at the end of World War II have shrunk or disappeared largely due to either a lack of entrepreneurial skill or the onslaught of a hard-charging newcomer.

Early in the 1960s, an Iowa cattle buyer by the name of Currier Holman, with no special talent or technology, grabbed the meat-packing industry by the throat. He outfought and outthought his competitors until, one by one, each of these giants—Cudahy, Wilson, Swift, and Armour—were bloodied or broken.

Holman's driving will blended with his tenacity and creativity to build Iowa Beef Processors from scratch into a multibillion-dollar business. He generated these fabulous results by introducing simple efficiencies and product improvements. He had no new inventions, technology, or breakthroughs—only sound ideas and better methods.

Entrepreneurs work their magic the world over, wherever freedom allows. The hallmark of the entrepreneur can be seen in the gleaming towers of Hong Kong and the exploding economies of the once-destitute Asian Basin. Wherever there is progress, improved living standards, and vibrant economies, entrepreneurs are free to work.

If Henry Ford was not the richest man of his day, he was close to it. He was a technological genius and a worldwide folk hero who deserves to be remembered as the greatest entrepreneur of the first half of the twentieth century. His automobile changed radically not only the way we live but where we live. Within his lifetime, and principally because of him, 80 percent of the population moved from the farm to the city. The horse and livery stable once found everywhere simply vanished. He built a massive industry the size and scope of which no one in his day would have dared to dream.

Year by year, he slashed the prices of his Model T. His aim was to make it affordable to everyone. He fastidiously improved quality and simplified the operation of his cars. For over a decade, during the period of the automobile's greatest growth, he made over half the cars sold on earth.

In 1914 he shocked the world as no man had ever before him. He doubled the wage of his workers to five dollars a day and reduced their hours. Every newspaper in America and most of those abroad chronicled this phenomenal event. The "five-dollar day" stands out as one of the most generous and perhaps the most influential acts in the history of commerce. It effectively doubled the wages of the work force.

Not only did Ford dramatically enhance the living standards of his workers through wage increases, he went far beyond any other employer to improve their lives. Ford paid a great deal of attention to the safety, health, and comfort of his workers. This had virtually never been done before. He set up a medical department with a hospital at the plant. He established commissaries where workers bought groceries, clothes, and drugs at favorable prices. He initiated a program of hygiene counseling and a legal department to assist workers. His concern for the many immigrant workers flocking to Detroit led him to start an English-teaching school in the plant. Immigrants were counseled extensively on such basics as economical shopping, home management, cleanliness, and temperance. He protected them from the exploitation that confused newcomers usually faced.

When the five-dollar day went into effect, Ford made a particular point of hiring the handicapped, giving jobs by the thousands to the blind, the deaf, epileptics, and those missing limbs. Most were unemployable anywhere else. After the war, handicapped veterans were welcomed. And at one time, Ford had as many as six hundred former convicts on his payroll, most of whom came directly to his company from the penitentiary.

Ford founded a hospital and a trade school and eventually a great museum that holds a fabulous collection of American antiques.

Such were the exploits of a man who built a vast enterprise from nothing. Forever in the limelight, he eventually displayed human prejudices that color our memory of his accomplishments.

As an entrepreneur, however, there has never been anyone like him. He was at the cutting edge of the most dynamic changes in American history. As a creator of jobs, prosperity, and social change, he has no peer. Sometime around 1915, he enunciated his marvelous credo, "I believe that I can do the world no greater service than to create more work for more men at larger pay."

If in every decade a country could spawn a few Henry Fords, then prosperity would be assured. Since we recognize their value, how do we encourage more entrepreneurs? I hope this book will help. For it is my contention that many people have the wherewithal to be business innovators.

All of us are motivated by the great American dream: economic freedom—the cash to be able to pay our bills, to spend some money frivolously without worrying about it, and to have enough assets to cushion us against reversals.

Just a few years ago when my business began to flourish, I wanted to buy a Suburban. I called the car dealer, got the price, told him to deliver it, and had a check for the total purchase waiting when he arrived. For the first time, I did not have to sit coaxing some junior loan officer at the bank into helping me; I did not have to listen to a lecture on the history of my last payment booklet, which had many late payments; nor did I have to worry that, as usual, I would come up a bit short at payment time.

Yes, it is this drive for economic freedom and the absence of financial pressure that triggers the ambition of would-be entrepreneurs.

David Ogilvy, the great advertising entrepreneur who founded Ogilvy & Mather, makes no bones about the motivational effect of pursuing money: "Many of the greatest creations of man have been inspired by the desire to make money. When George Frederick Handel was on his beam ends, he shut himself up for twenty-one days and emerged with the complete score of *Messiah*—and hit the jackpot.

"At the end of a concert at Carnegie Hall, Walter Damrosch asked Rachmaninoff what sublime thoughts had passed through his head as he stared out into the audience during the playing of his concerto. 'I was counting the house,' said Rachmaninoff."

Ogilvy goes on, "it wasn't until I tasted lucre on Madison Avenue that I began to work in earnest . . . when my salary was doubled, I tasted blood."

Your own enterprise serves your interests in significant ways.

Salary. Nothing can spin out money like a profitable company. You should, in time, be able to make a far higher salary than you could ever earn working for someone else. At the end of the year, a handsome bonus gives you *chunk money.* These large chunks are what you use for investments and major purchases. There's nothing like them.

Security. If you can consistently earn a big salary for many years running, you can take a long step toward security. Beyond that lies a company profit-sharing plan, a retirement program, started at the moment your firm enters the black, that will pile up a splendid asset for your later years.

Asset builder. As your company grows and becomes profitable, it takes on value. It becomes a separate unit which can be sold for a sum of money. Naturally, the more profitable it becomes, the more it is worth. In time, a company can be worth a fortune and its eventual sale can secure your future forever.

Perks. A company allows you the use of an automobile for business purposes, along with a host of other small advantages. It pays for your business travel and entertainment. It will make you a short-term loan or pay for your home security system.

Independence. Your own business can set you free from financial worries. As much as anything, however, it lets you chart your own destiny. It removes the necessity to be beholden to an employer. It allows you independence and freedom from bosses and supervisors.

Fulfillment. The excitement and challenge of your own enterprise makes life immensely stimulating. You derive a deep, psychological satisfaction from "doing business," and you banish boredom and restlessness from your life.

With all these attributes going for it, you might conclude that everyone would want to become an entrepreneur, but in fact only the tiniest minority of our citizens start their own ventures.

Why don't more people start up their own companies? It is mostly because they are afraid. The greatest fear centers on the possibility of forgoing a steady paycheck. Most people cannot stand the risk, the uncertainty, and the thought of no money. The idea of bills mounting up and no funds to pay them frightens many people.

Another reason so few people start up their own businesses is a lack of money with which to begin a venture. Many are stymied by a lack of working capital. Shortage of money is certainly an impediment to initiating a start-up, but there is an abundance of ways and means to obtain capital.

You always find ways to get through financial nightmares. In fact, they evaporate when you face them. If you persist, the money will always be there. Sounds like a fantasy, spiritualism, or one of those self-help dreamers, doesn't it? But bear it in mind. The most successful entrepreneurs on earth—past and present—would tell you exactly the same thing. Money problems always resolve themselves.

John Willard Marriott, founder of the hotel chain, knew

this when he said, "When you work for yourself, you become an innovator or you don't eat." In other words, money shortages force you to find solutions. And although it may be painful for a while, it is hardly unique. Most new ventures have capital shortages that are cause for grave concern.

I was at a party not long ago with an entrepreneur whom I knew was struggling with his venture. My precious metals, investment, and venture-capital business was also in the doldrums and I was living with a fair amount of pain. We talked and he explained how tough things were. "You must really be suffering," I said. He seemed to be surprised that I knew this. Apparently he thought that his pain was exclusive to himself. Hardly. There is a similarity of suffering among struggling entrepreneurs.

Life is going to dole out a share of pain to you no matter where you hide. A business friend I knew dropped out a few years ago and joined the hippie scene. Now he lives on nothing and feeds himself dope and booze daily. He suffers far worse than any business tycoon in the throes of losing an empire.

Yes, you should become an entrepreneur. Why not make the most of your life? Why not make all the money you need? Why not work when you want to and be free of others telling you what to do? This option is open to you. You don't need any special talents or abilities. All that is really necessary is enough bravery to begin.

Henry Kaiser, one of America's most courageous entrepreneurs, summed it up this way: "Live daringly, boldly, fearlessly. Taste the relish to be found in competition—in having to put forth the best within you."

As most people start in business to satisfy their occupational and money needs, we can conclude that the major element prodding the entrepreneur is self-interest. We produce, we risk, we strive for our own benefit.

Critics are quick to label this concern for self as no more than greed. They see only one side of the equation. For it is only in serving the self-interest of others that entrepreneurs prevail. A marketplace is made up of entrepreneurs meeting the needs of consumers. Buyers make a choice about the goods they purchase. When both parties agree to a bargain, they have satisfied their mutual self-interests. Only in serving the consumer does the entrepreneur achieve success. Buy an apple off a pushcart and you have made two people happy. Such is the magic of a system whose fail-safe mechanism insists that one party be pleased before the other is rewarded.

George Gilder, writing in his recent best-seller, *Wealth and Poverty,* suggests that faith is the most important principle of upward mobility. "Faith in man, faith in the future, faith in the rising return of giving. . . . All are necessary to sustain the spirit of work and enterprise."

Yet, although faith is indeed a crucial element to entrepreneurial progress, it is not the starting point or the only essential ingredient or the foremost element in success. Desire for money and position is the takeoff point from which the entrepreneur must launch his or her dream. A burning desire to do important things and to be significant, an obsession with great fortune and economic freedom—these are the starting points of enterprise. Without them there would be no beginning.

We recognize that faith and altruism are important building blocks of entrepreneurial progress, but it is also in our nature to think of ourselves. For this we need not apologize. Our wants and concerns give us the necessary desire to get ahead.

What kind of personality can develop this powerful desire to succeed? Is there a checklist of entrepreneurial character traits? Can we know in advance if we are entrepreneurs? Many articles on the subject imply that one must have certain inborn traits to be a successful entrepreneur: little or no anxiety, ability to take risks without worry, a great self-image, little self-doubt.

Perhaps there are entrepreneurs who start off so well equipped, but I don't think so. The writers who draw these conclusions have most likely researched well-established entrepreneurs. These qualities only evolve after years of experience. In reality, the successful entrepreneur of today is the scared kid of yesterday.

Entrepreneurs can come from backgrounds of poverty or affluence, broken homes or close-knit families. They can be popular or misfits, regular fellows or oddballs.

There are few clues to go on. I have, however, witnessed a few general characteristics worth mentioning. When my friend's son in his second year of college suddenly discovers English literature and consumes it with intensity, when my neighbor's boy in grade school becomes an expert on World War

II, when my own son pounds incessantly on his Moog synthesizer and reads, without prompting, volumes on astronomy, I recognize a certain intensity that I believe is a necessary ingredient for success.

This white heat of interest is the same ingredient that characterizes the entrepreneur's commitment and enthusiasm as he or she embraces a new business venture. Without intensity, the entrepreneur cannot get over the greatest hurdle: to pull it all together and start.

From biographies and literature on entrepreneurs, another quality emerges that seems common to most. Here it is expressed by J. C. Penney, the chain-store founder: "Early in my employment [salesman in a dry-goods store] the head clerk invited me to eat lunch with him. As soon as we finished I got up. 'Where are you going?' said my associate, looking at me with some curiosity, for he was going to sit in the park for a while with his cigar and the newspaper. 'Back to work.' 'Don't be foolish. Don't you know there's an hour off for lunch?'

"But my mind kept running over things at the store which needed to be done. . . . It got to be a saying of the head clerk's, 'Well, Penney never knows when it's time to quit.' "

The quality of giving extra, doing more than is required, is the common thread that runs through the careers of all successful entrepreneurs and their companies.

Most successful men and women seem to have this admirable quality innately. They give evidence of it from their very first employment. Andrew Carnegie rose to a position of no little importance with the Pennsylvania Railroad while still in his teens because he so impressed his superiors with his extra effort. If you instinctively do extra in your job or other pursuits, you possess a valuable talent for entrepreneuring.

This important quality can be learned, however. My first job as a caddy lasted two days. I quit because it was taxing and complicated. I flopped as a busboy, was fired as a construction worker, and was so slothful as an inventory counter at a hardware wholesaler that the president saw fit personally to keep an eye on me. My next job, at the U.S. Post Office, ended when I consistently failed the tests on how and where to sort the mail. Only later, as I pursued a career in sales, did flashes of this most valuable attribute begin to surface.

Beyond these ingredients may be murkier motivations—

the need to compensate for some inadequacy, to overcome a prior failure. But these weaknesses and fears are widespread among us all. Almost everybody would like to prove something to somebody. It's hard to believe that an entrepreneur was motivated to make millions because of having had acne as a kid. The more we look at entrepreneuring, the fewer limitations to assuming this role there seem to be. Many more people could become successful entrepreneurs.

If you are bored with your job, if you daydream about bigger things, if you are restless and feel dissatisfied, if you know in your heart you could accomplish big things—then you are a candidate.

If you want a lot of money, if you ache to build and create, if you hunger for success, or if orders from someone else bug you, then you might have no choice. Perhaps you *have to* be an entrepreneur.

More than anything, if you sense a fierce restlessness, you need to make a change. If you are possessed with a gnawing dissatisfaction, you need a challenge. If you suffer from a pervasive anxiety that life is passing you by, if you feel terribly unfulfilled, then you need to make up your mind on a different course of action.

Many workers and managers at the mid-to-upper levels of corporate America have these afflictions. The digits in their annual salary sound good, but for some reason they are not keeping up. Inflation has done more damage than they like to admit. They have salary limitations that forever fix their life-style in a conservative pattern. The big money will never be where they are now.

The economic distortions of the past two decades have taken a toll. Corporations have been whipsawed by inflationary booms and harsh recessions. These economic realities have changed things for those who aspire to upper-income levels. The life-style you seek may not be as attainable as it once was by working for a major corporation.

Business writer Robert Fierro comments, "There is no security in any job anymore. Teachers are fired. Middle management is washed up on the beaches of mergers. Recessions have wiped out whole hordes of public relations, advertising, and other media personnel. Twenty-five-year-olds are cutting the corporate throats of the middle-aged, and better paid, work force."

These factors are encouraging a boom in new ventures. Some of these firms are high-technology companies, national in scope. Most, however, are small, and can be started without great difficulty. Most enterprises start small, with one or two people, and stay small.

Two decades ago a kid with two first names, Howard Walter, came to Faribault, Minnesota, where I lived at the time. He took over a run-down restaurant on the main drag. It was the local greasy spoon, dirty and unprofitable. The townsfolk either smirked or felt sorry for him. My dad wrote up his fire insurance policy and gave his vote of no confidence, "We got the money up front on this one."

Despite the risks and his own apprehension, Howard Walter began his restaurant venture. He cooked, and his wife waited on tables. With two pleasing personalities, good food, good service, cleanliness, economy—it was no contest. In thirty days their café was crowded.

Twenty years later, the Holiday Café still hums. The success formula is still the same, but the line for a table is a little longer. Howard Walter has prospered. He still serves every meal with consistency and care, but now it's from love. His business and outside investments have made him free from financial worry.

At the other end of the business spectrum lie the "Super Entrepreneurs." Ray Kroc, for one, changed the way Americans eat and integrated his McDonald's into every city and hamlet. The underlying credo that assured his success was quality, service, cleanliness, and value. Note the similarity of this success formula to that of the small-town café owner.

McDonald's started as a single California hamburger shop. Starting at age fifty-two, Super Entrepreneur Kroc made his food chain an institution through uniformity and consistency. Generally even the Super Entrepreneurs start small, but they consciously choose to be big. Large companies don't arise by accident. They are the direct result of specific goals and dreams. But there is no requirement to build a megabusiness. Large or small, it is all in the entrepreneur's game plan.

Whatever one's entrepreneurial aspirations, there are no credentials required to start. You need not have a business degree or any special educational background. Anyone can start. Thomas Edison observed, "Business is a college more exacting than any of the schools and universities."

Educational mythology supposes that success without a diploma and degree is improbable. Nevertheless, there are numerous entrepreneurs who have never attended business school or college. Some of the most exceptional people I have known barely got out of high school. Ray Kroc says, "while formal schooling is an important advantage, it is not a guarantee of success—nor is its absence a fatal handicap."

Most business schools deal in the predictable and the quantifiable. They systematize plans and projections and measure the likely results. They dwell on the art of the possible. There is not much instruction on the sources of creativity, the roles of desire, faith, adversity, and experience necessary to the entrepreneurial miracle.

Risk and reward are not measurable quantities that can be fastened to business activity and understood. The entrepreneur's projects are often beyond measurable risk, the odds beyond comprehension. Some ideas may even run outside the realm of the known.

When Cob Burandt sat in my office and outlined his scheme to design a camshaft that would radically improve the internal-combustion engine, I was most uneasy. He needed capital to begin. At the time my business was bad; we were losing money, and we already had too many new ventures.

But gradually I was won over. Cob's enthusiasm, his faith in the project, his willingness to risk several years without much income, and his fondness for tinkering and inventing all served to make up my mind. He walked out with the first of many checks for $5,000 and a handshake. And that is how the relationship began that developed the most important automobile improvement since the automatic transmission, and which promises to boost Detroit's competitive edge.

What are the odds of such an awesome invention originating in an unheated backyard garage in a Minneapolis suburb, by an inventor who barely escaped high school and who had no engineering or automotive training or schooling? There is no way to measure such a long shot, no way to quantify the risk. How do these breakthroughs come about? By doing.

The education of the entrepreneur comes from hands-on experience: rejection in the marketplace, financial hardships, the need to solicit, bargain, research, negotiate, and encounter an endless array of setbacks.

B. C. Forbes, founder of *Forbes* magazine, gives this insight into the formula: "The only caste in America is merit. A price has to be paid for success. Almost invariably those who have reached the summits worked harder and longer, studied and planned more assiduously, practiced more self-denial, overcame more difficulties than those of us who have not risen so far."

While we examine ways to help novice entrepreneurs, society must examine exhaustively the economic environment most suitable for entrepreneurs to flourish.

When America's greatest black entrepreneur, John H. Johnson, publisher and owner of *Ebony* magazine and various other enterprises, said, "I think there is no such thing as security. There is no such thing as permanent success," he meant that wealth created by new enterprises can be rapidly diminished and swept away by subsequent bad decisions. For new ventures, risk is ever present. That is why capital should be nurtured, not taxed away.

The idea that we have a permanent wealthy class that can be taxed vigorously and a portion of their money redistributed doesn't wash. New wealth and old wealth are vigorously reshuffled every generation. Today there are poor du Ponts and wealthy Yokums. Investment skill or lack of it, entrepreneurial courage or cowardice ensure an ongoing redistribution of wealth.

From this existing pool of wealth (old money and nouveau riche) comes the seed money that funds new entrepreneurs. Without risk capital, there will be far fewer economic miracles and a steady trek into poverty. It has been our good fortune that entrepreneurs have been able to create wealth faster than we have been able to tax and destroy it.

Money and wealth must have incentives to leave the security of safe-deposit boxes and insured returns. Investments in entrepreneurs can offer the greatest returns of all, but not if they are taxed into oblivion.

Let any man or woman start from scratch and make something from nothing. Let them build what never was before. Let them pile up the wealth of Croesus to do with what they wish. In that way, and in that way only, there will be prosperity for all.

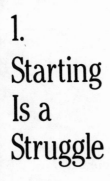

1.
Starting
Is a
Struggle

Never despair; keep pushing on!

—THOMAS LIPTON,
Founder, Lipton Tea Co.

My entry into business was neither carefully researched nor prudent. I was impatient to get started. I became wildly enthusiastic over a little company that claimed to have a revolutionary new water purifier. The promoters were eager for me to purchase a franchise, and they plied me with impressive scientific explanations, rosy projections, and persuasive promises.

My career as a small-town insurance agent rapidly grew ever more stifling, and I hastened to sell my partnership interest in the insurance agency for a small cash payment. I plunked a portion of it down on a "Crest Water" franchise for the Miami–Fort Lauderdale area of Southeast Florida. My market research consisted of a few phone calls to Miami, where someone assured me that the "water is lousy."

My abrupt departure from a secure job and promising future made little sense to anyone but me. I was following self-help guru Napoleon Hill's dictum, "Every person who wins in any undertaking must be willing to . . . cut all sources of retreat. Only by so doing can one be sure of maintaining that state of mind known as a burning desire to win, essential to success."

Furthermore, I had set a goal of attaining great wealth and my intent was to follow Hill's instructions to the letter, "*Wishing* will not bring riches. But *desiring* riches with a state of mind that becomes an obsession, then planning definite ways and means to acquire riches, and backing those plans with persistence which *does not recognize failure,* will bring riches."

The year was 1970 and Miami was a long way from Minnesota. I was in my early thirties and the task at hand seemed formidable enough that I wanted a partner. Throughout the summer I cajoled my closest friend, Jay Anderson, in an attempt to persuade him to throw in with me. He finally relented.

The harshness of the upcoming struggle escaped us. Our plan entailed allowing just a few months to set up the venture, with subsequent commuting between Minneapolis and Miami. Our familial responsibilities would remain in the North.

In early November, we started out driving to Miami. Our anxiety over setting up a business in a strange city was offset somewhat by our impatience to begin. Miami was a tough town for a new business venture. Furthermore, we were newcomers and came with a concept of dubious merit. We settled in a comfortable suburban apartment complex where the neighborhood reminded us of home. Our kitchen served as our office. We spent the first few days ordering business cards and buying bedding and dishes. We had targeted the upcoming Monday as our first work day.

The main thrust of our business, according to the instructions of our franchisor, was aimed at restaurants, which would be delighted with the idea of installing one of our units so they could serve our delicious water to their customers. (The franchisor always called the water *delicious,* and fairly smacked his lips.)

I consulted the yellow pages that first Monday morning for names of restaurants to call and explain our program of delicious water.

After a few calls, it became agonizingly clear that the rude rebuff I encountered indicated a flaw in the marketing scheme. Most café owners weren't the least bit interested in Crest Water nor, according to them, would they ever be. By noon I was fast slipping into a mixture of rejection and despair over the looming economic bind we were in. Suddenly, the dark likelihood of failure seemed very real.

Finally, I got up from the phone and lay down. Every possible negative thought flowed through my mind. I began to make plans to quit. I felt thoroughly defeated, depressed, overcome by anxiety, and terribly afraid. How could I have been such a fool to leave my comfortable little insurance business and deliver myself into such miserable straits?

That evening the words of Hill seemed hollow and meaningless to me. Yet I continued to read and reread. "The majority of people are ready to throw their aims and purposes overboard, and give up at the first sign of opposition or misfortune."

Such counseling did little good. My misery exceeds others, I thought, because my situation is far worse.

I struggled to control the dark and negative fears that dominated my thoughts, continued to work, and within a few days my state of mind switched to a more positive note.

Time and again over the coming months I would slip into sieges of rejection, anxiety, and negativism. I came to see how completely my mental state colored my perceptions of daily events and what I thought the future held. My circumstance could be good or bad, depending on my thinking process. Hill was right, "The positive emotions of thought form the side of the stream which carries one to fortune. The negative emotions form the side which carries one down to poverty."

In the meantime my partner, Jay, was struggling with a second part of our franchise—bottled water. The franchisor's plan had us setting up a drinking-water plant in a Miami dairy. Our low-cost water, packaged in paper cartons, would quickly dent the competition's market share.

After months of delay in obtaining the proper equipment, we were chagrined to find that the paper cartons leaked. When the Florida Health Department inspected our newly installed water plant, they would not grant us a water bottling permit in a dairy. That was the end of that segment of our business. At the time it seemed a grave injustice. Our franchisor, of course, promised to sue everyone in sight. A simple inquiry on their part months before would have saved us all time and money.

Because our restaurant purifiers elicited no interest, we decided to turn our attention to the condominiums and apartments of Miami Beach and North Miami. The restaurant unit was renamed to the apartment unit. Day after day I began to trudge through the labyrinth of condominiums in north Dade County. Our aim was to rent our units by the month. They would be centrally installed and the building members would come to the unit to draw their drinking water. We made zero progress. A hundred condominiums said no.

A health inspector tipped us off that Thoroughbred horses at the racetrack were drinking bottled water. Apparently a few trainers pampered their charges and kept them off the city water. My partner called at Tropical Park the next morning and made the rounds of the trainers. He got a few nibbles and within a few days an order.

Over the following weeks we spent our mornings at Hialeah, Gulfstream, and Tropical Park winding our way through stable boys, hot-walkers, jockeys, and trainers.

After two months in business we had installed three units at $30 a month each. The equipment for another few orders was woefully delayed, the racing season would be over soon, and our meager working capital was almost gone. Nevertheless, we were less fearful of our ongoing nightmare.

Clearly, our success hinged on penetrating the apartment and condominium market. Over time we had made inroads at several buildings in an area of North Miami where the water was foul. After interminable delays and excuses from the franchisor, we were shipped several units. To our chagrin, they were faulty and caused us no end of embarrassment.

The units stood upright and a button was supposed to activate a flow of pure water from the spigot to fill the user's jug. The flow from these first units shot straight out, hitting the customer on the chest.

Almost at once the units began to rust. The floor below them became stained with orange drippings. The machine cabinets became rust-streaked and ugly.

One day an apartment dweller looked into her water jug and noticed thousands of tiny black specks suspended in the water. The franchisor had failed to put screens over the carbon tanks that cleansed the water and flecks of harmless, but unappetizing, carbon were suspended inside the jugs.

Far worse was the fishy taste that frequently plagued our water when the deionization tanks wore out. These tanks used resins to remove excess minerals from the water. The franchisor used the wrong mix of resin. When exhausted, the tanks gave off an acid taste that spoiled the water.

When complaints started, we rushed to our units to verify the unpleasant problem. "I can taste my fillings," was the standard complaint.

One Sunday morning, a customer called lamenting that he had used our water to cook a chicken. "My chicken turned black," he cried. We raced to his building to placate him and change the tank.

These ongoing problems were psychologically devastating. The tiny market penetration we made was fast being eroded by events beyond our control. It was obvious that our franchisor knew nothing about water treatment. Faulty equipment that grievously embarrassed us and led to a steady stream of complaints sabotaged our efforts. Each complaint upset and disturbed us. Out of necessity, Jay improvised endless solutions to cure many of our equipment problems.

The rental income from a half-dozen units made a small bite in our expenses. As our money slipped away, our anxiety rose. To worsen our lot, the franchisor advised us of a month or more delay for any new units.

We switched our efforts to sales of a brand-new office unit. Our franchisor explained that this innovative piece of equipment would be ready for installation almost at once. The two of us worked the small businesses west of the Palmetto Expressway, where the water was unpalatable.

We ground out dozens of cold calls each day. The orders began to fall. We took checks for the first month's rent. We made promises of delivery dates based on our franchisor's directives. At last we had something going our way.

Unfortunately, no office units were ever sent to us. They had never been manufactured. The whole idea was no more than an unworkable pipe dream of the franchisor. After several months passed, we reimbursed those who had ordered and expressed our apologies for bothering them.

Meanwhile our bills were piling up. Our cash was gone. We

borrowed what money we could and sold off the last of our personal assets. We made partial payments to maintain our trade relationships. The phone company's blunt threats to cut off our service became a recurring monthly downer.

The Civil War general Stonewall Jackson advised, "Never take counsel with your fears." It was well we didn't, for we had no money, no orders, no equipment, and no prospects.

By late winter, I was fortunate enough to have gotten an appointment with Stephen Muss, scion of a wealthy real estate family with interests in New York and Miami Beach. Steve Muss was an entrepreneurial real estate developer who controlled many of the premier rental properties in Miami Beach. Today, he is mentioned in the Forbes 400 listing of America's wealthiest people.

In 1971, he was building a major condominium on Key Biscayne. I'd called his office a few times and finally got a chance to talk with him. I was plenty nervous but I asked for a brief appointment to explain our new product. For some reason, he said OK.

I was even more apprehensive by the day of my appointment. While driving over to Key Biscayne, I got a bad case of the jitters. I was on my way to call on a well-known millionaire and business tycoon, a mission that would intimidate most young entrepreneurs.

I was greeted cordially in his comfortable office at the construction site. I presented my case for a drinking-water unit on each floor of his apartment buildings. He pointed out the faulty economics of my plan. I tried a couple of other approaches. He immediately sized up weakness in each. Finally, I was stalemated. He questioned my market research, and we both concluded I should have done far more.

Our meeting wound down, and the results sounded grim. Almost as an afterthought I threw out the idea of a coin-operated water vending machine and asked his opinion. He liked the idea. After exploring the concept with me for a few minutes, he went so far as to give me the name of his general manager. If I got the problems with my machines straightened out and if I could build a coin-operated unit that worked flawlessly, I could test its results in one of his flagship buildings, Seacoast Towers.

I will always remain grateful to Stephen Muss, whose cordial manner and keen business perception solidified and encouraged my idea. I left that meeting with all I could have asked for —a new plan and reason to hope.

Despite the franchisor's continued botching and exasperating delays, we were finally able to get a vending unit perfected. We remained apprehensive about the likelihood of wealthy apartment dwellers visiting our unit to purchase a gallon of water. Whether they would accept the plastic jugs we supplied them and deposit their dimes to draw their own water was a dubious supposition. Several months later we put the first unit on-line.

We offered free gallon jugs and one week of free water. We installed the machine and slid notices under every apartment door. Almost at once, a line began to form at our unit. Virtually every resident responded to our free offer.

At the end of the week, we switched over to the coin-operated plan. We let it go a few days, then checked results. The coin box was partially filled. People liked the water; they would buy it. We had our breakthrough.

We went back to the franchisor with the good news. Sorry, they advised, there was no money to build machines, nor could they lease us any more units, as we had initially agreed. They had no money to make them and we, of course, had no money to buy them. And suddenly, on Miami Beach, there arose a demand for water vending units.

These were days of severe impatience and frustration. Our attempts to obtain equipment financing in Miami brought stinging rejections. My partner finally rounded up some fresh investors to give money to the franchisor. They manufactured a few units and found an angel to carry the financing.

We put the units in new buildings with continued positive results. The on-line machines were coughing out a solid flow of dimes. But we still agonized and despaired: we could get no real supply of machines. There was a demand we could not meet and that frustrated us terribly. Our financial plight was such that we were living hand-to-mouth. We borrowed and wheedled, fretted and worried, and somehow managed.

By early summer we had found an old gentleman from Minnesota who managed a wealthy widow's financial affairs. They agreed to finance our equipment. Through the summer the orders and installations progressed nicely. I went back to the many building managers and owners who had rejected my earlier sales presentations. Now they listened with interest; most had heard of our newfound success, and tenants were pressing them for a similar service. The entire beach fell, then Hallandale. I worked up through Fort Lauderdale and Boca Raton, all the way to Lake Worth. I was confident and strong. The rudeness and rejection I once so feared only made things more interesting now. The orders stacked up. The tiny flow of dimes had escalated somewhat and helped to meet some bills. Still, we were pinched and the financial pressure remained unbearable.

In late summer, we were rocked by a letter from the County Health Department. They maintained we had failed to obtain various licenses and permits. Worst of all, they indicated the state office at Jacksonville supported their decision to close us down.

The problem snowballed. A second county made plans to hang signs on our machines that read, "Closed by order of the Health Department." That would be the end of us. I pleaded with them to hold off until tests of our water proved our unit to be acceptable. They gave us some frustrating bureaucratic demands that were impossible to meet—but they held off.

Our water passed the health tests with ease. But that didn't seem to be enough. We were still to be shut down.

I flew to Jacksonville. For two days I ingratiated myself by flattering and chatting with health department underlings. On the third day I finally got to see the chief. It was clear from the start he did not like me. I sat in a room with the old boy while he contended that the city water needed no further treatment. I was a slippery opportunist, engaged in bilking the public.

He laid down a list of requirements. Our units would need extensive replumbing and major equipment revisions. The costs were prohibitive. Many other requirements were unworkable and damaging. We were finished. I went back to my motel and wept.

On the flight back to Miami, I tried to make sense of it, to overcome my anguish. The only thing that helped was a couple of Bloody Marys furnished by the stewardess.

I had called my partner and given him some of the particulars. When I got to our apartment, we went over the list in detail. We could comply with only one request: to encase the spout of our unit with a plastic cover. That made sense, but everything else was literally impossible for us to do. We couldn't knock down walls and dig up floors of apartment buildings.

I began to get the idea that we were done. It was almost a good feeling—at last we could quit. We could escape from this ordeal. It sounded better and better. I felt a flush of relief. We were going to go home. No more endless, early morning phone calls from upset customers and angry bill collectors. No more dealing with a franchisor who failed to keep promises. No more implacable rejection, frustrating delays, and unending financial stress.

When I confessed to Jay that I thought we were through, he stood up and began to rave and curse our bureaucratic strait-jacket. Finally he insisted we would continue as always and comply with but one small part of the onerous list. "The hell with them!" he shouted.

In a few hours I became convinced. Over the following month we put on the plastic covers, took out a vending permit, and neglected the other requirements. When the Plumbing Department refused us a permit, we forgot about them too. We never heard another word from the Health Department or anyone else.

It was early fall, almost one year later. We had fifty or sixty units out and a strong demand for our vending machines. Friction continued to grow between us and the franchisor, who had implemented a cumbersome inventory system that led to disputes each time we ordered a replacement part. Every little widget required extensive paperwork. Long waits became endemic. Even worse were the interminable delays in the delivery of the vending units—so important to everyone's success.

Due to our progress, the franchisor had sold several other franchises. Now, for some reason, we became an annoyance to him.

I obtained a second mortgage on my house, which enabled us to pry loose a few more vending units. Nevertheless, we needed many more to really prosper. Our income was improving and we had clearly begun to succeed. In our view, however, it was far too early to break out the champagne.

Our relationship with the franchisor broke down irretrievably, to the point where he refused to sell us any more of the units we needed. Just then, the gentleman who had arranged to finance our equipment made an offer to buy us out.

A few more months dragged by and our franchisor still refused to sell us units, threatening and blustering and eventually trying to take our franchise away from us.

Our potential buyer remained interested. We shot him back a high price that we thought would end the discussion. He agreed to it.

We began to think more seriously about selling out. We would never make big money in the water vending business. We had planned to sell off a part of our company anyway, to raise money to build our own machines. We still had the health department hanging over our heads. Our on-line machines were showing a reduced income each month. Plus, we preferred to live in Minnesota where we still had responsibilities.

Exactly fourteen months after we'd started, we sold out and pocketed about $60,000 each. To us it seemed like a lot of money. I would often look back and say we earned many millions of dollars from that experience—to be collected later on.

The franchisor failed less than a year after our departure, and all the other franchises went under. The company we founded lasted only two years after we sold it. The buyers dissipated our goodwill, and upstart competitors wiped them out. They filed bankruptcy.

How did we get through it? We lost all our money, yet we found money when we needed it. We had a worthless product, yet we found a way to make it worthwhile. We had no marketplace, but we found a market.

Napoleon Hill's advice on persistence holds the only explanation I know: "what we do not see, what most of us never suspect of existing, is the silent but irresistible power which comes to the rescue of those who fight on in the face of discouragement."

Starting up your own business is a tough, discouraging, anxiety-ridden struggle. It requires stubborn courage and tenacity.

Entrepreneurs must recognize the need to prepare for sieges of suffering that can be negotiated only with implacable persistence.

Napoleon Hill, after analyzing both Thomas Edison and Henry Ford firsthand for many years, concluded, "I found no quality save persistence, in either of them, that even remotely suggested the major source of their stupendous achievements."

SUMMARY

The new enterprise you start will have more than its share of problems, unique to that business. Every new entrepreneur has had to cut through a seemingly endless spectrum of difficulties. All these problems and setbacks can be solved. Those who stick around and push through the tough times emerge in the black.

Sometimes money is not an immediate reward. Experience, however, is better than ounces of gold. For it yields interest at a compounded rate, which you will inevitably draw upon. The longer your fortune is withheld, the greater it will be.

2.
Finding
a Business
to Start

"Do unto others as you would have them do unto you" and *"Give and you will be given unto"* are the central rules of the life of enterprise.

—GEORGE GILDER

The business you start up should, if possible, be a new idea. The way to find such a fresh concept or breakthrough is to concentrate on solving a problem or meeting a need of people that is currently unmet.

Your new enterprise will likely originate from something you know about. Your present job is a fertile source of ideas and concepts. Or perhaps you can invent a product while puttering at home in your spare time. That's how many household products begin.

Sometimes a hobby will lead you to an opportunity. Several years ago I began to collect guns. As I built my collection, I was frustrated by the lack of information on current prices. Were my guns a good investment? Had I bought them at a good price?

When I had collected coins, I used any number of market and price guides. Some were published annually and some weekly. I always had current information on what my coins were worth.

Not being able to find similar facts about guns frustrated me. Whenever you are frustrated by something, examine the reasons closely. If you find yourself wishing for or wanting something, analyze what that something is. Perhaps you will see an opportunity.

I saw a business possibility in my gun collecting. Consequently, I began to publish the *Blue Book of Gun Values.* This annual compendium of prices met little market resistance and we now publish 10,000 or more copies each year. They are quickly snapped up. The project makes a nice profit.

You can do exactly the same thing. But first you must analyze your daily circumstances and search for an unmet need. This mode of thinking must become a daily habit.

Get yourself a small vest-pocket notebook. On one page, write the heading, "Needs." On the next page, put "Errors." Each day jot down in your notebook the minor exasperations you experience. Record when you want something that's not there. Take note of shoddiness and poor quality. On the job, don't fail to sense a need for a missing product or a lack of information. Note where the management overlooks a market or mistreats a customer. To do this properly, you're going to have to think and have insight into yourself, otherwise you will miss these human needs and blunders. Every day you will find that you want something that isn't available. It flashes into your mind and quickly disappears. You need to capture these thoughts and write them down.

On the Errors page, put down examples of bad service and rudeness. When the telephone operator or receptionist shuns simple politeness; when a reservation clerk treats you rudely; when the gas station attendant makes you wait and then forgets to wash your windshield, jot it down. Enter them all, fill up your page. In the evening, review and contemplate the results.

By noting each day's foibles and peccadilloes, you are initiating a habit of thinking that is crucial to your ultimate success. I don't expect that in a week or two you will hatch an idea that catapults you to instant wealth and celebrity status. You will, however, lay the groundwork for critical business thinking. Once you adopt this method, you will be like a blind man who suddenly can see.

At twenty, I had little talent for seeing opportunities. My mind gradually became attuned to spotting these changes by concentrating on a search for them. By my early forties, I could not even take a fishing trip without pointing out the means for some enterprising person to profit. On a charter trip to Lake Michigan, our good fishing (everyone caught something) left us needing a photography service to take a professional picture, a taxidermist close at hand to pick up our trophies, a fish-cleaning and -smoking service or custom cannery to preserve our catch and mail it to us or to others as gifts. Small, part-time ventures, granted. Nevertheless, from such seeds of opportunity come profitable companies.

After a month, you can forgo the notebook. Your mind will be a bloodhound for opportunity. In time, the idea you need will flash into your mind. Then your venture can begin. The self-training you have given yourself in critically analyzing the methods and needs of others will help you in untold ways. Good management, good service, and good quality are the natural by-products of this focus.

Your needs are everybody's needs. We are far more alike than we are different. Your frustrations and desires are those of your neighbors. Your opportunity lies in your own self-analysis or your insight into others. If you are serious about your search for opportunity, your chance will come. When you are ready, the thing you are looking for will be there.

Innovation, breakthroughs, inventions, and new products are thought to be the special talent of a few lucky individuals. But it's not so difficult. Furthermore, once you have started a business, you will detect ways to benefit your customer that you would otherwise never see. It is experience and studying your customers' needs that lead to most innovation.

Alexander T. Stewart is somebody you probably never heard of. But in the last century he opened up a dry-goods store in New York and prospered. This success led to the opening of one of the commercial wonders of the world, the Marble Palace. When Stewart first got into the retailing business, prices on all goods were arrived at by haggling. Stewart established a pricing system with one uniform price for all similar items. At the time, this was a remarkable innovation and met with huge success. Stewart insisted that salespeople relate honest facts and discouraged the common practice of overpraising goods. He initiated a refund policy—an unheard-of procedure. He even went so far as to provide toilets for his customers.

Today we take all of these procedures and services for granted. They seem so obvious and simple. Yet, all were astonishing innovations in their day. Once in the dry-goods business, Stewart found new and better ways to please his customers. He wasn't born with any extraordinary talent for innovation. He started out as a schoolteacher. He looked for and thought about the needs of others. He listened to them and watched what pleased them and what didn't. That is all you must do. Many of these breakthroughs are simple and obvious. You can find scores of them in any business.

When I began to sell gold and silver to investors, I naturally bought some for myself. After placing it in my safe deposit box, I determined there was no insurance coverage available to protect my holdings. Bank boxes were thought to be quite safe, but nevertheless, I was concerned. After reading about a large bank where burglars looted the safe deposit boxes, I sensed an opportunity. There must be other people who shared my unease.

You can't just start up an insurance company in this country. Regulations forbid it without immense amounts of capital. The fact that this allows established companies to avoid new competition and become bureaucratic dinosaurs essentially devoid of innovation is not the subject of this book. Rather, the question is, How does an upstart get into the insurance business?

We started a *reinsurance* (insurance companies spread risk around so that it is shared by other companies) company in Bermuda. Anyone can do this. Then we formed a group that offered insurance on safe deposit boxes, among other services. We found a mainstream company to issue the original policy. Our Bermuda company shared in the reinsurance.

Then we offered memberships in the group to our customers. A number of them joined and thereby obtained the insurance coverage. Our company, The Monetary Protective Group, isn't setting the world on fire, but it does generate a nice little annual profit that adds to our nest egg tucked away in Bermuda.

From the simplest enterprise to the most sophisticated technological start-up, the rules are pretty much the same—you try to do something a little different or a little better than the way it is done now. Let's look at a very basic service, shoeshining. Many people would consider it a demeaning task. There are no human services that are undignified—they are all noble and worthwhile endeavors. When you meet the needs of your fellow humans, no matter how basic, you fulfill the fundamental rule of all commerce and all wealth building.

I wear a nice suit to the office, and some days on the way up in the elevator, I look at my shoes and wince. They look scuffed and dull. I whack at them with a brush from my desk drawer. When I pass through an airport, I relish the chance to get my shoes shined. I wish they could always look so nice.

Suppose that someone would be innovative enough to extend a shoeshining service from a stationary point to the customer's workplace. That would be a service breakthrough. Bring the service to the customers, rather than make them come to you. Any number of people in a given office building would respond to a pleasant, energetic individual whom they could count on to come by regularly once a week to polish their shoes.

That's what you are trying to do in any business. Go beyond the present level of service or the current way of doing things. Yes, it may take a measure of audacity and courage to advance your novel approach. There may be rejection and plenty of personal concern that the concept won't work. But remember that all unique strategies and breakthroughs were escorted to fruition by a worried entrepreneur. You get paid for devising a breakthrough only when you get it into the marketplace and customers pick up on it. It's not easy to make a lot of money, because it's not easy to have the tenacity and drive to get your product or service into the consumer's hands.

The business term for what you are looking for is known as a *market gap*. As it implies, a business venture should be the result of the discovery of some new, or better, or overlooked way of doing something—a gap or hole in the present methodology.

To repeat, what you are looking for solves a problem or meets a need.

Henry Kaiser, founder of a hundred companies, said, "You get ahead in direct relation to how well you offer services. If your aim is bold and high, you may search for new services that will fill the needs of others. . . . I confess that, wherever I see an unfilled need, I have an irresistible urge to do something about filling it. The opportunities to develop new products and services are as boundless as the ideas and desires of mankind."

A few years back, I took my family on a vacation to western Canada. One long day we wound through the British Columbia Coastal Mountains for hundreds of miles toward Vancouver. We came to the city well after dark and began to search for a motel. We had little luck finding one, but finally, after several phone calls, located an opening. As we drove through the strange city toward the motel, we were tired, rumpled, and hungry. It was late and we were apprehensive about finding a decent place to eat.

Suddenly, we popped over a hill in the neighborhood of our motel and were greeted with a familiar sight that flooded us with relief. "McDonald's," shouted my son. There they were—the golden arches, looking for all the world like a neon oasis.

What's the reason my little family of consumers reacted with such relief to see that McDonald's perched in a Vancouver suburb? McDonald's met all our needs. We wanted the assurance of good food and we wanted that food quickly. We didn't want to go in somewhere, sit down, wait, and worry about how we looked or what we were wearing.

Examine the market gaps filled by McDonald's, one of America's great entrepreneurial success stories:

QUALITY: always good food
DISTRIBUTION: found everywhere
SPEED: no waiting or delays
INFORMALITY: no need to dress
RELIABILITY: food always the same
SERVICE: attentive and fast
CLEANLINESS: nothing unappetizing
PERSONNEL: neat, polite, and attentive
MENU: kind of food you like
ECONOMY: reasonable prices

In the late 1950s and 1960s, Americans were more mobile than ever before. They moved, they traveled, and they often ate meals out. They would just as soon eat in jeans and shorts and they didn't like to wait long. They also knew what they liked— burgers and fries. Restaurant or drive-in chains varied from town to town, and individual restaurants could be fabulous or fatal. A clean, uniform chain that invariably offered good, popular food, served quickly and economically by neat, pleasant people met the needs of Americans. Seldom are so many market gaps filled by one venture.

You may not be planning to start a multibillion-dollar corporation the size of McDonald's, but the reasons that it prospered are going to be the same reasons any new venture takes off.

Kresge founder, Sebastian S. Kresge, discovered this reason while a young deliveryman and solicitor: "I began slowly to discover that progress, whether of the individual or of a business, depends principally upon giving the largest quality of service for the dollar."

Note that in a service business (a massive segment of our economy), the market gap or opportunity often lies in better service—from simple courtesy on up to a fundamental restructuring of consumer habits. Improved service, more service, new service—there are endless gargantuan opportunities in this sector.

"The service business is very rewarding," observes John Willard Marriott. "It makes a big contribution to society." William P. Lear, Sr., said, "I would say a young man has a better chance if he has an idea for a service. He won't require any machinery to execute his idea."

To repeat: get into the habit of noticing bad service. Sloppy, indifferent, slipshod treatment is commonplace. That represents opportunity. Furthermore, there are no existing businesses where service cannot be greatly improved. Time and again I have been able to break new ground in pioneering improved service to my customers. If you zealously search out these service breakthroughs in your business, you will find an ongoing number that, when put into practice, ensure the prosperity of your enterprise.

Listen to Henry Ford: "The trouble with a great many of us in the business world is that we are thinking hardest of all about the dollars we want to make. Now that is the wrong idea right at the start.

"I tell you the man who has this idea of service in his business will never need to worry about profits. The money is bound to come. This idea of service in business is the biggest guarantee of success that any man can have."

Then, when your business is up and running, you must become a service fanatic, a fierce advocate of new and better service, a driving perfectionist aiming to pamper and please your customers. Remember, *you are never giving, nor can you ever give, enough service.*

If you can't come up with a new service, then make an existing service better. Service innovations or breakthroughs fill gaps that your competition ignores.

Fortunately for you, most service companies are mediocre. You can beat them with ease. The average business operates carelessly. Many small firms are run by slobs. Every time I go into the bathroom of a gasoline station I get an insight into the slovenly way most ventures are run. Most of these so-called service stations are downright putrid. That's what you have going for you. Most of your competitors are going to have the equivalent of a filthy rest room somewhere in their operations. It symbolizes their ineptitude. You can outdo them by a wide margin. The world is screaming for excellence and impeccable service. That is your ticket to riches beyond any amount you will ever need.

As you get off the elevator at my company, you see a large plaque on the wall. It contains a quote from E. W. Statler, founder of the Statler Hotels:

LIFE IS SERVICE

The one who progresses
is the one
who gives his fellow-beings
a little more,
a little better service.

That is the essence of your success formula. Equipped with that simple secret, you may conquer the neighborhood or the nation.

In addition to service companies, product companies make up the other major segment of our economy. Goods—products or components—are made for sale to consumers and business. The market gaps lie in new designs, new technologies, new products, new inventions or advancements, and improvements of present products.

Historically, many business start-ups in these areas originate when several talented people leave an ongoing concern and start out on their own. Here, again, the present business provides the launching pad.

Charles Walgreen, founder of the drugstore chain, advised: "The largest opportunity for any average man is right in the line where he is already established. When he is already in a business, no matter how far down the scale, he can go ahead faster in that business than he can in any other. The average man who, like myself, has no special gifts, does better to stick to the line he knows."

Certain businesses possess qualities that can make them lucrative or easy to manage. They have secondary, or back-end opportunities for additional profits or proprietary angles that put you ahead of competitors.

In a service business, look for special ingredients that would discourage competitors or give you market dominance for a while—a trademark, a formula, a system. These factors also keep others who have been introduced to your business from going around you and starting a similar enterprise. Inevitably, however, the best weapons to discourage competitors are a superb reputation and supreme service that ensures customer loyalty.

Other good endeavors are royalty and licensing businesses (you give up use of your patent, product, or idea to others) which generate profits for the life of the patent or agreement. Renewal businesses (insurance, publications) also assure you of future income or commissions.

Some of the best businesses sell secondary items for use with their initial products. Videocassettes are the most profitable end for recorder manufacturers. Eastman Kodak generates most of its profits from film, not cameras.

An entrepreneur approached me with a new type of portable light he had invented for use by painters in the construction business (a market gap because painters inside construction sites had no standard, portable, first-rate lighting device). As we discussed his invention and its progress, I became convinced that he was missing the chief profit opportunity of his device.

The orders from major wholesalers were piling up. He had a small metals manufacturer making the units for him as fast as it could. His margin of profit, by necessity (he was a middleman), were small. Worse, his business was all one-time sales. Customers needed only an initial supply that lasted forever. If you sell something just once, you had better have fat margins. After all, you must do the same kind of promotion as a company fortunate enough to sell a repeater (most consumer products are repeaters).

We saw the light bulb as the key to making a good product an exceptional one. As bulbs burn out and must be reordered— probably for years—why not control that part of the business? A special bulb or an exclusive agreement with a manufacturer could tie up that ongoing need for good. The profit opportunities would multiply.

Look for means to double and triple the profit options. Look to start up businesses that have residuals. A magazine I started brought in subscriptions and advertising revenue, plus I could run free full-page ads for my own products. A franchise project for an energy-saving device of mine brought in a franchise fee, sold the raw material to the franchisor, and took in a royalty on all sales.

IBM sells hardware first, then sells everything a computer needs in order to operate (paper, discs, and so on) in addition to charging for whatever ongoing service is necessary. GM makes fat profits on replacement parts.

Here's another example. My mutual fund charges a sales commission; my management company that runs the fund gets an annual management fee; and most transactions from the fund portfolio are run through my brokerage firm.

Also, favor businesses where you get paid up front. The need to extend credit can be a weak link in your start-up. In any business, cash flow and profits are pinched from time to time. That's when a cash-and-carry business shines. Merrill Lynch, K-Mart, Delta Air Lines, and many great companies either get their money up front or they have exceedingly stringent credit criteria.

New companies have enough difficulty finding buyers, let

alone buyers with good credit. Whenever possible, set yourself up to sell for immediate payment. At the onset of the energy crisis, I was fortunate enough to step into the wood-burning stove business, which subsequently had quite a play. When we sold a stove directly to consumers, we got cash, but the dealers we needed to generate big volume wanted credit. The answer was no. We sold fewer stoves through fewer dealers, got paid in advance, and managed to make a few dollars. Those who extended credit to the many new and inexperienced dealers failed.

Ever since we had contracted for the manufacture of our wood stove, the Sierra, we had always been nervous about the possibility of a flaw in the unit contributing to a fire. Although that wasn't likely, there was always the chance that some careless person would burn down a residence and blame it on our stove.

Realizing this possibility made my decision to get out of the business much easier. Products liability insurance was expensive, and we knew a few lawsuits would cause us to lose our coverage. As the company grew in other directions, we saw this product's hazard as the Achilles' heel of our future prosperity. We bailed out and sold the wood-stove business to a small manufacturing firm and were lucky enough to collect annual royalties for six years.

The new business you select, whenever possible, should be free of these potential problems. Products liability lawsuits are a nasty drawback, as are problems of hazardous material, pollutants, worker compensation, or other liabilities that can water down your efforts and dissipate your profits.

Another negative aspect of the stove business was the horde of competitors. Anybody with a welding torch and a few slabs of steel could launch a stove business. Another flaw was its seasonality. Superimposed on that problem came the boom-bust cycle inherent in the inflation-prodded energy crisis. One particular year, hundreds of excited new entrepreneurs, all start-up manufacturers, dealers, and distributors, went into the fall season with maximum inventories and high hopes. By spring, it looked like a battleground strewn with the dead and wounded. The lesson: seasonal, supercyclical businesses that have a flood-tide of competition should be avoided. We were always amazed when late in the wood-stove boom, some eager beaver would call us for information on how to get started meeting the demand for wood burners.

It is true, however, that the first person to start a particular business reaps many benefits, no matter how competitive the marketplace eventually becomes. A Maine resident by the name of Eva Horton got an inkling of the potential in alternate energy, and she began to import wood stoves. Being first, she gained publicity, consumer acceptance, dealer demand, and superlative word-of-mouth advertising.

Eva had been brought up in Norway, and during the war her family heated with wood. With the energy crisis in the offing, she went back to Norway and made a deal with the company that manufactured Jotul stoves to become their exclusive distributor in the United States.

As she had little capital, she sold for cash. The attractive wood burners caught on and for years her only problem was getting enough stoves to meet dealer demand.

Eva had another precious ingredient to her success that was probably more foresight than luck. She climbed aboard a blossoming trend. To succeed in a big way, you need the proper timing. The ability to spot upcoming trends and growth opportunities comes from constantly looking out for them, plus having some experience.

If you like to read or can research avidly, you should cover a variety of subjects that interest you. If you read and believe the predictions and forecasts of others, you may be able to position a start-up to take advantage of a forthcoming trend. In other words, you can play off somebody else's vision and research. That's how I started my company Investment Rarities Incorporated. I read about the potential for inflation and believed the predictions of many of the so-called gold bugs.

When I first began to investigate precious metal as an investment, there was little or no interest in gold and silver. I thought the future of these inflation hedges to be bright, however, and went out into the world with my message. Few people listened; I was far from the mainstream.

Within a few years, that all changed. Over a billion dollars' worth of gold and silver went out our door for delivery to investors and refiners. We were fortunate to have had good timing.

There is no way that I or anyone else can give you a specific venture to start up. We could guess at what fields might offer the most rewards in the future, but it would be only a guess. Tom Fatjo, Jr., started Browning-Ferris Industries, Inc., and made as much or more money collecting garbage across the country as could any high-tech wizard. Opportunities are in your basement or your office; unfulfilled wants and needs are everywhere.

Over the past year I have had a number of new business opportunities presented to me by entrepreneurs in search of capital to start. As my company is up and running, I occasionally invest in new deals with some of our profits. Here's how we judged the merits of each of the following products. Each one can teach you something and help you size up the realities of your opportunity.

The decoy. A duck decoy is attached to a rope with a small lead anchor on the end. The anchor holds the decoy in place when you throw it into a marsh or pond. When you pick it up, you must wrap the anchor rope around the decoy. This procedure takes time, and in cold weather your wet hands become quite uncomfortable.

This new product has a device inside the decoy that automatically wraps up the rope when you pull the decoy from the water. In theory this is not a bad idea. It improves the current methods and, by making things simpler and easier, meets a need.

The entrepreneur had done a patent search. (There are attorneys who specialize in patents and patent law. A patent search determines what prior patents may have been made on your product or device.) The search indicated that at least six patents for similar inventions had been filed, some of them dating from the last century. The product had been thought of before but never perfected.

My view was that the major limitation of the device was that it must always work flawlessly. Anything that must work in water has a whole new set of problems. Plus it must work in mud and salt water and also in ice if it freezes. For the product to do all this and still sell for a reasonable price seemed like a remote possibility.

I suggested that once he had the device perfected, he apply for a patent and license it to existing manufacturers for a royalty. He was intent on building a small manufacturing facility, which I considered much too expensive for the potential rewards. I thanked him for showing me the invention but expressed no interest.

Several years ago I attended an inventors' convention. What a disappointment it was. Dozens of tables and booths were filled with prototypes of new inventions. Most of them were bad. I was dismayed at the clutter. Many of the inventors had been promoting their invention for years and getting nowhere. They were living in a dream world. Nothing good would ever come of their ideas.

If you invent a new device, don't get bogged down in the inventor's fantasyland. Do it the way the decoy inventor did it. Go out and show it to businesspeople, investors, and other experts. If you get discouraging advice, that's fine. You will be learning about the realities of your product. Use this information as a catalyst to move ahead.

The best thing you can do is to go ahead with your project. Start to make your product and begin to sell it. Before you succeed in a big way you will need many months and years of trying and doing. To begin—that is the one thing most inventors never do.

If the advice you receive is very negative, perhaps you should give up your idea and search for another. Better to move on to something else than to sit around for a decade wishing and hoping, as many inventors do.

Garbage into building blocks. This entrepreneur had supposedly perfected a way of chopping up garbage and mixing it with a glue to form building blocks. You could make almost anything from the blocks: buildings, fences, sidewalks.

This idea solved a big problem by doing away with landfills and other garbage-disposal methods. Most communities are looking for solutions to the garbage problem.

Unfortunately the plant and equipment needed to finish the product cost millions. Consequently the building blocks can't begin to compete in price with concrete. So what if you can turn garbage into bricks if nobody buys the bricks?

Avoid getting bogged down in major schemes that will solve one of the world's primary problems. They are always money hogs and most often can't be made to work. Start with small projects; they are demanding enough.

Statue of Liberty clock. This product ties in with the hundred-year anniversary of the Statue of Liberty in 1986. The promoter arranged a licensing agreement to make and sell a handsome bronze miniature of Liberty with a clock in its base.

I was lukewarm on this idea. As it celebrated an upcoming media event, it obliquely filled a need. However, once the anniversary is over, sales of the product end. All the work and effort needed to promote the Liberty clock would be better spent on a product that would continue to sell. You want a product or service that allows you an opportunity for long-term success.

There may be fads or gimmicks like the "pet rock" that make someone prosperous, but they are short-term phenomena. You want something you can keep building for ten or more years. That's when the real profits are made.

Nonalcoholic mouthwash. The standard mouthwash sold everywhere has a high alcohol content. Great numbers of recovering alcoholics are advised by their treatment centers to avoid using mouthwash. The entrepreneur's new product is a mouthwash without alcohol. Many people need such a product. It fills a significant market gap. This is the kind of clear-cut opportunity you are looking for.

Because it didn't take a lot of money and I liked the aggressiveness and experience of the entrepreneur, I put up the capital to start this company. Today we own 49 percent of Colorado Clear Corp., the maker of Morning Magic Mouthwash.

The book publisher and the bank. Several people proposed that we help them open a bank. Another fellow tried to interest me in starting a book publishing firm. Both ideas are bad. The world doesn't need another bank or another book publisher. These are good ways to lose a lot of money.

If the bank were to be located in a neighborhood where people were crying for banking services, or if the book publisher had some unique types of books, these ideas would be worth listening to. Neither, however, had the slightest uniqueness or need. Far too many businesses are started as mindless imitations of the competition. This is the formula for frustration and failure.

Always avoid squaring off against a well-entrenched business. Unless you have something unique, they have a huge advantage.

The drum company. A drummer had devised several new concepts. The first was a metal grommet that fastened the drum to the drum stand. This eliminated the vibrations that detrimentally affect the sound and clarity of the drums. He had solved a big problem for drummers.

He had also invented a portable drum set made only of drumheads. The set sounded great and could be folded together into a slim carrying case—great for practice or minor gigs. He had solved another problem.

He took his ideas one step further. He combined the drumheads with the antivibration device and made a line of drums for marching bands. They were lightweight, easy to carry, and sounded great.

Here were three breakthroughs that made a drummer's life better and easier. I liked this venture, but before I had decided whether to get involved, someone else put up the money.

The inventor of these products was looking for not only capital but also a business manager, someone to run the company. If you have little talent for inventing but shine at sales or management, this kind of partnership could be what you're looking for. Sometimes an inventor will sell out to you for very little or take a royalty on future sales. These kinds of opportunities are available once you begin to search for them.

Rent an expert. This service business allows companies to tap the expertise of leaders and educators in fields such as cryogenics, metallurgy, and scores of other disciplines. This seems like a handy service for the many corporations who don't have access to or can't afford these consultants on a full-time basis.

Although this service meets a need, there will probably be a long period of maximum effort before it noses into the black. This is a big project for a tough-minded entrepreneur. You have to have a little extra tenacity, perseverance, and will for this kind of a task. It's not the kind of big endeavor you want for your first fling. In this case the entrepreneur was adequately financed from the sale of a business and never got around to asking me if I wanted to invest.

The autophone directory. This idea centers on a plastic case to keep phone numbers in your automobile, for people who own car phones. This may be a growing area, but it didn't seem large enough to kick off a business.

Furthermore, the product is so inexpensive it would be hard to generate much profit on such limited sales. Competitors are common in this type of business. It does meet a need, but demand doesn't seem to be great enough.

The entrepreneur who makes a commitment to this kind of product will likely come up with something else along the way. There's nothing wrong with this; better to start with a mediocre product than never to get going. In the final analysis, it is not the product that will make the company a success. It is the person behind it.

As you can conclude from the preceding examples, there is an infinite variety of business opportunities available to you. Each has its own subtleties and of all these ventures, small service businesses are the quickest and easiest to get rolling. If you have no special talent or great scientific discovery and you have limited capital, a small service business is the ideal starting point. You will gain a fund of necessary experience and, should you want to go further, this will serve as your launching pad.

I have stressed over and over again in this chapter the need for entrepreneurs to provide quality goods and to give service above and beyond the call of duty. This attitude facilitates like no other the discovery of market gaps. Opportunity is no more than a better way of serving and providing for humanity's needs. "As you give, so you shall receive, equally."

John H. Patterson managed a business in which he constantly had to watch out for clerks who stole cash. To thwart them, he ordered a newfangled cash register made by a local saloonkeeper. Receipts shot up. Patterson quickly recognized the opportunity and jumped at the chance to buy the cash register business.

His device, no great technological breakthrough, was tough to sell because its merits were hard to grasp. He overcame this drawback to teach and educate storeowners and shopkeepers the world over about his unit. Thus, he built National Cash Register into a giant.

Patterson was a legendary disciplinarian. This tough, demanding perfectionist numbered among his alumni Tom Watson, the principal architect of IBM, Henry Theobald, founder of Toledo Scale, and Charles Kettering, co-founder of Delco. He taught them all how to think in terms of the customers' needs.

John Patterson spotted an opportunity just as you can. He became a highly influential entrepreneur. How he did all this can be emulated by you today.

While some businesses are clearly superior to others, the continued search for the perfect venture can turn into mere procrastination.

Your idea for a new business may or may not have merit. You won't know for sure until you have been at it for a while. The key is to get started. Make the decision that you are an entrepreneur. If your plan doesn't work, if your business fails, you are that much closer to ultimate success. The direction in which you start out can be switched many times. Henry Ford started out to make a tractor. Thomas Edison first invented a telegraph device. It's highly unlikely that you will succeed with exactly the same plan you begin with.

You must desire a lot of money and acknowledge that you are an entrepreneur in search of this reward. You must stick with it. Remember, the big winners suffer and ache through five, six, or seven years of highs and lows. You may wind up in a business far from your original venture, but success is inevitable.

For example, Conrad Hilton, the hotel-chain founder, had saved some money, had developed a few associates with investment capital, and was intent on making it big in the banking business. A friend told him about the fantastic oil boom in Texas.

> I had been looking for my dream. A big one. The pieces suddenly fell into place. Here it was, My own frontier. . . . Where there's oil there's activity . . . banking. . . . A string of banks in Texas. . . . If you want to launch big ships, go where there's deep water. Go to Texas, Connie, and you'll make your fortune.
>
> If a stranger in Kansas City had stuck by his word

. . . I would have bought a bank in Texas. Granted, that's what I set out to do. Granted, I tried my best in Wichita Falls, in Breckenridge, in Cisco. And if I had succeeded, I would, I know now, have been a very mediocre banker and gone broke besides. Within a few years when oil, the banker's security, dropped from $3.00 to $1.00 a barrel, most of the banks went broke.

The minute I stepped off the train in Texas I knew there were fortunes to be made in Texas. You just had to find a good thing.

The first thing we saw was a town roaring like a blast furnace. It was hard to get meals, next to impossible to get beds, and inconceivable that a man could think of buying a bank.

I put the question squarely to the president of the first bank I saw. I was eager. "The price?" the man said icily. "Why, it isn't for sale at any price." I should have been discouraged. I wasn't. Evidently business was as good as it looked—and it looked good. Here was boom town vitality, jostling crowds, a whirlwind of excitement that was as stimulating as an icy shower after the drowsiness of the Rio Grande Valley.

There were oil men in laced boots and flaring trousers, each one a potential millionaire. The nearby Burkburnett fields were pouring black gold into their veins. There was the colorful riffraff that follows in the wake of sudden money, smooth-faced gamblers, smooth-tongued promoters, a sprinkling of painted ladies, more obvious than smooth. Between the two, catering to all, were the banks, false-front emporiums, over-crowded restaurants and hotels.

There were no saloons. The Eighteenth Amendment had closed the package store. But there was a seemingly endless supply of corn liquor, quite disreputable stuff, and alcohol with which those lucky enough to have a bathtub made what they deceitfully called "gin." Men were still protecting their lives and possessions with guns.

It was lusty country. Tall men. Tall tales. Giant laughter. Feverish work. Fierce fighting. I wanted in!

Wichita Falls was too "high on the hog" for my bankroll and I moved on to Breckenridge, west of Fort Worth and not far from the Ranger fields. It was the same story in Breckenridge. Even the drinking water was loaded with oil, and there was nothing for sale at any price.

I headed for Cisco, farther south but comfortably close to the Ranger fields. Here was a new kind of Romance, a search that knocked everything else from my mind. I thought, dreamed, schemed of nothing but how to get a toehold in this amazing pageant that was Texas.

It was waiting for me in Cisco. Cisco was a cowtown gone crazy, but basically still a cowtown. I had a feeling it had been there yesterday and would be there tomorrow, that there had been citizens on the street when only children bothered to dig holes in Texas dirt. Besides, it looked closer to the size of my stake, and it had four banks. Call it hunch again, but Cisco felt right.

I went straight from the railroad station to the first bank I saw. It was for sale. I had a mounting sense of excitement. There was no trouble about examining the books and from what I saw there the price was right. The absentee owner wanted $75,000. Better and better. A bank, at the right price, in Texas!

The difference between the price tag and the amount pinned inside my coat didn't bother me. You could, I thought confidently, always get money on a good thing. For once I was too impatient to bargain. I dashed back to the railroad station and wired the owner in Kansas City that I was prepared to buy at his price.

Then I cruised around town. I was dreaming big. I had visions of laying the cornerstone of my banking empire right here, and went back to wait restlessly until the owner should deliver it into my hands.

He did nothing of the kind. Instead, the telegrapher handed me a message which read: "Price up to $80,000 and skip the haggling." There it was. The telegram that changed my life. The stranger who went back on his word . . . and in such an arrogant fashion that I saw red. "Skip the haggling?" Why I'd already, against all my instinct and training, skipped the haggling. I didn't like that kind of a raise. Once, many years later, I was to stand raise after raise from a man named Healy to get the biggest hotel in the world. I didn't like it then. I didn't like it that day in Cisco.

In fact, I wasn't going to stand this raise. "He can keep his bank," I informed the startled telegrapher vehemently. Then I strode out of the station and across the street to a two-story red brick building boosting itself as the "Mobley Hotel."

The Mobley Hotel, when I first saw it, looked like a convenient place to sleep. Nothing more. I wasn't through with Cisco. I was playing out my hunch. But I figured I'd play a steadier hand if I could rest in a bed for a few hours. The milling press in the hotel lobby acted like sardines clamoring to get into the can. From behind, from the sides, the crowd tried to push into the tiny funnel around the desk clerk. Since I was tall, in excellent condition and determined to get a room, I plunged right into the spirit of the thing and was within speaking distance of the clerk, when that harassed individual slammed his book shut and hollered: "Full up!"

For a stunned moment the crowd milled in a circle, I with them, and then, like children playing musical chairs, dove for the few seats the lobby boasted. I wasn't expecting it and lost out. Leaning against a painted pillar I tried to decide what to do next.

A granite-faced gentleman was making his way methodically about, giving here a push, there a push, trying to clear the lobby. Finally he worked his way to my side. "Sorry fella," he said, looking anything but sorry. "Come back in eight hours when we turn this lot loose. You may have better luck. But we don't allow loitering in the lobby."

I was hot under the collar. First I couldn't buy a bank. Then I couldn't get a place to sleep. Now I was accused of loitering. I was about to explode when a thought struck me. "You mean you let 'em sleep eight hours and then get a complete turnover?" I demanded. "That's the idea. Three times every twenty-four hours, day in and day out. They'd pay to sleep on the tables in the restaurant if I'd let 'em."

"You own this hotel?"

"I do," he said bitterly. "I am tied to it with an anchor and chain. Every nickel I've got is sunk in this glorified boardinghouse when I ought to be out there in the oil field making real money."

"You don't seem to be doing so bad."

"Not," he said shortly, "if you're willing to settle for the hotel business when guys are turning into millionaires overnight. If I could get my stake out of this place . . ."

"Are you saying," I spoke slowly, fighting to keep any trace of excitement out of my voice, "that this hotel is for sale?"

"Fifty thousand cash and a man could have the whole shooting match including my bed for the night."

"Mister, you've found yourself a buyer," I said.

He gave me a suspicious look. "You don't get the bed 'til I get the cash."

"I don't want it," I retorted. "I want to look at the books."

Three hours later, after a careful inspection of the Mobley books, I thought a man would be crazy to want oil. If they told the story, this had banking beat all hollow. I watched the lobby for another hour, wary of planted "guests." If Mobley had salted this mine, everyone in town and his brother had to be in on the act.

I wired L. M. Drown (a prospective investor) that I'd found something and then slept on a bench in the station. Drown came running, arriving on the noon train. He was pretty excited. When I explained the deal his eyebrows went up. "I'm a banker, man. I don't know a thing about hotels."

"I've had a little experience," I said, possibly stretching a point, considering the size of the family hotel in San Antonio, "and when you've had a look at this, you'll be ready to learn."

I escorted him to the street and pointed proudly to the Mobley. "That," said Drown, "is a hotel?"

"It is a cross between a flophouse and a gold mine," I replied. "Just be glad the people around town have so much oil in their eyes they can't see it."

After looking things over carefully, Drown shook his head. "The man who'll sell this is either a crook or he's crazy."

"Oil-crazy," I said.

"It's a good thing," Drown said. "I'd sure like to get in on it. But I can't swing it."

"You are in. I'm cutting you in," I told him. "You can

be manager of the Mobley. What we've got to do first is buy it."

We needed to know exactly how much we had to raise. That meant bargaining and I rolled up my sleeves. Mobley was a gem, a worthy opponent. He knew when to howl, when to run, and when to clamp down. It was a first-class bout and we could both enjoy it because we never let the deal get out of hand. He wanted to sell. I wanted to buy. At $40,000 we shook hands. Mobley gave us one week to "transfer funds."

"But not one day more. I mean it!"

Then I began to put together my first buying group. I had one-eighth of the money on me. Drown moved another $5,000 when he turned up with an oil man, one C. P. Smith, who was looking for an investment. Mother mailed a check for $5,000 and a rancher friend in Socorro came in for another $5,000.

We had used up four days. With half the purchase price in my hand, I approached the Cisco Banking Company. I had rehearsed my sales talk on Smith and Drown. I could have saved myself the trouble. The president knew all about the Mobley, his bank was loaded with money and, since we would outright own a half-interest, they were more than prepared to give us the necessary loan. It was almost too easy.

Then the rancher's check bounced. When the notice came to me by mail, we had twenty-four hours to close the deal in cash, or bow out. It looked like we were through. We couldn't find another $5,000 in town, and it would take too long to get it from New Mexico, even if we should turn up another partner.

One thing I knew I had to do immediately was inform the Cisco bank. Their loan was being made on our $20,000. We didn't have $20,000. I set off for the bank feeling as if I were going to a wake. I could taste again the bitterness, the defeat I had felt (from past failures). . . .

Anyone following me to the bank would have thought I'd gone crazy. First my steps lagged, while I tried to make the dream last. Then I'd increase my pace almost to a run, to get it over with. Lag. Run. Lag. Run. Finally, there I was. There was nothing to do but go in.

I sent a fervent, if confused, prayer to St. Joseph, approached the bank president, and dropped my bomb.

Nothing happened. He didn't throw me out. He just pressed the ends of his fingers together, swung his chair from left to right, and thought. I was thinking, too, feverishly.

Finally he spoke. "It's rough. You had a bonanza right in your hand." Then an idea came. Startling, but worth a try. "This rancher friend of mine," I said. "He owns his ranch in New Mexico outright. A conservative valuation would be $20,000. Why don't you loan him the $5,000 on his ranch 'til he gets a liquid position? I'll wire for his power of attorney to act for him. The money'd be here. The check would be good. We could go through with the deal."

For a moment he didn't say anything. The Mobley was hanging in the balance. Then he said, "Fair enough."

And that was the way it happened. I raced off to the telegraph office, leaving Smith and Drown in a coffee shop gazing steadily at our hotel, as if it might vanish if they took their eyes off it.

The following day, at noon, the Mobley changed hands. I was in the hotel business. And I hadn't been in the hotel business five minutes before I knew this was it.

Like many business beginners, Conrad Hilton bought an ongoing enterprise rather than create one from scratch. If you have the money, this can be a fast, low-risk way to get started. You probably save a year or two by stepping into an ongoing company. However, it takes every bit as much entrepreneurial skill as does a raw start-up to make the company you buy expand and flourish. You must create a breakthrough in this company, just as you must in a start-up.

In his book *How to Become Financially Successful by Owning Your Own Business*, Albert J. Lowry lists six advantages of buying a business:

1. You may possibly get it for a bargain price. Circumstances sometimes force an owner to accept less than his business is worth in order to sell it quickly. (Health, personal, and domestic problems are examples.)

2. You bypass start-up problems, which can be unforeseen and costly. You save the time and trouble of buying equipment and supplies. Operating methods are proven. Customers are already buying from the company.
3. Guesswork is minimized. If you start a new enterprise you can't be sure about the right location for it, right-size building, right forms of advertising, right prices, and so on. An established owner already knows most of the answers.
4. The owner can give you valuable information about competition, demand, seasonal fluctuations, community attitudes, and other variables.
5. You get a time-tested list of suppliers and service people.
6. Often you inherit trained employees who will stay on and help you learn the business.

Therefore, if you can't think up a new opportunity, consider buying a small existing enterprise. Scores of small companies are for sale, from tiny service outfits to manufacturers. Look in the want ads. Call a small-business broker. Examine these deals with an eye for a potential opportunity that the current proprietor misses. You should probably look at dozens of these ventures. If you find one that appears to have growth potential or can be improved dramatically, you have a candidate for purchase.

Remember, you are looking for entrepreneurial opportunities when you buy a small business: the chance to give superior service, to improve quality, to take bold, direct actions that will build sales.

Don't buy something you can't make grow. Avoid deals in areas with shrinking populations, bad reputations, or obsolete products. Talk to some of the current customers. Investigate the product's potential by calling competitors anonymously. Pay a visit to the company's banker. Discuss the business with vendors who serve it.

If you decide to buy, make a ridiculously low offer. If it is turned down, ask for a counteroffer from the seller. In this way you will get an idea of what the seller will accept. Your next offer should be a bit lower than the seller's price. That will likely seal the deal. Remember that buying right takes skill. Many businesspeople never learn to buy right. *The first rule of making a good purchase is to get the seller to commit to an asking price first.* Then you can bargain from there.

Unfortunately, most business opportunities listed for sale are bad deals or money-losing traps. The final act for many failing companies is a belated attempt to sell out. Many companies offered for sale have slumping sales and bleak futures. The owners want to bail out and escape the misery. Some companies purge money-losing divisions. Others sell slow growers or capital-intensive subsidiaries.

Consequently, you must look at these companies with exceeding care. You will hear rosy projections and optimistic chatter. Ignore the sales pitch and get current financial data. By current, I mean up-to-the-minute facts. Most companies for sale are late with the current financials. They will have a statement six months to a year old. Enormous deterioration can happen to a balance sheet in thirty days. You should get audited financial information, and it should be recent.

Stick your nose into the books. Grill the bookkeeper. Check the receivables. Inspect the payables. Closet yourself with the accountant and get a good financial picture of the company. You need to have reliable facts on sales, margins, and profits before you consider any purchase.

Whether you buy a business or a building, use time to your advantage. The economic bias leans toward more inflation. Make the smallest down payment possible. Extend the payment contract for as many years as you can. Don't buy anything with a floating or inflation-indexed interest rate. Try to get a fixed rate and at the very least put a cap on how high the interest charge can go.

Make sure that the seller sticks around for a month or two. You must be grounded in the fundamentals of the business. You need to be introduced to the customers and the suppliers. Don't despair if you don't immediately find any breakthroughs to improve the business. A strong commitment to serving others will quickly translate into imaginative concepts that benefit your customers.

If possible, buy your business when it's in the doldrums. The price will be cheap. In our cyclical economy, this means buy during a recession. Sales will tend to increase and business improve in the months ahead.

Don't buy anything at the pinnacle of the business cycle: you'll face a long-term business slump. You will pay too much by buying at the top. Furthermore, high interest rates will make borrowing impossible and your payments intolerable.

SUMMARY

If you study closely your own needs, wants, and minor frustrations you will uncover an opportunity. At home, at work, or even at play you must, day by day, pay attention to your reactions. Why are you displeased, what irritates you, what are you wishing for, what do you desire? Your needs are everyone's needs.

You must also study others. What problems do they have on the job or at home? How can you solve their problems? How can you meet their wants and needs?

In order to prosper you must find a market gap. Then your business will have a purpose. It is futile to duplicate a competitor's efforts. Find your own niche. Serve others. Make life better, easier, happier, or more profitable for consumers, and you will be rich.

A service business is easier to start than a product business. In a service company, excellence may be the only breakthrough you need. Begin to notice bad service and you will see untold opportunities.

A company with a new product must stress quality. Try to develop a product with more than one profit option. Look for residuals and repetitive sales.

Whatever you start may not be your permanent task. Once you have started, new ideas and opportunities emerge which offer even greater rewards.

You may decide to buy a business. If you have the capital, this can offer definite advantages. To succeed in a big way, however, you will still need the entrepreneurial ingenuity to discover breakthroughs.

3.
How to Start Your New Enterprise

I believe the true road to preeminent success in any line is to make yourself master in that line.

—ANDREW CARNEGIE
Founder, U.S. Steel Corp.

The classic entrepreneur (whom this book hopes to nurture, perpetuate, and multiply) creates out of nothing an ongoing enterprise. According to economists, entrepreneurs develop and apply new combinations, which is another way of saying they innovate.

But how does a novice entrepreneur develop the powers of innovation, the alertness to profit opportunities, and the skills necessary to create and build a new venture? By doing. Experience gives form to the newcomer. The secret is to begin. Do the thing and it will be yours.

Let's start out with the most elementary concept of what successful business is all about. You, the entrepreneur, must present your particular product or service, within the framework of the marketplace, alongside all other competing products and services, to be examined by a group of people who are the kings of the marketplace. They pick and choose what appeals to them and ultimately spend their money on those things. These kings of the marketplace are the consumers. They decide who wins or loses, who succeeds or fails. They are shrewd and discerning, self-serving and unforgiving. You must please these rulers of the market with goods and services that offer advantages to them. Successful business begins and ends with providing these sovereigns of the marketplace with superior products they will choose willingly.

One of the world's great inventors and entrepreneurs, Charles Kettering, observed: "In business the one fellow you never think much about, whom you don't know, sits back and controls the whole thing, and that fellow is your customer.

"I have often said that all of the profit and loss on any manufacturer's books are the applause and hisses of the customers."

Your goal is to bring to the market a new product or service that brings you this financial applause. To do this you need some basic ingredients.

First you should put together some sort of written business plan. What will your service or product be? Once you have decided, you need to list a few objectives and goals. This helps you crystallize where you are going. Having an outline of what you are planning to do may make you more likely to do it.

Then you must set up a budget for your first year's operation. This should tell you how much money you're going to need. Most of this will be guesswork. Nevertheless, you need to fix in your mind an amount of money that is necessary to fund your new enterprise and get you started.

Determining exactly how much you will need cannot be reduced to a simple formula. You should have at least one year's working capital, which includes a salary for you to live on. The tendency is to underestimate this requirement, but that only means you will be out of money at some time. This predicament is common to all entrepreneurs. Those who are most successful seem to have been at their creative best during such bleak periods. They praise these periods of adversity for developing in them skill, ingenuity, and creativity.

Next you will need to find the money, get a lawyer, set up some kind of legal business entity with a name, and master some foolproof fundamentals on how to gather information and improve your skills in human relations. You have much to do.

You will probably have to start your new venture on a modest basis. This works to your advantage. By starting small, you spend less money and you learn thoroughly the fundamentals of your business. Over the years, a humble beginning will favor growth and profits.

In the biography of his grandfather, Cyrus Hall McCormick, inventor of the mechanical reaper (International Harvester), the younger Cyrus McCormick writes, "All the early machines were built in the blacksmith shop on the Walnut Grove [home] farm. Cyrus had no other factory. He not only had to supervise such workmen as he employed, but he must himself do any work that required particular care. To sell his product, he had to ride for miles and days over mountain roads. He had to learn to watch credits and supervise collections. He, alone, could secure materials, arrange for drayage to the nearest canal, do all those things that now require the services of department heads and organization."

Cyrus Hall McCormick had no choice but to become grounded in the fundamentals of producing and selling his invention. Nothing else explains his ultimate success. Inventors are often flops in business ventures. These people are entrepreneurial up to the point of creating a new device. Alexander Graham Bell and his assistant, Thomas Watson, could have done far better financially on their invention of the telephone. Thomas Edison, the colossus of discovery, rated average at business. They did not have either the interest or the opportunity to secure a lesson in the fundamentals of commerce.

Cyrus McCormick's difficult but valuable early lessons enabled him to attract farmers everywhere to his mechanical reaper. His device freed them from hand labor and opened up the midwestern farm belt. McCormick laid the foundation not only of modern agriculture but of modern industry and business as well. He pioneered early mass production, waste saving, and standardization in manufacturing. As if that weren't enough, he was the first person to advertise or to demonstrate and sell a product aggressively. What's more, he established the first broad warranty of a product. He came up with the idea of servicing the equipment he sold. He developed the first widespread distribution system. Then he started the first broad application of credit. All these practices were unheard of in his day and shocked his contemporaries.

Through his invention, Cyrus Hall McCormick wiped out the last vestiges of starvation (still common in the mid-nineteenth century) in what was then the modern world. Further, he enabled pioneers to settle the vast prairie and to climb up from bare sustenance to prosperity.

This mind-boggling list of accomplishments originated in the humblest surroundings by an inventor whose early struggles forced him to grasp the fundamentals of commerce, which he would ultimately embellish as no man before or since.

As did McCormick, when you start small, you have nowhere to go but up. Aside from learning by necessity the fundamentals of your undertaking, you can operate on a low budget and conserve capital.

Harvey Firestone, founder of the company that bears his name, points out the greatest benefit of starting small: "I lacked capital. Because of this I was forced to keep down overhead and watch every expenditure.

"In fact, I feel that if I had had all the money I wanted when I founded my present business, it never would have become so big as it is. I never would have found it necessary to make such a close study of details to promote the efficiency of the organization. I would have accomplished less because I would have lacked the prod of necessity for surefooted, painstaking accomplishment and the elimination of waste."

You don't necessarily have to jump into a new venture full-time to start. Many entrepreneurs work a job and develop their ideas on the side. George Eastman, founder of Kodak, started his film business while employed elsewhere. Curt Carlson, founder of the multibillion-dollar Carlson Companies, built his Gold Bond trading stamp business up to a point where he was forced to quit his job and run the stamp venture full-time.

At the other extreme comes advice from William Lear: "Lots of people wonder, if they're starting a business, whether they should go in hock to get the business started. I'd say it depends on how intelligent a fellow is. If he is really sure about his business, he should mortgage his house. I've mortgaged everything at times to stay in business. As a matter of fact, I can remember a time when it seemed I owed everybody in the country." Sooner or later you're going to have to make this kind of commitment, no matter how you start.

I've used up my savings, remortgaged my house, and sold off every asset I had. You will probably have to take similar steps. When you use your own money, you don't waste much capital. Splashy start-ups that squander money are out of the question.

Whenever I see a new company setting up a plush layout that looks sleek and prosperous before they've earned a dime, I blanch. That prime clue is all you need to know in order to forecast their outcome.

In the late 1960s, a small group of so-called entrepreneurs raised $300,000 in the hot new-issue securities market in Minneapolis. They rented lavish suites and appointed them sumptuously, leased Lincolns, and hired staff. They set an interesting record of sorts. Of all the companies with public offerings during that speculative period, they went broke the fastest.

The DeLorean Auto Company spent money on the perks that supersuccessful companies are accustomed to. They started at the top and as one analyst commented, "had nowhere to go but down." Whatever the travails of Mr. DeLorean, he violated two rather substantial principles of start-ups. He began on a grand scale and he had no market gap.

In military terms, the DeLorean venture would be called a frontal assault on a well-entrenched enemy. In business and martial history, this approach has frequently proved suicidal. There are well-established, skillful auto manufacturers too numerous to mention. When RCA took on IBM, head to head, in the computer business, they suffered the greatest single loss in history. Apple Computer got the edge on IBM in the small home units only because they avoided futile confrontations and concentrated on a market gap where they could win.

As I said earlier, lack of money keeps many potential entrepreneurs on the sidelines. The fear of no steady paycheck, or of a period without income, tends to paralyze even the bravest souls.

However, this fear of the financial woes associated with a new business tends to be exaggerated. You can get along on far less than you might think. Once you begin, there always seems to be just barely enough money to enable you to scrape by. You learn to live with financial worry, fight it off, and evolve the ingenuity to get you through. Lack of capital forces you to scramble, to cope, and to emerge from the struggle far tougher. You become more resourceful, in both staying power and the discovery of sources for money.

How do you raise capital? What are the best sources for money? Small product or service business start-ups can usually be funded (and most often are) by a loan from a relative, friend, or lending institution.

Naturally, it's far better if you can rely on your savings, sell off some assets, or use some other of your own resources. However, if you have to borrow, do so. It is vital that you get started, whatever your financing arrangement.

By far the quickest and easiest means of raising capital is through the sale of an interest in your new venture. Here you can tap friends, relatives, present customers or clients (they are best), and outright strangers or referrals. This effective strategy assures you of all the money you need to get going.

When the decision was made to start up my company, Investment Rarities Incorporated, we easily raised the money we needed. We turned to seven investors who had been clients and, for $64,000, sold them 20 percent of the new entity. A steal for us at the time, it later turned out to be a bargain for them, too.

My partner in this new venture was the late Bernard T. Daley. Bernie had been a professional finder and knew how to raise money. We followed his suggestion to capitalize or set up the company with a million shares. "If you start out with a hundred shares in your company and sell 10 percent, your investor owns ten shares. With a million-share company, he owns 100,000 shares. Sounds better," he would say. Bernie theorized that this was an easier sale—it sounded as though you planned on the company's being large, and the investor could multiply 100,000 shares by any dollar figure he projected the stock to be worth. Furthermore, it didn't cost any more to handle it that way.

People invest in new ventures with the hope of hitting a bonanza. They dream, wish, and fantasize over the fortune they might make. Unfortunately, as we all know, these hopes are often dashed. Nevertheless, this yearning and the promise of fulfillment gives cause to the gamble. If you are going to raise money, your investors must see the potential for a windfall. They must see a fortune awaiting them as the reward for their risk.

I used this carrot with great success with my initial investors. It implies no dishonesty. You must believe in where you are going, and your destination must be significant. Then you must disclose a portion of your dream, along with an invitation to invest. In this straightforward manner, you will find it simple to raise the money you need.

It seems easier to raise smaller amounts from several people than a big chunk from one or two investors. Large sums usually bring in attorneys and accountants to review the deal. They tend to cool off investors on the kind of high-risk investment that start-ups represent.

Prior to starting Investment Rarities, Bernie and I had begun to start a mutual fund. We tried to raise a large amount of money from two individuals. Bernie had suggested we start up a fund that would invest exclusively in gold stocks. At the time there was only one major gold fund, and we were convinced that inflation would soar and gold with it.

Over the next few months, Bernie began to make the arrangements to bring out the new fund. He contracted with an uptown Minneapolis law firm to register the deal with the Securities and Exchange Commission. He convinced gold expert and author Donald Hoppe to seriously consider managing the fund. We mulled over marketing plans and plotted sales strategy. Finally, we combed through our customer files and acquaintances to come up with potential sources of venture capital. We needed $150,000 to kick off the fund, and we were willing to part with a third of the venture in exchange for the money.

A friend introduced us to two potential investors, brothers-in-law who had sold their company to a large New York Stock Exchange firm. We drove down to see them in their small community just south of Minneapolis. We talked about our mutual fund and our need for capital. They were somewhat interested and asked for more data along with our projections. We promised to get back to them.

On our way back to Minneapolis, we were flushed with anticipation. They were clearly interested. Not only that, they possessed substantial sums that were being directed into high-risk ventures.

Over the next few weeks, Bernie was busy putting together a *pro forma*. This is a set of projections of sales volume, expenses, and future profits that accompanies the structuring of new venture financing deals. Bernie was fastidious about the details. I was totally in the dark. I couldn't comprehend the wizardry of putting two years' worth of future figures on paper. "Jimmy," Bernie would say, "these figures don't mean a damn thing, but we've got to do it."

We dropped in on our prospective investors once again, talked a while, and left them the pro forma. We set up a meeting for a few weeks later. They were likable enough, and we got along with them well. We were excited about the possibility of our forthcoming alliance. Bernie seemed to think we had a good chance. I remained awed by the huge amount we were asking for.

On the day of our meeting, the four of us clustered in their office and discussed the deal with intensity. It sounded good. One of the gentlemen pulled out his checkbook and wrote out a check for $75,000. He handed it to Bernie. The other took out his checkbook. We talked a bit more. He was somewhat cautious and more reluctant about the commitment. Finally, he said, "Ah, what the heck!" and started to write. He filled it out, but before signing he looked up and said, "I'm going to call the lawyer and tell him what we're doing here. It will just be a minute." With that he picked up the telephone and called their corporate counsel in St. Paul. Briefly he told him about the deal. There was a long silence while the attorney responded. He hung up, looked at us, and explained that a meeting was necessary at their law firm. They would hold off for a few days until after we met with their law firm's expert on mutual funds. Bernie and I left somewhat chagrined, but still with hopes intact. We had given the check back and although it had hurt, we knew we were still very close.

Three days later we gathered together at the law firm. The lawyer, although presented as a well-seasoned securities and mutual fund expert, was youthful. He wasted no time. His main theme was the potential our investors had for director liability, in other words, would we do anything with the company that would get them in trouble? He further accentuated the risks of undertaking a new mutual fund, emphasized our lack of experience, and concluded there was a high probability of our failing. We pointed out the inability of any new venture to be able to procure director liability insurance. We suggested our investors refrain from sitting on the board, and we belittled the likelihood of potential liability. The meeting wore on. The lawyer continued to sow seeds of fear and uncertainty. One of the investors had to leave for another meeting. The situation deteriorated further as we argued with their counsel. Finally, the remaining investor suggested he take the matter under advisement and let us know in a few weeks. The meeting adjourned. We were dead and we knew it. It was a terrible disappointment.

A new venture can't stand up to the scrutiny and logical onslaught of doubting lawyers. As they are paid to offer opinions and give advice, they relish such opportunities to gush out critiques. You can expect somebody else's lawyer to poke holes in your venture. Lawyers know the rules of the game. In some ways they are like referees or umpires. They are far more at ease with the substance of legal tradition and the concreteness of rules than with risk or the faith and optimism of entrepreneurs.

The fact that they often take a jaundiced view of new enterprises does not negate the fact that you must deal with them from the inception of your new concern.

When we started our corporation, we ignored legal counsel. Always a sharp bargain hunter, Bernie knew a guy who would incorporate us for one-third of the usual cost.

Bernie had experience with new corporations and thus our cheap incorporation made some sense. As for me, I didn't know that directors' meetings must periodically be held, that shareholders generally met once a year, or that a minute book logged the results of these meetings. I had a vague familiarity with how a corporation worked, but nobody had ever sat me down and explained how the officers are chosen and what the relationships are between directors and shareholders. Some of my directors may suggest I still don't know.

Consequently, I strongly advise beginning entrepreneurs to consult with an attorney on initiating their corporation. You should be grounded in the fundamentals of corporate legalities and basic law. Your attorney's function, among other things, is to explain thoroughly the benefits and procedures of a corporation. Expect and request this intensive briefing. Attorneys need to pay closer attention to giving this constructive advice, rather than just treating the damages of ignorance later.

The choice of legal counsel will have a profound bearing on your entrepreneurial career. You need good advice, competent execution, and someone with an understanding of your nature.

The relationship you have with counsel should mellow over time into friendship, mutual trust, and respect. If you have the good fortune to pick such an individual you will be spared untold exasperation. You don't need to be put off, ignored, talked down to, shorted on advice, or given less than preferential treatment.

My corporate attorney, Roger Frommelt (Frommelt & Eide, Ltd.) of Minneapolis, is an expert on new ventures, entrepreneurs, and securities law. He gives this advice about legal counsel:

> Generally a lawyer that will serve the entrepreneur well needs to be versed in general business and corporate law, and capable of assisting in the drafting of various contracts. The guy down the street who handles house closings and wills may not do. In addition, if the entrepreneur foresees that he will need to raise capital from outside sources (other than through normal commercial business sources), the lawyer should understand the practical and legal ramifications of raising capital, which requires a familiarity with the various state and federal securities laws. I am sorry to say that while many lawyers will profess to be proficient in all of the above areas, few are. I am continually amazed at how often lawyers I work with are unaware of basic corporate law, and how sloppy they are in the preparation of contracts.
>
> First, the entrepreneur should obtain a clear understanding of the fees of the lawyer he intends to use. The most expensive lawyer on an hourly basis may in fact be the cheapest in the long run. In other words, although the entrepreneur should shop around, don't skimp on fees. If the entrepreneur can't afford the fees, he should tell the lawyer. There are a number of lawyers who will show the entrepreneur how he can save on legal fees and who will work out some sort of payment schedule. I enjoy working with entre-

preneurs and sometimes offer to assist with reduced fees in their beginning struggles, but nothing makes me madder than a client who doesn't live up to his commitments.

The entrepreneur might ask the lawyer about other clients with similar businesses. This will help find a lawyer whose experience will provide a certain amount of efficiency in dealing with legal problems unique to the entrepreneur's business. With most clients the legal problems are quite similar regardless of the industry. However, if the business is one with unique problems or is highly regulated, a lawyer with experience may be important, particularly in highly regulated industries, such as securities or banking.

If the entrepreneur doesn't get a good lawyer, he is probably still better off with any lawyer rather than seeking amateur assistance or going for do-it-yourself kits as an alternative. An experienced lawyer can assist the entrepreneur in getting organized, and warn of pitfalls. Do-it-yourself legal work usually costs the entrepreneur more in the long run, when he must employ a lawyer to straighten out the mess.

If you sell off part of your company to raise money, be somewhat tightfisted in handing out shares. A good, optimistic promotion of your company's chances should enable you to sell fewer shares for more money. Value your company highly, and keep the major interest for yourself.

Frommelt confessed to me that he is appalled by the frivolous manner in which some business newcomers pass out stock. He believes that a new company's stock should be coveted. The idea of giving stock for services and expenses encountered by the start-up is folly.

"I have often been confronted by entrepreneurs asking that I take stock in their enterprise instead of fees. I usually have to bite my tongue, because normally I would love to share in the entrepreneur's success. However, once I become a shareholder or partner, conflicts can immediately arise. I am no longer in a position to be totally objective in my advice.

"Furthermore, the entrepreneur may find that giving away stock will cause future problems both with control of the company and intervention from minority shareholders."

Frommelt covers another potential hazard:

I am particularly sensitive to the problems that entrepreneurs get themselves into in selling securities. More
often than not, they (as well as, I am sorry to say, many
lawyers) are unaware that the various securities laws affect
every issuance of securities. Failure to follow these laws
may result in civil, as well as criminal, penalties. If the
entrepreneur misses out on good legal counsel, the issuance
of stock to himself or herself and a do-it-yourself incorporation is probably not going to create a calamity. On the other
hand, the minute the entrepreneur intends to take on a
partner or shareholder, or raise capital through the issuance
of stock, debt, or any other instrument (the definition of a
security is quite broad), he should run, not walk, to his
nearest competent attorney, and that attorney should be
fully aware of applicable federal and state securities laws.

Not only do you need to be fastidious about securities laws
when you raise money and sell shares, you must also have some
idea about the future ownership and structure of your company.

"Bear in mind, Jimmy," Bernie would counsel when we
were raising money, "investors want to know how they're getting out. There are three ways: we go public, sell out to a big
company, or buy the shares back ourselves. We're not going to
have any dividends for a long time. Nobody wants to be locked
into a private company forever and have nowhere to go with the
stock."

The major issue here, for you and your stockholders, is
whether you intend to go public or stay private. With a public
company, you have three major benefits:

1. Your personal shares are liquid
2. You can more easily raise money
3. You can go back to the public again and again with
   numerous financing options that raise more money.

The drawback is that each time you sell this newly created stock
to raise money for the company, you water down your own
interest.

Hand in hand with your public or private decision lies the
issue of how many shares you intend to sell. In other words,
what percentage of your company are you going to give up?

Henry Ford was forced to take a minority share of the Ford Motor Company when he formed it with a group of investors. Typically, they drove him crazy. Over the years he bought them out and, after a bitter lawsuit with the last of them, wound up with complete control. Thereafter, he deplored the thought of relinquishing a single share. Ford had found it to be an enormous frustration not to control his company.

William Lear, developer of the Lear Jet, gave this advice on selling stock:

> The principal thing most of them do wrong is selling [stock] out too early in their effort to get money into their organization. A stockbroker will propose a stock offering to raise five hundred thousand dollars and these guys say, "This is absolutely great. Now we'll have all the money in the world to work with!" They forget that when they're getting this five hundred thousand dollars they're going to end up with only fifteen percent ownership in the company at that stage of the game. If they would hold on longer and suffer a bit longer and work more midnight hours they might be able to get five hundred thousand dollars for, let's say, fifty per cent of the company. But if they held on two, five, or ten years, that stock in their company grows, because of their original effort, their intelligence, their hard work, and that stock could easily be worth a million dollars to each of them.

An early conglomerator, Royal Little (Textron Corporation), advised, "If you don't enjoy being sued, my advice is: Don't get involved in publicly owned companies the way I have —stay private. I'll guarantee that if you are active in business for sixty years as I have been and are an officer or director of a public company, sooner or later you'll be involved in some kind of class action or derivative suit."

However, staying private with a small group of stockholders usually leads to minor conflicts. Attorney Roger Frommelt comments,

> Having one or several shareholders can be as troublesome as being public and having 500 shareholders. In a public company, shareholders don't seem to have as much of a

tendency to think that they have a voice in the operations of the company as do shareholders in a closed corporation. Minority shareholders who receive shares in a closed corporation soon realize that those shares have little or no value. They are entirely dependent upon the whims of the controlling shareholders. Often those minority shareholders begin to feel cheated. If employees own stock in the company and arrive at this same conclusion, that too can serve as a detriment to the business.

If the corporation is public, the shareholder has a ready market for his shares; that is, the shareholder can see that his shares have a current value, and the success of the business will directly affect that value. This is also why public shareholders are less likely to bother management; if they don't like management, they can sell their stock.

More than a few entrepreneurs have launched brilliant corporate success stories that Wall Street fell in love with, only to find that in less glamorous times they were assessed to be lacking in foresight and management skills. They were ousted. They had given up control through stock sales, and somebody else held the votes.

Fortune magazine quoted Ray Dolby, president of Dolby Labs (Dolby Stereo-Dolby Sound), on why he owns his entire company: "This way I can do what I want," he said. That sounds simplistic, but it's not. Freedom to do your own thing is one of the reasons you're an entrepreneur. Shareholders, in either a private or public company, will nullify your ability to do what you want if their shares total more than yours. Minority shareholders will also try to impair this freedom, and in any company, they can be a nuisance. We all know the courts are full of shareholder litigation.

I started out with a shade less than 40 percent of my company. Several years later when my partner, Bernie, left, the shareholders purchased and split up his interest. I wound up with 47 percent of the company. A year later I asked the directors for a *stock option* (an opportunity to buy more stock) that would give me control.

When I pushed for the option, they balked. I threatened to move down the hall and start up a new company in the same business. A nasty squabble broke out. In a tense and tempestuous shareholder meeting, we fought it out. My bluff worked. They caved in and granted my option.

Later, there would come a time when my insistence on control of the company appeared to have been providential. For without it, I would surely have been booted out by an alliance of shortsighted shareholders, directors, employees, and officers whose perceptions at the time have proved to be distorted.

My experience tells me that entrepreneurs should maintain control of their companies. No business will run smoothly forever. In today's cyclical economy, when uninterrupted growth and prosperity are improbable, a majority interest becomes imperative. Otherwise you may face the challenge of those who, although deprived of your insight, are emboldened by their power to bring you down. *Always keep 51 percent until you've tired of the game and it's prudent to sell out.*

While going public seems to be the "end all and be all" for most companies who've advanced beyond the ma-and-pa stage, my sentiments are less enthusiastic. You are subject to shareholders who can be serious pests. You have more government regulations to put up with. You're subject to far more snoopers. You have no financial privacy. You are more likely to relinquish control through stock issues. I prefer a majority interest in a private company, because this absolute control means no one else can tell you what to do.

Initially, you may not have control of your start-up because you elect to begin with one or more partners. I started my first and second corporations with partners who owned equal shares in the new company.

Involving another person or other persons in your venture can be a valuable asset. Partners bring differing sets of talents, and they tend to pump up one another's courage when the going gets choppy.

One of the best arrangements exists between a skilled businessperson and an inventor or scientist. It combines the necessary business moxie and technical know-how for success. Arthur Vining Davis, salesman and industrialist, teamed with researcher and inventor Charles M. Hall. This splendid team developed aluminum and founded the Aluminum Company of America (ALCOA). Many technical experts and inventors need to find a good businessperson to hook up with.

A partner may very well make the difference whether you go ahead with a planned start-up. Psychologically you may need this other person to start. If you are a business novice, having a partner makes even more sense. New ventures require all the talent and help they can get. A partner can cut down on this painful initiation period. Another huge plus with the right partner is the wealth of learning you can pick up from someone with different education and experience than you. I strongly advocate two or even three partners at the outset of your first new undertaking.

There are exceptions, generally due to the background and age of the entrepreneur. Forty and over seems to be a magic age for success. The proper mix of experience and application proves fruitful. A start-up at that point by a veteran entrepreneur probably won't gain that much from a partner—certainly not as much as you would give up by splitting ownership of the deal.

At this point in my personal business evolution, a partner is the last thing I want. Why have a partner when you don't need one? Without my years with partners, however, I would not have endured long enough to mature as an entrepreneur and eventually be able to stand alone.

Partnerships generally break up in time. They are strong in infancy and intimate during adversity, but with prosperity they weaken and erode. Human shortcomings and perceived inequities eventually exasperate one partner, culminating in arrangements of necessity or outright dissolution. Bonds are broken and through such shuffling new opportunities arise; fresh undertakings are devised; greater strengths and larger victories accrue to the combatants.

An entrepreneurial business career brings you into numerous alliances. You will likely have many associates in various deals. Many of these undertakings will fizzle or flop. They are part of the necessary learning process that allows you eventually to get hold of the gold ring.

These associates may be investors, partners, stockholders, advisers, agents, or representatives. They all share the goal of reaping profits from your product or service. You will learn from them all.

Leo Baekeland gave this advice to chemists like himself who

wanted to start up a company. However, it applies to all entre-preneurs.

In selecting business associates for my new industry, I took less into consideration any money they were willing to introduce as stockholders, than their exceptional personal qualifications and business experience. This point of view, on which I put great stress, is too often overlooked by chemists who start in a new enterprise where they are primarily confronted with the problem of finding the nec-essary funds. Frequently they make reckless connections with almost anybody who can furnish them the first money, regardless of whether they are the proper persons to help or advise or inspire them in their work, or whether they are men utterly uncongenial or who do not see in any enter-prise anything but getting quickly as much cash as possible out of it, regardless of any other consideration.

If in the enterprises with which I have been connected, I managed to get along pretty well, I can attribute it, to a large extent, to the fact that in each instance I had the good fortune of being surrounded with congenial partners or collaborators, who, instead of causing friction and irrita-tion, aroused my highest enthusiasm.

Better not attempt much if you have as business associ-ates only men whom you cannot trust, or who do not trust you, or who irritate or depress you, or who are dangerous by their greed, their recklessness, their superficiality, their weak character or their general unreliability.

Business opportunities are endless. Once you get estab-lished and have a few dollars, the word quickly gets around. The phone calls and appointments start. If your door is open to new deals, you will meet an ongoing parade of characters who will try to entice you into a venture. Some may have merit, but most lack potential.

You can avoid wasting a lot of time if you don't get involved with super-big deals, because they are generally time wasters. Ventures far outside your normal operation and expertise should also be shunned.

There are plenty of frauds around. A few phone calls and background checks can tell you a lot. When you see any history of bunco, dishonesty, or questionable practices on the part of the principals, forget the deal. Learn to rely on history and past performance when analyzing people and their proposals. Practice this rule routinely with a new deal or you will be sadder, although somewhat wiser.

Royal Little gave this advice, "Whenever an investment opportunity from Texas gets all the way up to New England after having been offered to the smart money in Texas, St. Louis, Chicago, Philadelphia, and New York, BEWARE! If the project had been any good, the New England investor would never have had the opportunity even to see it."

After several years, my partnership with Bernie Daley, the co-founder of Investment Rarities Incorporated, broke up. This time of momentary bitterness was soon patched up and we continued our friendship. But from the split came new opportunities for both of us which were turned into separate tales of success.

We learned much from one another. In many ways, Bernie was my mentor and in some ways I was his. One of Bernie's great talents was his ability to gather information. At the beginning of a new venture it is mandatory to acquire reams of information. The new company with the most information stands the best chance of succeeding. When investigating a potential business or after beginning one, you need to pile up data on many topics. The key to your success will be uncovering sources of supply, vendors, raw materials, or whatever else you need (at favorable prices) to make up your service or product. On the other end, you need to know the complete lowdown on the distribution system for your business (direct sales, distributor, manufacturer's reps, wholesalers, trade shows)—how it's done and who does it.

That information can be exceedingly hard to extract. Only after a full year in the gold business did we finally reach the initial source of supply. Bernie used the telephone to gather this kind of information. He would get a lead from a trade association or similar source, make the call, and strike up a conversation. All the time he chatted, he filled a notepad with valuable information. From that referral would come other referrals and in time we would have a data bank of gossip, opinions, history, and valuable facts.

All new ventures should make heavy use of the telephone to gather information. Get on the phone and start calling some people. You will uncover reams of necessary input that will be vital to your success.

Bernie honed his phone skills to such an extent that after our parting, he could start a new business with the phone as his only resource. He initiated a company with an eye on selling energy-saving products nationally. For months, over his WATS line, he combed through the companies that manufactured energy items. From weatherstripping to caulking, he developed competitively priced sources for over a dozen practical energy-saving products. Then, using the telephone again, he sold these goods to wholesalers, power companies, and government agencies. He hired a room full of telephone solicitors and began to push up sales. It took him five long and arduous years to do it, but at last the profits came. At the moment of his untimely death at age forty-eight, he looked fit, acted cheerful, and appeared happy, for he had weathered much adversity, and, philosopher that he was, could now dispatch his varied storehouse of wisdom wearing the credentials of success.

The type of pleasing personality that Bernie possessed helped him immeasurably, not only to gather facts but to sell his products. Bernie had the kind of graciousness that E. M. Statler, the hotel-chain founder, emphasized: "Any business enterprise, I don't care if it is a hotel, a department store, or a livery stable, must put *graciousness* at the head of its rules of conduct."

Most new ventures require you to do some selling. A good personality, coupled with the knowledge of how to please and influence people, serves as a springboard to selling success.

One book stands out as the premier instructor on how to master human relations and garner many of the fundamentals of selling. I don't believe there is a single successful entrepreneur who has not either read this book or been exposed to the lessons it gives. The book, *How to Win Friends and Influence People*, by Dale Carnegie, is an absolute must for new entrepreneurs. *Buy it and read it.*

As I became a polished salesman, I relied on Carnegie's advice almost exclusively. When making calls, I would question my prospects, urging them to talk about themselves and their interests. I developed a genuine interest in hearing their stories.

Often, I would walk out with the order as though it were an afterthought.

A. P. Giannini, founder of the Bank of America and Transamerica Corp., a man with a fine personality, insisted on meeting and getting acquainted with his customers, getting out of the office and hearing what they had to say. He instructed, "The way to build up clientele is to go out among them and present to them first-hand the advantages offered by your business."

Another important aspect of a new venture concerns financial forecasting and planning for future capital needs.

My attorney, Frommelt, gives more advice:

> The most common error which I see entrepreneurs make is in the area of financial planning. I am no longer astonished to find that the entrepreneur who is asking me to represent him has made no financial plans whatsoever. Often the first advice I give him is to seek out the assistance of a good C.P.A. [Certified Public Accountant] and prepare a comprehensive financial plan, including a monthly cash flow projection for at least eighteen months.
>
> The area of financial planning which seems to cause the greatest problems for entrepreneurs is their failure to recognize reality and plan accordingly. Every good and successful entrepreneur I have run across is a dreamer and believes he or she is going to be successful. If they don't dream and don't believe, they will fail. Dreaming and believing, though, don't preclude good planning, and the most prevalent error I have observed over and over again is that of gearing up for sales. That is, the practice of buying equipment and hiring employees in anticipation of sales and production.
>
> I have reviewed literally hundreds of financial projections prepared by entrepreneurs. Each time I am presented with one of these projections, I am assured by the entrepreneur that the sales forecasts are conservative. They almost never are. Entrepreneurs are often struck with the belief that if you build a better mousetrap, the world will beat a path to your door. It doesn't happen that way. Although good products and good services are important, they don't sell themselves. I would advise every entrepreneur to allow

the sales to drive his overhead, not vice versa. I believe it is better that the entrepreneur lose a few sales because he doesn't have the equipment or staff to fulfill them, than to go out of business because his expenses ate him up before he could generate any revenues.

If your new enterprise is a service company, you have a more direct path to your first sale than you would with a product company. You need only advertise and solicit to begin.

A product can be far more complicated. Once invented, your product must be protected and then it must be manufactured. Suppose you develop a new product or a dramatic improvement of an existing device. I strongly advocate you apply for a patent at once.

The entrepreneur who showed me the new type of light for use by painters failed to apply for a patent. I confessed surprise and advised him to apply for this protection. Design patents are relatively easy to get and helpful to a start-up.

A successful product without patent protection comes under immediate attack from competition. Before you know it, they start being produced in Hong Kong. Even some patented products that are manufactured in the East will turn up illegally, all over the world.

Even worse, someone else can patent your device if you don't. Leo Baekeland, father of the plastics industry, had a rare combination of inventive genius and entrepreneurial skills. He warned, "If you do not patent your inventions and if you prefer to work them secretly, you take the risk of having your work interfered with at any time, not only by others copying it, but by somebody else taking out very disturbing patents, which afterwards may cost you much time and money in litigation."

A patent assures you of a reward (assuming the product is a success) for your originality, time, and investment. This protection encourages the flow of dynamic new products and technologies.

Once you come under the guidance of a patent attorney, you can begin to think about manufacturing your item. It takes significant capital to produce a product (for tooling, lines, and production equipment, for example). You may want to have another shop make your first products. Why manufacture when you can farm out this function? You can always manufacture later, should there be either a necessity or an opportunity of doing so.

The development of a new and successful product offers an awesome challenge to the entrepreneur. I evolved the rule of "five and ten" for considering significant new service or product ventures. *It takes five years to get into the black and ten times as much money as you initially budget.*

These costs may be such that you are better off licensing your product or improvement than attempting to market it. This becomes especially true with devices that improve old-line products. For example, the party that invented the coolant recovery device for car radiators was better off licensing it to the auto companies than manufacturing and selling it.

With a new product, you must pay fastidious attention to the details that assure its excellence. Quality and reliability are to a product company what good service is to a service company. Andrew Carnegie, king of the entrepreneurs, said, "The surest foundation of a manufacturing concern is quality. After that, and a long way after, comes cost." Virtually all great consumer goods companies or technological and industrial firms serve up products of high quality and reliability that are perceived as good values. When there is service connected with their products, these companies are best at that, too. In fact, most great companies tend to perceive themselves as service companies first.

Thomas Peters and Robert Waterman, Jr., writing in their book, *In Search of Excellence,* give us insights into the corporate philosophies of our best firms. Here are a few glimpses of attitudes that show a commitment to quality, service, value, and reliability. More than any other factors, these ingredients account for the fabulous success of these companies.

IBM. "In time, good service became almost a reflex in IBM. . . . Years ago we ran an ad that said simply and in bold type, 'IBM MEANS SERVICE.' I have often thought it was our best ad. It stated clearly just exactly what we stand for. We want to give the best customer service of any company in the world."

(THOMAS J. WATSON, JR.)

Frito-Lay. "What is striking is Frito's nearly 10,000-person sales force and its '99.5 percent service level.'"

(PETERS and WATERMAN)

Boeing. "We came to a realization that, if we are going to succeed in commercial business, the important ingredient was the customer."

(*Vision* magazine)

Disney. "In . . . scores of . . . ways, overkill marks every aspect of Disney's approach to its customers."

(PETERS and WATERMAN)

Ogilvy & Mather. "In the best institutions, promises are kept no matter what the cost in agony and overtime." (DAVID OGILVY)

Caterpillar Tractor Co. "The company's operating principles seem to be an individual version of the Boy Scout Law: The main principles are excellence of quality, reliability of performance, and loyalty in dealer relationships." (*Fortune*)

"Forty-eight-hour parts service anywhere in the world or Cat pays." (Caterpillar Tractor Co.)

McDonald's. "If I had a brick for every time I've repeated the phrase Q.S.C.&V. (Quality, Service, Cleanliness and Value) I think I'd probably be able to bridge the Atlantic Ocean with them." (RAY KROC)

Digital Equipment Corp. "Growth is not our principal goal. Our goal is to be a quality organization and do a quality job, which means that we will be proud of our work and our product for years to come. As we achieve quality, growth comes as a result." (Digital Corporate Philosophy)

Maytag. "Maytag built its reputation on solid dependability, not jazziness. . . . It makes things good and simple"

(PETERS and WATERMAN, *In Search of Excellence*)

"Ten years trouble-free operation." (Maytag)

Hewlett-Packard. "A quality focus is ubiquitous at HP because the employees don't seem to be able to separate it from anything else they are doing. If you ask them about personnel, they talk quality. If you ask them about field sales, they talk quality. If you ask them about management-by-objectives, they talk about quality-by-objectives."

(PETERS and WATERMAN, *In Search of Excellence*)

Schlumberger. "While sometimes a competitor will be first with a given item, when Schlumberger introduces the product, it will be more complete and of better quality."

(*Dun's Review*)

The overriding themes that pervade these successful, well-known corporations are the same elements mandatory to victory with any product. Entrepreneurs who manufacture, produce, or sell an item must instill this fervor for excellence from top to bottom. This is the mortar that holds together a winning enterprise.

It also makes sense to mention that our economy continues to move away from production, manufacturing, and capital-intensive types of industry. Experts tell us not to worry about this trend (tell that to the mayors of northern cities). However, entrepreneurial solutions to the problems of our basic industries and the accompanying social spin-offs may well be the most lucrative market gap in America today.

The problems of declining industry represent just one of the many distresses afflicting mankind. The energy crisis, food shortages, economic recession, population burdens, exhaustion of resources, pollution, unemployment, and other limitations to growth supposedly mandate our imminent decline. In reality they offer the greatest opportunities to the most imaginative venturers. Your small start-up may eventually come to grips with one of these massive dilemmas.

Edwin Land, founder of Polaroid, said, "Work only on problems that are manifestly important and seem to be nearly impossible to solve. That way you will have a natural market for your product and no competition."

When you hatch your first fragile idea for your own undertaking, you are vulnerable to many forces that will break down your resolve. In fact, that's as far as most people ever get—a frail, momentary conception.

A neighbor, laid off from his job, considered taking over a local service station. He had a pleasant personality and would likely have flourished. When approached on the deal, he rolled it over in his mind until his wife insisted that he could *never* run a gas station. Of course, he never did. He heeded her advice and settled for a career as a delivery boy.

Remember that when people offer advice, whether or not solicited, they predicate their conclusions on how your idea affects them. When you ask people, "What do you think of my idea?" *the answer will be based on their perception of whether your idea and its implications are good or bad for them.*

Robert L. Shook, writing in his book *The Entrepreneurs,* summed it up as follows:

> The first requirement for any individual about to embark on a new business venture is a strong conviction about his concepts. In all probability, most of his well-meaning friends and relatives will try to discourage him. Mary Kay Ash invested her life's savings in Mary Kay Cosmetics when she and her husband founded the company in 1963. A month later he died, and she was advised by her attorney to liquidate the business immediately and recoup whatever cash there was or she would be left without a cent. Her accountant advised her that the company's commission structure made success impossible, and he too recommended that she quickly dispose of the new business. Rather strong warnings. . . . for a newly widowed woman to receive. Had she listened to their advice, one of America's leading cosmetics firms would never have been more than a dream.
>
> Another widow, in her early twenties, was given practically identical advice when she was about to open her first service station. "Everyone advised me not to go into business," Mary Hudson [Hudson Oil Company] recalls. "Of course, this was back in 1934, and we were right in the middle of the depression, with unemployment around 12 percent. In those days women weren't supposed to work." A local businessman told her, "Look, little girl, during the

past year this station was opened and closed twice. Now, if those smart men could not be successful, I'm sure you're going to fail. And you don't look like you can afford to lose your money at this point in your life."

Such strong warnings would discourage many people in similar circumstances.

Nevertheless, she plunged ahead. She built small station buildings, stressed low prices, mid-block locations, wide driveway, and good lighting, and outsold—three to one—the majors, who eventually copied many of her innovations.

An entrepreneur's conviction is often such that he or she is willing to risk financial ruin if the new business venture fails. Robert L. Shook asks, "Why were these individuals willing to assume such great personal risk? They had conviction. They knew they would succeed. And, although some of them had failed in previous ventures, none would ever accept permanent defeat. They were too resilient to be conquered by discouragement. Joe Sugarman (JS&A) shows this when he talks about an early business failure: "That was just one of my incredibly big disappointments. There were other times I felt so sure that I was about to become a millionaire that I started reading the classified ads for mansions and picked up brochures on Cadillacs. Then in the next moment I would totally lose the dream. I would be back to zero and have to start all over again. Thank God I was able to bounce back."

Time and again, in the formulation of my start-ups, I faltered and became fearful when advised that somebody else was planning or already doing what I intended to do, or had tried it and flopped. That is the kind of ongoing input a new entrepreneur lives with and eventually must learn to ignore. *Remember that on any new venture you start someone will bring you news of a company already doing what you're planning to do.* Shake it off! They will never duplicate exactly what you are attempting.

If people aren't telling you you're too late, they're telling you your idea won't work. In one of the most understated and inspiring commentaries ever written, Henry Ford described his entry into the auto business:

The Edison Company offered me the general superintendency of the company, but only on condition that I would give up my gas engine and devote myself to something really useful. I had to choose between my job and my automobile. . . . I quit my job on August 15, 1899, and went into the automobile business.

It might be thought something of a step, for I had no personal funds. What money was left over from living was all used in experimenting. But my wife agreed that the automobile could not be given up—that we had to make or break.

There was no "demand" for automobiles. . . . At first the "horseless carriage" was considered merely a freak notion and many wise people explained with particularity why it could never be more than a toy. No man of money even thought of it as a commercial possibility . . . there was hardly anyone who sensed that the automobile could be a large factor in industry.

There, in the humble reflections of the man who changed the world as much as anybody and who built its greatest industry, unfolds the drama of every new entrepreneur. It takes great courage to strike out on your own. But if the world thought the automobile was a joke, how much credence should you give to those who disparage your ideas?

If the greatest entrepreneurs of our past, such as Henry Ford, could give you personal advice, they would sound surprisingly similar. These great business pioneers would tell you that to become a successful entrepreneur you must not be overly concerned about what others think of you or your ideas. Most of these men gravitated to large cities where they had a certain anonymity. They were not easily influenced by the negative comments of others, nor did they fear criticism of the novelty of their concepts. To become an entrepreneur, you must shrug off the fear of being gossiped about and ridiculed. *The favorite subject of mankind is the shortcomings of others.* You might as well be talked about for doing something new with your life.

A singular quality that all these entrepreneurs had was the ability to think a bit differently from those around them. They would all tell you that if just once you hold a thought in your mind contrary to popular belief and act on it, and make it work, you will never think the same way again. Do one little thing that others scoff at or discourage, and you are changed forever. You will think differently about everything. That was the key to Thomas Edison's incredible string of inventions. He always thought in terms of things never before done. His thoughts were outside popular prejudice, sentiments, and beliefs. *Do just once what others say you can't do, and you will never pay attention to their limitations again.*

Some of the best advice that insurance magnate James S. Kemper, founder of the Kemper Companies, was ever given came from his grandfather: "When you see most of your associates or most of your contemporaries or competitors in business or most of the people of the country headed in one direction, go off by yourself in some quiet place, preferably the sort of place where you can commune with nature, and ask yourself this question—'Why are they going in *that* direction—Is it the *right direction?*' "

You are always going to be faced with advice on why something won't work. You have to go ahead and do what others discourage you from doing. You have to believe that you can accomplish what others can't or won't.

Adolph Ochs, the entrepreneur who built *The New York Times,* stressed the simple virtues it takes to make it when he said, "Success you discover is won simply by practicing the ordinary virtues—hard work, intelligence, enthusiasm, self-reliance, honesty. The resources of this country are so illimitable, the opportunities so innumerable, and the means for educating and equipping one's self so plentiful, waste and neglect so prevalent, that there is really little excuse for failing to attain not only dollars-and-cents success, but success in the fullest sense of the term."

The great entrepreneurs of the past would also tell you that you will be sorely tested. The founders of new ventures must undergo spells of adversity. These experiences tax your willingness to keep going. They force you to persist and have faith. They build inner strengths of profound worth. No man or woman can achieve greatly without suffering through these bitter bouts of adversity.

You need some sort of inspirational, guiding philosophy to

start out as an entrepreneur and most of all to keep going. I suggest several of the books by Napoleon Hill, a writer who spent twenty years studying the great entrepreneurs of his time. From his studies of business personalities, such as Ford and Carnegie, he concluded that success followed predictable and distinct patterns. He suggested that all men and women have similar options open to them. He argued that great success and achievement are available to any and all who choose to follow certain requirements that he spelled out clearly in his writing.

I have no special talents, and in high school I was far below average. I believe that the writings of Hill sparked my rise, changing the way I thought about my inadequacies and removing many self-imposed limitations. I have no other explanation for the startling success of a person who had been so mediocre.

SUMMARY

Once you have an idea for a new business, write it up as a plan. This will serve as an outline for the future.

A budget should identify how much money you will need for a year's operation. Then you must raise the money. Finding capital to start a new venture is easier than you think. You must make investors believe in you, and they must see in you a large profit opportunity.

If you start small, you have nowhere to go but up. It takes much less money than starting big and enables you to master every fundamental of your business.

You need a good attorney early on. There are a number of options for you to decide about your new company. I recommend, however, that you stay a private corporation.

A partner can be an asset early in your business career. However, partnerships generally wind down over time. At a certain period, you can get along without a partner. Some of the best, long-lasting partnerships couple an inventor or scientist with a sales or management type.

One of the first things you must do in your start-up is to find information. You must learn about competitors, pricing, marketing, and distribution, to name a few things. The telephone will do this for you.

Your fragile idea for a new enterprise will quickly become the subject of ridicule from those around you. It has always been so. No sane person thought Henry Ford's invention could be anything more than a gimmick. You are in good company when your idea draws doubt or scorn.

4.
How to Develop and Run Your New Company

Business is never so healthy as when, like a chicken, it must do a certain amount of scratching for what it gets.

—HENRY FORD

Once you have started a company, you must then keep it going and manage it. Mastering the fundamentals of your business allows you to hire others to handle these tasks. Added sales volume leads to new people and expansion. Part of your ever-growing job will be to hire, train, and supervise new employees. Ultimately, when your company flourishes, you will have special people to handle these functions, but in the early stages it will be up to you.

Most well-known success stories follow a formula of hiring others to do jobs initially handled by the pioneering founder. Two of the world's richest men, John MacArthur (perhaps the first billionaire) and positive thinker W. Clement Stone, both founded life insurance companies. They sold the first policies themselves and hired others to emulate their trailblazing. They learned the fundamentals and then taught others how to sell their product.

Along the way they also learned much about hiring, training, and human behavior. Henry Ford thought these lessons about human nature were the "one principle which a man must follow if he wished to succeed."

A business writer once referred to the initial set of employees in a new venture as the "founders' team." That has a certain glamorous ring, ripe with commitment. In reality, nobody ever has as much intensity or concern as the founder. Furthermore, a high percentage of your team will inevitably desert, move on, or be fired.

A salesman of mine once came in to shake hands and say good-bye before going to work for one of my competitors. He thanked me for the opportunity to work and learn at my company. I replied that our relationship was really fifty-fifty, a two-way street. The modern employer-employee relationship is one of mutual and very near equal benefit. When my employee walked out the door, I didn't owe him anything; neither did he owe me. He had exchanged his time and labor for compensation and learning. We had both benefited.

Some of your employees will stay with you for the duration. The highest percentage by far, however, will find other opportunities. At certain times, some will be extremely valuable and at other times, expendable. Some will rise under your tutelage, others will fall. A few will drift into bad work habits or develop personal problems that interfere with their jobs. Others will become dissatisfied and demanding. Ultimately, some will go out against you as direct competitors.

Employees, like entrepreneurs, pursue their own self-interest. You are their vehicle, and they yours. The best human relations are mutually self-serving. The extent of your concern for them is generally repaid in the degree of their loyalty to you.

Employees are the lifeblood of your enterprise. They make it go. Some will serve as your right arm, or will move mountains for you—you could not achieve the same success without them. Yet, none is indispensable. All serve their own masters first. If that appraisal sounds too harsh, remember that from this partnership of self-interest springs feelings of care and concern. The loss of good employees can bring you sorrow and melancholy. Some of the saddest moments in the infancy of my company came when my best secretaries left to follow their husbands who were transferred away.

The best way for a start-up company to find personnel is through an employment agency. My firm developed a good relationship with one by happenstance. Were I to do it over again, I would screen a few of these agencies and allow them to present arguments for contracting their service. They should be strong in selecting applicants most suitable for your needs. They do this by testing and interviewing. They should not throw just anybody at you. Some, however, are enormously aggressive and put their placement needs in front of your special requirements. You want bright, energetic people whose talents and experience fit your job description. The right person at the right agency can accomplish this for you.

In times of economic stress you may be able to forgo the expense of an agency. More people than usual are looking for jobs. A well-written want ad can bring good results.

You need to interview these first applicants with an eye to your needs. My company doesn't necessarily hire based on an armload of educational credentials, but intelligence does rank at the top of desirable qualities. A simple written test of twenty-five questions (math, spelling, general knowledge, business terms) can give you important insights into your prospective employees. Naturally, there are exceptions. Not all jobs require whiz kids.

A brief discussion with applicants can give you a few rough clues about their merits—whether they are extroverts or introverts, slow or quick. You can quickly appraise their general appearance and bearing. A high percentage of applicants will be suitable for most jobs. From the best of these hirings will come your future managers and superstars.

David Ogilvy instructed his staff, "If you hire people who are bigger than you are, Ogilvy & Mather will become a company of giants; if you hire people who are less than you are, we shall become a company of dwarfs."

It may be that the best employees and the highest caliber work force follow the innovative, fast-growing companies. In the 1920s it was the automobile business. Today it may be high technology or breakthrough consumer and financial companies.

In a growing entrepreneurial company, you can seldom bring in an outsider to fit a specific job. Nobody has experience that exactly parallels the tasks your company requires. All jobs have subtle but significant differences from company to company, even if they bear the same title. I once hired an outside expert with a pile of credentials, whose only interest turned out to be where he would eat lunch. I couldn't get rid of him fast enough.

Henry Ford preferred amateurs to experts. When the company needed a metallurgy expert, he pointed to a worker sweeping the floor and instructed his managers to make him the company metallurgist. Oddly enough, that individual went on to become a highly regarded authority on metals. Henry Ford distrusted outside experts: "The moment one gets into the expert state of mind, a great number of things become impossible." He believed experts were too familiar with the reasons that something couldn't be done. For several decades, Ford operated in an entrepreneurial mode defined by economist Joseph Schumpeter as the ability to "act with confidence beyond the range of familiar beacons."

An entrepreneur should generate a truly fabulous work environment with an immensely favorable climate of opportunity, advancement, and personal growth. When given a chance, most people fit into the job. They respond, grow, and master the task. Progress and excitement are all part of an entrepreneurial company. The people within such a concern meet and conquer every challenge. Wimps become giants. Average souls spin out stellar feats and worthwhile accomplishments.

For every newcomer and outside professional who came to us, an equivalent number within the company was promoted or took on difficult new responsibilities. An entrepreneurial organization always holds out the promise of challenge and advancement to current staffers.

In my company, telephone operators became brokers, shipping clerks advanced to managers, and secretaries turned into vice-presidents. In half a decade, four-figure incomes became six figures. The talented, the ambitious, the extra-milers flourished. They fostered excellence and drubbed the competition. As the company grew, so did they. Expertise originated from within, spurred by the crucible of dizzying growth.

The ability to assess people for employment takes no special talent. An interview gives you only a superficial glimpse into the character of the applicant. Consequently, you make some mistakes. Experience helps. The obvious measures of background, references, and testing results superimposed on your general intuition in the interview generally work out well.

Always check your applicants' references. Many companies make only a superficial background check. You should dig a little deeper. At the very least, talk with past employers. Make all new hirees pass a physical at a nearby clinic. You will reduce your workmen's compensation rates if you don't hire chronic back problems. These days a chemical-dependency check can also save you considerable grief. Earlier in this century generous unemployment and worker's compensation benefits were nonexistent. Today they have an impact on your employment tactics. Your worker's compensation rate will go up if you hire injury-prone workers. Unemployment charges cut into your profits if you hire people who get fired or quit so they can laze around and draw benefits. Your hospitalization insurance rates will soar if a few employees are prone to sickness or injury. We are still paying for a typist who hurt her back several years ago. She claims she can never work again.

In some cases, you are competing with government assistance programs for workers. Many people who receive free government checks turn up their noses at low-paying, entry-level positions. I once had an employee quit a good-paying sales job after one week, refusing his paycheck because it might have interrupted his unemployment benefits. A few decades ago, he would have had no choice but to stick to the job and earn a living.

You will see a number of applicants who know they can fall back on the government. They will frequently quit soon after employed. They will come in late, have little discipline, and show no real interest in their work. A number seem to have significant problems with chemical dependency. The dole allows them to get along despite these problems. They need not take the remedies that a competitive world would force on them.

These safety nets lead to reduced productivity. They erode discipline in the work force. They weaken resolve and character. One of the best ways to solve this problem is to pay exceedingly high wages, providing your entry-level workers enough incentive to shun the enticements offered by the government.

Employees don't always have to come to you through normal channels. I like to keep my eye out for exceptional people everywhere. One summer day several years ago my car had a flat along a highway bordering a large northern Minnesota lake. There were no gas stations among the cabins along the route, so I pulled into a resort. My mechanical ability is such that a tire repair is a major trauma to me. I once had a car fall off its jack, and on another occasion had to walk for help because I couldn't jack the car down. At the resort, all parties regarded my plight with total indifference. Furthermore, when I attempted to take off the hubcap, a special antitheft locking device foiled me.

Suddenly, a kid on a motorbike pulled up. Within moments he volunteered to help and was soon at work reading the manual, mastering the antitheft device, and changing the tire. My gratitude was immense, and I gave him a handsome tip. Then I invited him to apply for a job at my company should he ever wish to do so.

Weeks later we hired him as our part-time custodian and maintenance boy while he finished high school. He stayed with the job for a year or so after graduation, and now, after pestering me for six months, has become one of our brokers. The chance to reward merit and give people an opportunity brings a high degree of personal satisfaction.

A somewhat puzzling factor in our expansion and hiring was the fact that whenever we needed a particular task done, someone inevitably showed up. I have no logical or sound explanation why it is that time after time when I needed a special talent, a rare individual or special person to get the job done, that person turned up. Some blossomed from within the company and others seemed to appear magically on our doorstep. I am convinced this same phenomenon must extend to all who are striving to build a vital enterprise.

When I needed to incorporate my present company a decade ago, I met a jack-of-all-trades by the name of Jesse Cornish, who would incorporate you for one-third the cost of an attorney. (It is a poor policy to forgo legal help and advice.) A former African trader and raconteur, Jesse would later become a vice-president of my company and gain national recognition as an investment speaker and media personality.

In my darkest hour, Jesse came through for me. The precious-metals business had sunk from sight in 1975, and with the energy crisis only a year old, as previously mentioned, I had jumped into the wood-burning stove business. A metal works contracted to build our first twenty-five steel-plated stoves. In the meantime, I had lined up orders to sell all the stoves. Unfortunately, they had to be delivered to many different states and as we were in dire financial straits, we had to collect the money for each one upon delivery. I turned to Jesse for help. He rented a big van and loaded up the heavy wood burners. Alone, in heavy winter weather all the way, he wound through ten states, wrestled out the four-hundred-pound stoves and collected the money for every one. We were good for another sixty days.

All new human relationships go through a brief honeymoon period. Everyone is on his or her best behavior. Both parties have a tendency to see the other with rose-tinted shades. Inevitably, reality seeps into the affair and human frailties and weaknesses are registered. All employees will have at least one major flaw and likely a few lesser ones. Poor employees may have even more drawbacks. There are no perfect people. You will inevitably spot this weakness or characteristic in your employees and generally excuse or work around it. Your employees are making the same adjustments to your shortcomings.

Since the honeymoon period exists also in relationships other than employee-employer, it can provide you with important clues to the future of all your dealings. If you are contemplating a new business alliance with someone and early on there are misunderstandings or erratic behavior, you should reconsider. Relationships seldom get better. They degenerate further and bad traits are seen even more vividly later. I have backed away from a pending deal when only a slight flaw popped out in the other person. If you spot aberrations and inconsistencies during the honeymoon period, you are seeing the tip of the behavioral iceberg.

With certain new employees, it is wise to make an employment contract mandatory. This rule applies to salespersons or others who have access to formulas, secrets, and especially to customers. Many such contracts contain noncompete clauses that attempt to prohibit your employees from eventually going into competition against you or working for a competitor. These clauses are difficult to enforce and seem undemocratic. Consequently, we forgo any attempts to thwart former employees from competing. Competition keeps you sharp. Entities devoid of competition (bureaucracy and monopoly) are generally wasteful and arbitrary and render poor service. You shouldn't fear competition nor should you attempt to strangle it.

No would-be competitor, however, should have the right to customer lists, trade secrets, or new technologies developed on your payroll. An employment contract should protect what is yours; no more and no less.

Employment contracts, as well as all other agreements, should be composed by your attorney. Some entrepreneurs draft their own documents. Others rely on verbal agreements and handshakes. There are subtleties and nuances in even the simplest, most basic written agreements that require legal supervision and drafting. Although it appears cheaper to do it yourself, it's a sophomoric business practice that invariably backfires at the very worst times.

An incalculable number of deals are agreed to and never put down on paper. These arrangements have a much higher chance of winding up in the tank. No two participants totally communicate the exact nature of their understanding. Opinions differ, memories fail, perceptions vary, and acrimony inevitably breaks out. Unless your purpose is to have a loose and cloudy arrangement subject to misunderstanding, legal counsel should pin down in a contract the exact nature and scope of your agreement. Otherwise you will not be able to enforce your right to what is justly yours. Verbal deals are amateur deals. A written contract keeps the other side straight. If you are going to be in business, you are going to have to operate smart to succeed. Let counsel spell it out for you.

Get into the habit of passing all important documents and agreements by your attorney before signing them. Never ink a contract without counsel's approval, no matter how toothless you think it is.

Send copies of important correspondence, advertising, and corporate policy to your attorney routinely. Counsel will not only ensure you get your just desserts but keep you out of trouble so you can enjoy them.

No less a mogul than Ray Kroc violated these commonsense principles when he made a deal with the McDonald brothers to franchise their drive-ins across America.

In his book, *Grinding It Out,* Kroc relates an eventful meeting with the McDonald brothers who had started a single fast-food outlet in California.

> So I asked Dick McDonald—when he wondered aloud who they'd get to open a lot of similar restaurants for them— "What about me?" The response seemed to surprise him and his brother momentarily. But then they brightened and began discussing this proposal with increasing enthusiasm. Before long we decided to get their lawyer involved and draw up an agreement.
>
> In the course of this conversation I learned that the brothers had licensed ten other drive-ins, including two in Arizona. I had no interest in those, but I would have rights to franchise copies of their operations everywhere else in the United States. The buildings would have to be exactly like the new one their architect had drawn up with the golden arches. The name, McDonald's, would be on all of them, of course, and I was one hundred percent in favor of that. I had a feeling that it would be one of those promotable names that would catch the public fancy. I was for the contractual clauses that obligated me to follow their plans down to the last detail, too—even to signs and menus. But I should have been more cautious there. The agreement was that I could not deviate from their plans in my units unless the changes were spelled out in writing, signed by both brothers, and sent to me by registered mail. This seemingly innocuous requirement created massive problems for me. There's an old saying that a man who represents himself has a fool for a lawyer, and it certainly applied in this instance. I was just carried away by the thought of McDonald's drive-ins proliferating like rabbits with eight Multimixers in each one. Also, I was swayed by the affable openness of the McDonald brothers. The meeting was extremely cordial. I trusted them from the outset. That trust later would turn to bristling suspicion. But I had no inkling of that eventuality.

When you rely on somebody else's attorney to draw up a deal while you represent yourself, you are making a colossal blunder. Kroc goes on:

My troubles started the minute I got together with my contractor and went over with him the plans furnished by the McDonalds' architect. That structure was designed for a semi-desert location. It was on a slab, no basement and it had a swamp cooler on the roof. "Where am I going to put the furnace, Mr. Kroc?" he asked. "Damned if I know. What do you suggest?"

He suggested a basement, pointing out that other arrangements would be far less efficient and that I would need a basement for storage anyhow. I couldn't just leave my potatoes outdoors as the McDonalds did, for example, and there was no room for a back building on this lot, even if I'd wanted one, which I didn't.

So I called the McDonald boys and told them about my problem. "Well, sure you need a basement," they said. "So build one."

I reminded them that I had to have it documented by a registered letter. They pooh-poohed it; said it was all right to go ahead, they weren't much good at writing letters and they couldn't afford to hire a secretary. Actually they probably could have hired the entire typing pool at IBM if they'd had a mind to. I hung up hoping that they would have second thoughts and send me written confirmation, but they never did.

It was a messy way to start, being in default on the first unit, but there was no choice. I went ahead with the building, telling myself that when I got breathing space I would fly out to see the McDonalds and get all the contractual wrinkles ironed out at once. That would have worked, had the McDonalds been reasonable men. Instead, they were obtuse, they were utterly indifferent to the fact that I was putting every cent I had and all I could borrow into this project. When we sat down with our lawyers in attendance, the brothers acknowledged the problems, but refused to write a single letter that would permit me to make changes.

"We have told you by telephone that you may go ahead

and alter the plans as we discussed," said their attorney, Frank Cotter. "But the contract calls for a registered letter. If Mr. Kroc does not have that, he is put in jeopardy," said my counsel.

"That's your problem."

It was almost as though they were hoping I would fail. This was a peculiar attitude for them to take because the more successful the franchising, the more money they would make. My attorney gave up on the situation. I hired another and he quit, too, saying I was plain crazy to continue under such conditions. He could not protect me if the McDonalds should close in on me. So I said, "Let them try," and I plunged ahead.

Misunderstandings that lead to legal hassles are common in business. From time to time you may be forced to sue somebody. You will, no doubt, be subjected to similar attacks.

My attorney always makes the other guy's lawsuit sound so potent, as though I might be clamped into the electric chair momentarily. My suits, however, always seem weak and shaky.

I once called an attorney in Florida who welched on a large order and caused us a $25,000 loss. I told him I would report him to the Florida Bar Association if he didn't pay. Then we sued him. Before it was over, I wound up, on the advice of various lawyers, paying him $9,000. My threat to report him to his association constituted extortion.

With today's crowded dockets, a suit is seldom tried before two years roll by. When our phone equipment failed incessantly and caused enormous problems, I replaced the system and refused to make any more payments. The phone company sued. Several years later they settled for one-third of the original amount. That's the way it works in today's legal system.

A dentist cheated us out of $24,000 on a large trade he'd welched on. We sued. When the case came up two years later, the judge ruled it wasn't in his jurisdiction. We appealed for another year. If we sue in the dentist's home state, it will be another two years. The whole system is slow, tedious, and somewhat slovenly.

The best advice on legal hassles comes from Harvey Firestone:

Settling disputes through the course of the law has never appealed to me as a pastime. Lawsuits are not only expensive, but they do not, and cannot, settle anything which could not be better and more quickly settled through putting all the cards on the table and having a frank talk. A man who wants justice does not often have to go to the courts to get it. In fact, he will compromise with something less than justice to keep out of court. A fair man is drawn into court only when the other side refuses to face the facts. I avoided a lawsuit with a company by going to the president and saying:

"You and I know all the facts and we ought to be able to make a better settlement than any judge and jury, because they will only know such facts as we tell them. And in addition to that, we shall have our lawyers to pay. If we go to law, we shall drag along for several years and in the end, no matter which one of us gets the verdict, both of us will lose. Why not put everything right down on paper now, and strike a balance?"

One last piece of advice about legal counsel: when you are in trouble, or are a one-time client, or have an emergency, you should get a firm cost estimate. In times of high anxiety and troubles some attorneys maximize their charges. Keep close tabs on the hours and the rate.

Another tool that forestalls misunderstandings and ensures smooth, professional operations is the heavy usage of written correspondence. Use letters to frame early dialogues that lead to agreements, verify preliminary understandings, cover minor matters, and clarify a host of business circumstances. A letter is a record. A good entrepreneur writes a lot of them. They are the simplest and best way to cover a magnitude of corporate affairs.

Telephone communications have obvious importance and need significant managerial attention. There is nothing more basic in business than good telephone manners. Nevertheless, the frequency of the rude and indifferent treatment on the telephone that all of us experience is astonishing. The first introduction of a potential customer or client to your company often comes on the phone. Outline an answering routine that highlights enthusiastic politeness and stresses "please" and "thank you." If this seems elementary and obvious, try to provide a consistently upbeat answering routine and you will find how difficult it can be. You must train, preach, and admonish. Make politeness on the telephone a hallmark of your company from day one.

The following letter from one of our customers verifies that clients take note of phone service:

> I recently placed my first order with your company, and I want to pass on an observation. There are few experiences left which I classify as a "brighten-your-day" kind of event. Even fewer which would cause me to sit down and write a letter and persuade my wife to type it. However, I did have one such experience in my dealing with IRI. I have spent thirty-four years in business in administration and supervisory positions. During these years I've made my proportionate share of phone calls. I believe the conversation with the telephone operator is a vital part of every contact. It, to a large degree, sets the tone and climate in which an ensuing conversation is carried on. My observation is this: that the young lady or ladies who make this initial client contact for your company are, in my opinion, unexcelled. They are courteous, gracious, efficient, very professional and perceptive. I have a very peculiar name. On two occasions I have given my name and number for a return call. In each instance the operator replied to the effect "I'll give him the message, Mr. McEachern," without once asking me to repeat the name. I have some reasonably close friends that I've known for years who can't pronounce it properly! It's a real tribute to these operators that in the three / four seconds you are in conversation with them they have an ability or personality that creates the feeling that one is dealing with a real class organization. I don't know how one quantifies the relative contribution of this function to an organization, but if you could I'll bet you'd be surprised.

I once paid a visit to a particularly obnoxious government bureaucracy, where slackness and indifference were pervasive. The phones rang incessantly and went unanswered. Finally, in frustration, I asked why someone didn't answer the telephone.

They were insulted by my inquiry, but explained they were understaffed. "Take them off the hook, then," I replied. "There's a person on the other end." Needless to say, our meeting failed to accomplish much.

In my company, a phone will never ring more than three times. With a trained ear, you can hear someone's phone ringing across the corridor and down the hall. If you have to, go answer it yourself. That will soon solve the problem. Phones should be off the hook or the switchboard should be able to advise immediately when no one is there. Remember, common sense is not so common, and your customers can easily be put off by a ringing phone that someone in your company ignores.

Anyone calling at your company in person should also receive a warm greeting. They should all be made to feel that you are glad they are there. I love to walk through my waiting room and find several smiling people chatting with a gracious receptionist—that's pure class.

Many of these visitors will be salespeople who want to see you. I try not to turn anyone away. When I was a young salesman, I vowed that should the situation reverse, I would be receptive to all callers. In the early period of your enterprise you pick up much valuable information from salespersons and can acquire products and services that help you. Later on, you can steer these solicitors to your managers. For the same reasons, you should also talk with all who call you by telephone. As your enterprise becomes larger, however, you will have no choice but to have your phone calls screened. As a company grows, you are forced to sacrifice a measure of outside contact.

One type of incoming call that you can never be too busy to answer originates from customers. Charles Revson, the founder of Revlon, would take a call from a customer no matter how full his schedule. While other calls stacked up, Revson would chat with a woman in the Midwest about a tube of lipstick. Besides coating over complaints and soothing livid customers, fielding gripes is a powerful management tool.

Early in the life of a business, you can personally ask for the complaint calls. Later you can use devices that direct these irritations to you. I ask my customers in all our mailings to write to me if they are not totally satisfied with my company's service. My customers know they can count on me if they have a gripe.

The complaint card used by hotels and restaurants is another effective vehicle to steer problems to your attention. Walter P. Marriott, founder of Marriott Inns, read every single complaint card from all hotels and motels until he was into his eighties.

When you begin your transactions, include a postage-paid customer complaint card addressed to you. You don't need compliments—limit the card to complaints. Follow this practice and you will have the most effective management tool yet devised at your fingertips. This is the way to perfect your company no matter how big or how small. For executives who take over the management of a firm, this is the quickest imaginable way to get a handle on its weaknesses.

If your product or service doesn't lend itself to complaint cards, then devise some other method to see that customer complaints are directed to you. They pinpoint problems in your organization. You can go right to the source of your difficulty and solve it. A more powerful insight into the failings of your company does not exist. Furthermore, when you take a complaint to heart and mollify the client, you save a customer and stimulate powerful word-of-mouth from an ardent new fan.

The president and guiding force behind Sears, Roebuck, Julius Rosenwald, was at his desk when a department manager walked in carrying a ragged sweater. He said it had been knitted by a woman who'd ordered the wool from Sears and she'd sent it to the company with a complaint about the quality of the material. She said that her husband had worn the sweater for only eighteen months and that its present condition indicated that the materials sent by Sears were faulty. The manager asked what to do.

Rosenwald said he should send her another consignment of wool. He also dictated a letter to the woman expressing his personal regret that she had wasted so much time knitting a sweater that proved unsatisfactory. He enclosed a check for five dollars that he said he hoped would partly reimburse her for her labor.

The woman was from a community of only three hundred residents. Business for Sears had never amounted to more than fifty dollars a year from the whole town. But the following year receipts from the town were more than nine hundred dollars.

Never be afraid of your customers. Meet problems with them head-on. If you can't deliver as promised, be up-front about it and let them know. One of the key differences between a winner and a loser is how customers are handled during problems and crises. A casualty insurance agent I once knew could never bring himself to advise his policyholders forthrightly when they didn't have coverage for a loss. He would put off, backtrack, or otherwise delay giving his clients the bad news. By the time they found out, they would be so angry they would cancel their policies with him. If he had gone directly to them and conveyed that their policy excluded coverage for such a loss, they would have understood. He reacted like a loser. Handle your problems promptly and directly or they become far larger.

Fear of customers reflects itself in other ways. One of the basics of business relates to the manner in which you collect the money owed you. If you don't get it up-front, it becomes an accounts receivable. Volumes have been written about collecting accounts receivables. Printed notices and dunning formulas, which help you collect, are for sale. If you fail to bring in your receivables because of sloppiness, procrastination, or careless management, you court financial doom. You must become a tenacious collector.

A common reason for poor collections may be fear of the client. This is especially true of a large and important account. There's a tendency not to press the "big guys" for fear of ruffling them so much that they drop your services. You are intimidated to the extent that you allow them to use your money. Should they go under, however, you go down with them.

My dad was a great accounts receivable manager and collector. He would put handwritten notes on every overdue bill for small amounts. On larger accounts he would call on the phone, always getting a promise for at least a partial payment. He could differentiate between the deadbeats and those with the temporary shorts and was adroit at using whatever leverage he could apply. He would threaten cancellation or plead for help. "Get the money," he would emphasize to me. He knew that in collecting receivables, "the wheel that squeaks gets the grease," and his wheel squeaked with a persistent clamor.

A large furniture manufacturing firm comprised one-quarter of the premium volume of his small insurance agency. When it failed to pay within thirty days, he offered them a premium financing option which they refused. He had the guts to cancel all their policies and sacrifice this big and valuable account. The furniture firm came back to him and arranged for reinstatement. This time they paid. Before the year was out, they unexpectedly filed bankruptcy. Had he not collected the premiums but ridden along with the big receivable, he would surely have been out of business too.

Fear of losing customers manifests itself in an even more important way—reluctance to charge enough for your product or service. A surprising number of start-ups choose to operate on the cheap. They are afraid they won't get business unless they practically give away their wares. Under no circumstances are you going to get all the business. Thus, you should not be afraid to miss some. It is far better to do a smaller volume at a good profit than a larger volume at a minimal profit. It is entirely possible to operate with good, solid profit margins and, by dint of good service and quality, capture a dominant position in your line. In fact, a lion-sized market share will become even more possible in time because the cushion of past profits protects a company from future recessions and slumps. When others fail, you survive.

Why operate for less than a generous profit? You deserve to be paid well for your efforts. All good companies take down a fair margin of profit. When I structured IRI to be a national retailer of gold and silver, I used a commission schedule that, although not excessive, allowed me to profit. Often we were told that our products could be purchased cheaper elsewhere. Some dealers temporarily thrived on paper-thin margins. One day the band stopped playing, and the volume died off. One by one those low-margin dealers failed. They had no cushion.

Every business makes mistakes, squandering some profits in the good times, making a few costly blunders. These errors and impracticalities, when coupled with a shrinking volume and a constant overhead, are more than many firms can tolerate. If they have not storehoused some capital to build reserves, to secure a level of financial insurance that protects against the hazards of a slump or a falling business cycle, they will fail.

Any business is fraught with devilish twists that could suddenly devastate profits. That is why solid margins are needed. If you are afraid to secure the markups necessary to wind up with a positive bottom line, you won't last through the inevitable downturns. Furthermore, all sales don't stick: orders are returned, payments don't come in, goods are faulty—the list is endless. I can preach this ever so important business practice and those who need to apply it most will read it and rationalize why they can't raise prices. If you can't charge enough to moth-ball some money, what value has such a timid enterprise?

Set your profit margin first. Then add your operating expenses (difficult to do with a new product). Have an amount in mind that you want to make on each line or on each dollar of business, preferably expressed in percentages. Naturally, you can't get too far out of sync with the market. Your competition's pricing and charges will provide guidelines. On similar products or services you should be priced at or slightly above the average. You don't want to charge the highest or the lowest prices. It isn't mandatory to beat the competition's price, but you must beat their service and quality.

Your accountant should be able to assist you with these early decisions on your company's pricing policy. In fact, you'll need to rely on your accountant for a host of information on balance sheets, operating statements, cash flow, and other useful yardsticks of your company's progress. There's a lot you don't know about this specialty, even if you've studied it.

Expect your accountant to sit down over the course of several days and give you a graphic, thoroughgoing explanation of the rudiments of finance. Too many business beginners want to appear knowledgeable and so refuse to ask basic questions about accounting. Entrepreneurs who succeed in a big way can't afford to bluff. If you wear your accountant out with questions, you will capture much useful information.

Your accountant should also provide you with sound tax advice. You must be familiar with Internal Revenue Service requirements for payroll taxes, reports, and other claims on your enterprise. They begin on your first day of business. Allow your accountant to acquaint you with these necessary procedures and the fail-safe means of implementing them. A lot of people are going to assume you know all this hocus-pocus. That's how you get into trouble. Ask!

When profits eventually roll in, your accountant really earns the seemingly exorbitant charges levied on you. Within the framework of the tax law your CPA firm should be creative and flexible. Your objective is to pass on to the government as little as possible and to keep the maximum amount allowed within your control.

From my perspective, a small accounting firm serves a start-up best. You want someone who will consider you an important client and who wishes to grow along with you. Certainly, you can establish relations with individual accountants in large firms, but they tend to court large, established companies. Furthermore, you will be frequently subjected to personnel changes in a large firm. A relationship with an accountant should be nurtured and grow in much the same way as that with your legal counsel. They should be long-term arrangements.

Accountants tend to be direct opposites of entrepreneurs. They are cautious, skeptical, rigid, thorough, realistic, sensible, and logical. They register high levels of anxiety and worry. As such, they are valuable counterparts to entrepreneurs and their ventures. They offset your overexuberance, focusing on reality and rendering accurate assessments and practical judgments. They give valuable advice, and you need to rely on them. Nevertheless, they are not entrepreneurs and at times they are bound to think you are crazy. If your accountant never shakes his or her head in disbelief, you're doing something wrong.

Quite soon in your start-up you will need an internal book-keeper and ultimately a controller. Your bookkeeper or controller is really an in-house accountant who keeps track of results, pays the bills, and manages the company's money. Through this person you need to establish a reporting system that keeps you closely attuned to the company's operating results and financial well-being. While all this information merits your scrutiny, the foremost measure and guide you rely on should be the amount of money you have in a liquid state. This becomes particularly important when and if you slide downward. A handle on your net liquid cash is one of your most effective management tools.

Don't assume you're getting 100 percent accurate financial information. Numbers often seem to lie, to change dramatically when some oversight is uncovered. Hound your financial people for flawless facts. Keep the following rule in mind: *when you're going up, you never make as much as you think you are making; when you're going down, you always lose more than you think you are losing,* and at a much faster rate than you believed. When you're flat, you're usually putting a little something away, especially after a down leg.

Another professional you should spend an afternoon with is your insurance agent. There are two kinds of agents. One sells fire and casualty insurance. You need to be indoctrinated by your agent with details on your present and future insurance needs. You should come away understanding the basics of physical protection against fire, crime, and other perils. Make your agent explain your needs for liability coverage and workmen's compensation, bonds, and umbrella policies.

You should expect a good agent to visit your firm periodically, oversee corporate changes, and update your coverage needs. Changes in a company mean new and varied exposures that require additional protection. If your agent fails to service you fastidiously, find a new broker. Expect this agent constantly to look out for your needs. Use what your agent has taught you to audit his or her program. Allow other agents to check your program as well. If they can poke holes in your coverage and point out unprotected hazards, give them the business.

Casualty insurance might be an area you'd like to scrimp on. That's a mistake. Buy sound coverage with high limits of protection. Insurance is a form of mistake avoidance. I operate my business as though I had no insurance, but maximum safeguards against crime and other perils are in place. *The best insurance lies with company strategies that stress the avoidance of losses and claims.*

An entrepreneur also needs a second, knowledgeable insurance person. A life- and health-insurance agent helps put the company benefit package together. Health insurance and possibly disability or life insurance make up this employee perk. These agents also design life insurance to protect the corporation against the loss of key people, and manage the personal insurance affairs of the entrepreneur, plan for the estate, and protect heirs. You need a business-insurance professional in this complex area. Life-insurance agents seem to be more aggressive than casualty agents, so you should have a handy selection to choose from.

Your company will also be served by a host of vendors selling supplies and services (printers, office equipment, and so on). Many of these sources will lowball price on first-time orders to get your business. Later they'll raise the tariff. You need to monitor these vendors from time to time and later teach this lesson to your purchasing people and your advertising or art department. Price, however, should not be the sole criterion for buying. Establish good working relationships with vendors, keep them honest, and don't jump at every price deal that comes in the door. The crucial judgment on vendors comes when you need special service or treatment beyond the norm. If they respond favorably in a crisis, stretch to the limit to meet a deadline, or make a tough delivery, then you have a most important ally.

At an early date in your new venture, an alliance with a public relations firm will serve your interests. Initially, you can handle PR yourself. Draft short one- or two-paragraph announcements regarding new products, new services, or anything of commercial interest. Make a list of publications in which exposure to your item will be of benefit. Send them periodic announcements. Include a sharp black-and-white picture. This helps get new products into the media limelight.

You may contact writers or editors of publications for free publicity. A Texas inventor I know got his fire screen written up in a national newsmagazine by calling a New York editor.

A regional farm publication that chronicled new products wrote up my wood stoves at my bleakest moment. The article sold just enough wood burners to pay the rent and phone bill.

A small public relations firm may help you. A minimal monthly allotment to them can often get you a host of articles, interviews, and media exposure worth far more than what your ad budget could deliver.

One of your principal relationships will likely be with an advertising agency. Small start-ups frequently use newspapers to put together ads. They often look tacky. A professional job by an agency enhances your image. Start out by asking them to make up your logo (trademark or motto). Then, when you need it, they can formulate your first ad. A good ad agency account executive can also give you direction and insight into your market and its distribution channels. Use your agency as an important teacher of advertising and marketing techniques that will be useful throughout your career.

In time, you will need to establish an art department within your company to facilitate a myriad of small jobs that every venture requires. The extent of its involvement in lofty corporate promotions depends entirely on the skill and expertise of the people you hire. Good art, copy, and layout people are a fine asset, particularly if they are careful, watch costs, and minimize mistakes in printed material and ads.

Your ad agency can be a one- or two-person house, or a monolith. Your primary concern should be to make sure they have a feel for your product or service. This requires your participation in ad planning meetings. Lend all the talents you can to the advertising process. In fact, if you have skills in this area, do what you can yourself. Only you can fine-tune the gist of your ads. If the agency is to develop a feel for the company's products and mission, the entrepreneur must scour their efforts and critique copy and layout. This can be bruising to the agency. Nevertheless, make them overwhelm you with talent before you are satisfied.

You want a good agency. The big guys won't be too interested in you when you start. A lot of small guys won't be either. I once contacted a former big-agency hotshot who had split off to start his own company. He turned up his nose at my piddling account. He wanted major corporations. He failed to understand that growing up with small accounts can be a superb formula for a new agency to follow. When my company boomed, he began to call me. By then my ad needs had been met and I was too busy to talk to him.

Sometimes small agencies that have been around a long time have stayed tiny because they were no-talent operators or outright chiselers. Like any business that serves people, an agency must be looking out for your interests first.

There are a lot of part-time ad people, creative floaters, and short-term entrants in the advertising field. You may be able to strike up a profitable relationship with one of them; but a young, aggressive, small house, willing to gamble somewhat on your future, seems more suitable. It should see in you not just present income but an opportunity for you both, where their contribution will help to enhance and build your company.

Sometimes, because of expense or inexperience, a new company fails to advertise. No company, large or small, can get by without advertising. If you wish to survive and grow, you must advertise. If you plan to have a truly entrepreneurial, first-rate growth company, advertising will speed you toward that goal. The best means of appreciating the value of advertising is to go ahead with it. You will see immediately that advertising brings results. You need to spend at least 5 percent or more of your gross income on advertising.

A mandatory requirement of your advertising is that it be truthful. Practice full disclosure of all the facts, good and bad, in your promotions. Julius Rosenwald made sure that the Sears catalogue faithfully described the merchandise it offered. He instructed, "It may take courage to say plainly that the embroidery on the sleeve of a woman's coat is of artificial silk, but it is better than to have even one of a hundred women find out for herself."

A new company should forgo institutional-type advertising. You need specific offers, return coupons, lead generators, and response vehicles. Your ad promotions should cause people to take action—to call, to write, to buy, to investigate, to come by. You're trying to uncover customers and interest them in what you have to offer. Entice them to make a move.

My company has outpaced its competitors by providing information and education constantly in its advertising. We send out special reports, booklets, and educational pieces on all our investments. We try to teach and instruct. We give knowledge. We dispense facts. If we help our customers to make better decisions, then they will prosper. If they do well, then so will we. This philosophy should permeate your whole operation and particularly your promotion and advertising.

I am touching here on a vast subject, and it would be presumptuous to reduce it to a thumbnail presentation. I believe a truly successful entrepreneur must in time become somewhat of an expert on advertising. Through trial and error, an understanding of the art evolves. The Appendix of this book lists several books about advertising, written by the masters, to supplement your actual experience. They will guide, suggest, and inspire. If you do not contribute directly to the creative process of your advertising (copy, layout, media selection, or campaign), then you must at least recognize and sense what is powerful and what is weak.

Advertising is frequently bad, generally average, and occasionally great. The best of it (which you want for your company) comes through a process not unlike the entrepreneurial experience. Good ads come through innovation and creativity spawned from deep commitment and total understanding of both product and market. Good advertising catches the spirit of the entrepreneur. It breaks new ground, seems fresh and different, provocative and new. It will be imitated quickly by others; for, above all, it will work. A breakthrough company supplemented by breakthrough advertising will dazzle the marketplace. Couple entrepreneurial genius with advertising genius and no competitor is safe.

The bottom line on advertising lies with its integrity. You must perform as you say you will. These words come from the great nineteenth-century merchant and entrepreneur John Wanamaker: "What we advertise we must do. Tell the customer the exact quality of the goods, if he does not know it, and don't let him be satisfied with a poor fit or with a style that is manifestly unbecoming. Don't you see that his women folk will make him dissatisfied? Then he won't come back."

Advertising forms part of the overall marketing strategy of a company. What exactly is marketing? How important is it? Peter Drucker answers, "Because its purpose is to create a customer, the business enterprise has two—and only these two—basic functions: marketing and innovation. Marketing and innovation produce results; all the rest are 'costs.' . . . The economic success of Japan . . . rests squarely on an acceptance of marketing as the first function of business and its crucial task. . . . True marketing starts out . . . with the customer, his demographics, his realities, his needs, his values. It does not ask, 'What do we want to sell?' It does not say, 'This is what our product or service does.' It says, 'These are the satisfactions the customer looks for, values and needs.'"

With any new product or service you must determine to whom you are going to sell it. Is your product suitable for the buyers you have in mind? Will they buy it? Initially, you may not have these answers. You can implement a variety of market research methods or use outside consultants. The best method, however, is to get on the phone and talk with anybody and everybody related to your project. Although you get, on balance, negatives to most fact-finding phone sessions, they are the best way to learn a lot fast.

Most entrepreneurial products (breakthroughs and innovations) don't lend themselves well to standardized market research. New concepts are invariably greeted with disparaging commentary. Inevitably, you must make a commitment to them in spite of all the negatives you hear.

The old "better mousetrap myth" implies that the world will beat a path to your door when you perfect and display a superior device. But rarely, if ever, does a product sell itself. For the entrepreneur, selling is the guts of marketing. Selling and marketing are not opposites, they are one and the same. If you don't get out and sell, you aren't going to make it with a new venture.

An old sales motivator, Red Motley, used to say, "Nothing ever happens until somebody sells something." There is a lot to know about running a company. But before you learn and practice most of it, there must first be sales.

There are reams of material on effective selling techniques. I shall repeat A. P. Giannini's sage advice: "The way to build up clientele is to go out among them and present to them first-hand the advantages offered by your business." Either you or some exceedingly competent associate must go out and sell your service or product.

If you do the selling and marketing in your company's infancy, you will be able to instruct others easily on how to do it later. Your product or service has its own individual strong points and weaknesses. If you sell the product first, you know how to emphasize benefits and overcome objections. Then you can teach these tactics.

My definition of *marketing* is *promoting your services.* Business writer Brooks Fenno carries this a step further—"An effective marketer promotes a product in ways that relate to the needs of the buyer."

This is exactly what IBM chief Tom Watson was angling at with the formulation of IBM's influential and successful marketing philosophy. Mack Hanan, in his book *Fast-Growth Management,* tells us:

> When IBM was young and in its entrepreneurial phase of development, Tom Watson stood before his people and laid down policy. Assets would thenceforth flow chiefly to marketing. Customer knowledge would be the company's most important resource, the base from which all products and

promotion would flow. The sales force would sell as consultants to their long-term clients. *The consultant sales force objective would be to improve customer profit, not sell computer systems.* For this, IBM would command a premium price. Premium profits would follow. The entire organization would live as it sold—by being the most cost-effective processor of information about its markets and then marketing the output in the twin forms of the product and selling style.

This philosophy must surely have emanated from National Cash Register's founder, John Henry Patterson, who instructed employee Watson and others, "Don't talk machines, talk the prospect's business."

Hanan goes on to refine further one of the most powerful marketing strategies ever devised:

What is the one best way to grow your business? There is a single answer. Grow the value of your customers' businesses. Help them make more profit as the result of doing business with you. Teach them to be profit-making investors in the rewards you offer. Then teach them how to reinvest their return in adding still greater values to their businesses through applying more of your products and services. Demonstrate the unique benefits of a planned partnership with you.

If you do these things, your customers will be unable to escape growth. Their growth will leave you no recourse but to grow in response.

Customers have already been described as sources of funds. Now we can amplify that definition. Customers are the sources of growth funds. They are the true sponsors of your profits. You are, in effect, in their employ as a grower of their businesses just as much as you are in the employ of your own business. Without them, you cannot speed your growth. Without you, they cannot speed theirs.

Perhaps this is what old-time entrepreneurs mean when they say, "Take care of your customers and they will take care of you." A good growth relationship with your key customers is essentially a mutual aid pact: You help me grow and I will help you grow.

Customer growth must also be the basic positioning of your business. Why are you in business? "We are in business to help our customers speed their growth." And you yourself, in your style, your policies, and your role as definer of your business, must speak out clearly for customer profit enhancement at every opportunity.

This is a marvelous marketing credo for you to follow, but what exactly are the marketing steps you must take to get sales? Let's follow your start-up through the various marketing elements.

1. Your market research should first be done by telephone. You want to pinpoint potential customers. Who are the buyers? Who are your competitors?

    It's crucial that you also uncover the distribution system. How are such products or services sold? By mail? By phone? Through reps? Via salesmen? Dealers?

    My partner, Bernie, called his lengthy sessions on the telephone "brain picking." He was constantly searching for new products, fresh opportunities, market gaps, and breakthroughs. When he found one he zeroed in on all the marketing dope over the phone.

2. The library offers many publications that are imperative for you to look over, for example, the Thomas Registers, which give listings of every company in scores of manufacturing and product lines. The library has lists of trade associations, trade shows, manufacturers' reps, and endless other rosters that you can use to contact other companies. Lists of suppliers, distributors, and wholesalers are invaluable to new ventures.

3. There are two fundamental rules of selling that must be followed religiously. The first rule demands that you listen to your prospect, let the customer talk, ask questions, discuss business needs, personal affairs, or whatever the other party wants to converse about. All of us love to talk about ourselves. The second rule dictates that the first sales call to the prospect should be the opening stanza in a five-part solicitation. First calls invariably bring negative responses. Follow-ups sell. Your sales so-

licitation must be comprised of a minimum of five separate calls.

4. Effective marketing requires close coordination among product availability, timely shipping, and sales. Your product development must ensure that the goods be available for timely delivery following the sale. The start-up often has problems perfecting the product, thus losing many orders. Development and manufacture of new products mean delays, incredible frustration, and more delays. In this period you will either learn patience or you will go mad. When selling new products, it is wise to allow more time for delivery than normal.

5. Once you have sold and delivered a few orders, you should develop a postsale follow-up. If your product requires service, it must be done with speed and timeliness. A personal contact to determine satisfaction makes sense. Some sort of excellent, unique follow-up must be devised.

Tell your customers from time to time that you appreciate them. Letters or mailings can convey this message. A small gift of information or advice also shows your gratitude. Then your customers will begin to sell for you. If you overwhelm them with appreciation and concern, they will tell others about you. When that begins to happen, you will be exceedingly busy.

John North Willys was a remarkable entrepreneur. He built the Willy-Overland Company from next to nothing into a highly successful auto company in a brief span of time. Back in 1917 Willys passed along these gems of marketing and distribution wisdom:

I once picked up a book on business and, turning to the chapter on distribution, I read these satisfying words: "It is always best to sell your product to the jobber because he will, in turn, dispose of it to the retailer." In the mind of the author of that volume the whole problem of distribution was contained in—"just get the goods out of the shop."

It would be delightfully simple if real life only worked out in some such way. But the businessman today knows that distribution cannot be so easily dismissed—or dismissed at all. A good part of the success of any businessman depends on how his marketing is done—how the man acts who comes into direct contact with the ultimate consumer.

All of us are quick to recognize that the wrong kind of an agent has in him the potentialities of much harm—he is the direct representative of the maker, and whatever he does comes back squarely to the maker. But the independent dealer is just as important as the selling agent. If a dealer misrepresents, no legal liability attaches to the manufacturer; but the avoidance of mere legal liability is not the modern way of doing business. The new doctrine is: *"Nothing is sold until it is well sold."* Bear in mind this rule, the dealer becomes a part of the manufacturing organization, and, although he is not in the same financial relation as an agent, he should be guided, inspired, and rewarded just as an agent is guided, inspired, and rewarded. Only thus can the very best results in ultimate sales and goodwill be achieved.

Help your customer. Help your dealer. The same theme is the marrow of all exceptional companies, large or small. John Willys said, "I cannot too greatly impress the fact that big business is only the result of hard work in small business—the elemental facts of small business and of large business are the same."

The goal of your growing concern should be to capture the dominant position among all competitors in the marketplace. If you follow the sound business principles I outline, if you are innovative both in product and service, and if you build reserves from profits to weather cycles and setbacks, then you can pick off this premier position.

Just as my company has gained market leadership in hard-asset investments by implementing sound strategies, so may your company. You will see this begin when competitors imitate your innovations. They will duplicate your marketing techniques and copy your products. Your competition will react to you. Ray Kroc said, "My way of fighting the competition is the positive approach. Stress your own strengths, emphasize quality, service, cleanliness, and value, and the competition will wear itself out trying to keep up."

As your volume grows and you capture larger slices of the

market, you must be certain your profits keep pace. Mack Hanan advises that "leadership in profit on sales is the acid test of market preference. It validates the market's value-to-price perception of your product by proving that premium value merits a premium price."

Mack Hanan also stresses the need to make customers out of the biggest users of your product. He states that "20 percent of all your customers . . . contribute up to 80 percent or so of your profitable sales volume. This is a precarious base. It means you must capture all the heavy profit contributors you can persuade to do business with you. Once captured they must be kept. Few in number though they are, they are your growth source. They are not just your market; they are your business. To build it, build them."

Another relationship that may have a great bearing on the outcome of your enterprise is that with your bank. It would be nice never to have to turn to a lender for help. Unfortunately, your entrepreneurial career will likely be punctuated with bank loans. In a critical early juncture when my liabilities mounted and assets drained away, I went to see my banker for help. He advanced me $7,000 against my only remaining personal asset, a coin collection. With it I paid my secretary's salary and the rent, phone, and a flock of other bills. That loan kept my embryonic company going. Without it, the phone company would likely have unplugged my service. I always considered that unbecoming event an undeniable indication that the end was near.

I don't think you can ever be totally comfortable when your company owes money to the bank. Even when your accounts receivable or a nearly liquid inventory serves as collateral for your loan, you are paying a percentage of your profits out in interest. With contemporary interest rates fluctuating in wide swings and peak rates coinciding with recessionary slumps, borrowing makes little sense. It's wiser to curb expansion than to fund it with usurious loans. If you are extended and you miscalculate on future volume and then feel the pinch of rising rates, you may not survive.

F. W. Woolworth claimed that Dutch businessmen of straitlaced Puritan stock taught him how to flourish in business without borrowing money. "They ran their stores on the same policy for more than half a century; they did not progress, except as a tree progresses in size. They grew wealthy slowly, but surely. They never went into debt; they always paid for what they bought, and paid with cash. They bought at the lowest price, and they bought not a cent's worth more than they actually needed. When they put money in the bank—salted it away—it was put away to stay. There are no liens on anything they owned. These Dutch farmers taught me to manage my own business and never to let my business manage me."

Bankers are generally leery of start-ups. Your optimistic projections sound like hallucinations to them. A banker will give you money only if your collateral is liquid and far exceeds the amount you are requesting. You would probably be better off selling the collateral and forgoing the loan.

Walt Disney once wrote of bankers that "they are fellows who don't understand your business. . . . They'll get you down." Banks look at you in a mercenary and emotionless fashion. They don't like risk. Banks that gamble or don't do their homework go out of business. Bankers' reputations and careers ride on the success or failure of their loan portfolios.

A raw entrepreneur represents a risky prospect to them. They may see a future in your venture, but before helping you, they want a secured deal and a good customer. Bankers first want to know what you can do for them, not what they can do for you. If you want a banker's help, you must first have all your business accounts in place at that bank. Then you must have some money going through the account. Bankers love cash balances. They draw interest by lending out these overnight surpluses. The more money going through your accounts, the more stature you have at your bank.

Harvey Firestone advised that he "made it a rule to keep a substantial balance in the bank. No matter what the difficulties," he said, "a businessman should never withdraw all his funds, leaving no bank balance."

Bankers get squeamish at the sight of overdrafts. Whatever happens, don't let yours become a problem account. If they perceive you as a deadbeat, you'd better shift banks. Start out with minimal office-equipment financing or a small test loan. Pay your interest on time. Give the bank some history. They love to review a record of timely payments, kept promises, and accurate assessments of your future.

Harvey Firestone stated this business truth: "The most important fundamental asset of the man who would succeed in business is credit. With good credit to begin with, chances for ultimate success are better than simply with ready money, for good credit will enable a businessman to solve the money problem and to establish a financial bulwark against the needs of the future."

You waste your time walking into a brand-new bank searching for a loan. Bankers want a known quantity. Successful relations with a bank are built up over time. You must first establish a beachhead with your business and then convince them of your good character. The auto company pioneer John Willys said, "Tell only the truth to your banker and make him believe in you. Bluffs to your banker mean ruin."

All your business relationships should bear the stamp of character. You must speak the truth, fulfill your promises, evidence reliability, and ensure that your word is kept. That leaves no room for chiseling, petty finagling, or constant misunderstandings. If you are of strong character, your company will reflect that same quality. *You will find that honor opens many doors and trust favorably influences the outcome of all your dealings.*

This ethical posture will filter down throughout your company. *New York Times* entrepreneur Adolph S. Ochs commented: "Subordinates take their cue from their superiors. Secure the confidence of the rank and file in the integrity of its head and you have an invincible army for carrying forward any great enterprise or people massed for good purposes."

Real estate multimillionaire John W. Galbreath builds some of the largest housing projects on earth, including a fabulous development in Hong Kong. One of his early business experiences explains why he succeeded on an international scale. He states, "I can remember one time when I told an institution that there was an extra bathroom in a house. Later they were taking an inventory and they discovered that there was only one bathroom. When they told me about it, I didn't say a word to them, but instead I went out and built another room on and put a bath in it, without ever telling them until it was completed. Then I went to them and said, 'You look at it now. It now has two baths.' Well, that mistake cost me . . . but I had to do it; a man's word has got to be the law."

Men and women of great accomplishment in business today are generally of lofty character. Along with this integrity, however, entrepreneurs need other favorable qualities. A person who hopes to build a major enterprise needs harmony among the workers, which requires the ability to be fair. You must spot grievances and straighten out inequities. You need to be an equitable arbitrator when arguments break out among workers. Employees must trust you. Nothing can hurt your company more than a perceived injustice. If one person doing a job similar to others receives favoritism or special financial rewards, you have a real discrepancy for employees to rally against. An entrepreneur must be an astute judge of what is fair.

One of the early employees of the giant Swift meat-packing concern had this to say about its founder: "I worked for G. F. Swift for twenty-seven years. He was the squarest man I ever worked for. All that time I never asked him what he was going to pay me. I never had cause to complain. If you worked well for him, he saw that you got what you deserved in money and in every other way."

You must also learn to stand up to people—stockholders, directors, employees, vendors, and sometimes even customers. Within your company you must ask embarrassing questions about jobs that weren't done properly. You must speak up, criticize, rebuke, and have sticky confrontations that embarrass and fluster. You must butt heads and resolve issues in your favor.

You should also learn to manipulate your prima donnas. Every company has superstars who outperform the others. Their egos become sizable. These "big hitters" should be rewarded with perks. A plush office, a luxury car, or a title will often suffice. Prima donnas are restless. They complain and become indignant far more often than other employees. Generally, you learn to tolerate them. They are big producers and some sort of uneasy truce between them and you works to your interest.

Some of my best salespeople are quiet and genteel. I never slight them in favor of the temperamental ones. Rather than antagonize the hotshots I try to accommodate both types equally. You must maintain discipline, but top producers should, whenever possible, be kept happy.

Many entrepreneurs have attributes that draw criticism. Many entrepreneurial giants have been described as willful, stubborn, demanding, and autocratic by bystanders and commentators.

Great entrepreneurs strive to perfect their companies. Ray Kroc said, "perfection was what I wanted in McDonald's. Everything else was secondary for me."

Fairly or not, entrepreneurs may expect employees or vendors to super-perform in much the same way they do. When workers fail to meet these high standards, there is a tendency for the entrepreneurs to boil over. The ultimate exasperation for many entrepreneurs comes when imperfections have been pointed out but remain intact, when mistakes are repeated, and when patterns of overt carelessness continue. Andrew Carnegie once instructed Charlie Schwab, "You can make as many mistakes as you like, but don't make the same one twice."

Clarence W. Barron, founder of *Barron's National Business & Financial Weekly*, was known for driving his employees relentlessly. He believed "in shaking the man up, giving him a jolt. . . . The men who love me the most I sometimes think are the men to whom I have given the biggest shakeup."

In sharp contrast to Barron and others, a far less common style is that of Charles Schwab, who once said, "For twenty-two years I have never spoken a harsh word to anybody in the entire organization of the Carnegie Steel Works.

"The way to develop the best that is in a man is by appreciation and encouragement . . . I have yet to see the man however great or exalted his station, who is not susceptible to the approval of his fellow men. . . . And the severest criticism that can come to any man is not to find fault with him, but not to notice him at all. I believe in the doctrine of encouragement. . . . Mr. Carnegie practiced the rule and taught it to me. . . . If I go through a department and find it slack, I say nothing. Silence is a heavier censure than words. When I cannot praise, I do not blame."

Great entrepreneurs draw comparisons to great generals. In many ways a business and an army have parallels. Upon touring entrepreneur John Wanamaker's great emporium in Philadelphia, Ulysses S. Grant said, "It takes as much generalship to organize a business like this as to organize an army."

Stonewall Jackson would have been a great entrepreneur.

When necessary, he was stern and demanding. He drove his troops yet loved them. They responded with a degree of excellence, bravery, and fortitude that stood out above the other contingents of a great army. He managed to transfer his feelings and ambitions onto the ranks. They sensed his intensity and concern. A humble man of great faith, "Old Jack" positioned himself as a leader among equals. An innovative, daring soldier, much stirred by the struggle, he touched his army with an intangible greatness and rarely lost in battle.

Great men worthy of emulation can be found on the battlefield or, as David Ogilvy notes in his autobiography, *Blood, Brains and Beer,* in the kitchen. For several years, Ogilvy worked under a noted French chef who taught him "exorbitant standards of service" that he applied to his business.

The head chef at the Majestic was Monsieur Pitard, and a more terrifying martinet I have never encountered. He worked at a desk in the middle of the kitchen, his beady eye always upon us. One day he noticed that the tops of a batch of brioches were crooked, and fired the culprit on the spot. When he overheard me tell a waiter that one of the dishes on the menu was finished, he bawled me out. "A great kitchen must always honor what is on the menu."

"But, Chef," I pleaded, "it was roast chicken, and it would have taken forty minutes to roast another." "Don't you know that you can roast a chicken in fifteen minutes if you heat the oven to six hundred degrees?" "Suppose the plat du jour is coulibiac, which takes all day to prepare?" "In that kind of emergency, come and tell me. I will telephone to other establishments until I find one which also has coulibiac on the menu. Then I will send you to fetch it in a taxi."

My next post was in the garde-manger where I prepared hors d'oeuvre, a minimum of twenty-six different varieties for each meal. I also made the mayonnaise. The rule was to break each egg separately into a cup and smell it before adding it to the others. One morning I was in too much of a hurry to observe this precaution. The fifty-ninth egg was rotten and contaminated all the others. I had no choice but to throw the whole batch into the garbage. If Pitard had seen me, he would have fired me.

That afternoon the chef garde-manger sent me to the chef saucier with some raw sweetbreads which smelled so putrid that I knew they would endanger the life of any client who ate them. I protested to the chef garde-manger, but he told me to carry out his order; he knew that he would get in hot water if Pitard discovered that he had run out of sweetbreads. I had been brought up to believe that it is dishonorable to inform. But I did just that. I took the putrid sweetbreads to Pitard, and invited him to smell them. Without a word, he went over to the chef garde-manger and fired him. The poor devil had to leave, then and there.

SUMMARY

Once you start you must keep growing and managing the company's affairs. You must do the initial hiring and build your founding team. Your employees will help build the company, but most faces will change over the years.

You must learn how to maintain a policy of hiring the best people. Most people will grow in the entrepreneurial environment. Promote from within whenever possible.

All human relationships go through a honeymoon period. If you spot flaws during this period, it's only the tip of the iceberg.

Use employment contracts, but don't try to kill competitors. Never clinch a deal without a written agreement that your lawyer has drafted. Learn how to use the courts and how to control legal expenses.

Write lots of letters to get your business going. Ensure that your company's phone manners are unsurpassed. Make heavy use of complaint cards—customers' complaints are the best management tool.

Never be afraid of your customers. Meet problems head-on. Charge enough. Collect your money. Keep margins fat.

Call on your accountant to teach you the fundamentals. Demand accurate financial data and always question them.

Have your fire- and casualty-insurance agent teach you the insurance fundamentals as they apply to your business. Make an alliance with a public relations firm. Learn advertising from the experts. Demand great ads. Serve others with your advertising.

Marketing means promoting your services. Relate to the needs of the buyer. Develop a marketing strategy that helps your customers grow. Show your appreciation to your customers. Strive to be the dominant company in your industry.

Bankers are not much help to entrepreneurs. Build your banking relationship slowly and carefully. Guard your credit and reputation. Maintain lofty character. Ensure fairness.

5.
Three Keys
to a Successful
Start-up

I began to visualize what I felt would be the ideal store. The formula for it was simplicity itself. The store merely would have to combine four things—service, fair price, attractive-appearing goods, and first quality.

—BERNARD H. KROGER
Founder, Kroger Food Store Chain

A sound operating philosophy not only defines the intended scope of a company, it lays down bedrock principles that govern corporate conduct. First among these is integrity. No aspiring entrepreneur can afford to scrimp here. Sadly, all too many business start-ups employ shortcuts and neglect a commitment to total integrity.

Unfortunately, most discussions about honesty come off sounding like clichés. Nevertheless, we must dwell on it at length here because it is a crucial quality for entrepreneurs. You must emotionalize your honesty; feel and sense your commitment. It must transcend words and emanate from your core.

Lack of integrity comes in various shades: outright fraud, simple advantage over the customer, ignorance of the law. Whatever the nomenclature of this ethical breakdown, the powerful truth remains that no company can flourish for long if it practices dishonesty. Only totally honest companies will prosper over the long term. I repeat, as long as we have free markets, integrity remains an essential element of success without which corporate growth will be stymied.

Thomas B. Walker, friend of the legendary railroad entrepreneur James J. Hill and lumber millionaire (he owned over 900,000 acres of timber in Minnesota and California), said, "Not only can a man be honest and grow rich, but it is almost impossible for a man to grow rich unless he is honest. It is honesty, integrity, and uprightness that make people trust you and that attract trade and stimulate business relations."

We wouldn't have to dwell on this issue if it weren't such a problem. Too many new ventures seem to place their own interests ahead of their clients'. And there are many opportunities to cheat customers. The bluntest sort of fraud is the antithesis of service and value. In fact, such shabby acts comprise a surefire formula for failure. If you practice these crimes, you will ultimately flop and probably be imprisoned as well.

A number of companies that sold highly speculative margin transactions in gold and silver sprang up in my area during the 1970s. These were "paper capers," where the buyer never got the actual precious metals in his or her possession, but supposedly gained leverage by putting up a small amount of money to control a large amount of gold or silver. In one seamy example a business would simply take the money, buy nothing for their customers, and hope the markets would drop. They gambled recklessly with their clients' funds and, naturally, enjoyed a regal life-style.

It was bad enough that they sold a dubious, high-risk paper transaction as an inflation hedge; on top of this they added flagrant fraud and deception. The inevitable collapse left their investors empty-handed. Most of the culprits were imprisoned.

Contrast my company's philosophy with that of these rip-off artists (also, witness the astonishing market gaps that required filling in the early 1970s):

DIRECT DELIVERY (investors wanted actual physical possession, gold and silver coins and bars, in their hands, not on
paper)
ABSOLUTE INTEGRITY (people desperately wanted an honest,
straightforward national source)
QUALITY (many dealers sold inferior bars or coins; buyers
wanted the best)
SERVICE (people wanted quick delivery and fast payment)
RELIABILITY (clients wanted a source to go back to again and
again)
INFORMATION (customers wanted information and advice)
SAFEGUARDS (people wanted to send money in for payments
without worrying)

While companies pushing highly leveraged margin transactions flourished, we stuck to our conservative methods. Business
was slow but growing gradually. Fraud, greed, and bankruptcy
leveled many of our competitors. Inevitably, our excellent reputation gained wide favor. In the hectic markets of the late 1970s,
forty thousand to fifty thousand phone calls a day poured into
our switchboard from people eager to buy gold and silver coins.

Many of these long-departed competitors recognized the
opportunities in precious metals that lay ahead. They had the
right timing and foresight. They could have done exactly as my
company did. Yet their need for a quick hit, their absolute insen-
sitivity to their clients' interests, their bad judgment, and their
outright fraud doomed them to failure and imprisonment. How
foolish to fumble away such great advantage for want of a decent
level of integrity.

Jacob Schiff, who directed Kuhn, Loeb & Company, to huge
success, said in 1898:

> My own experience in what is termed "Wall Street" covers
> a period of more than thirty years. During this long range
> of time I have seen many firms, who thirty and twenty
> years ago occupied the front rank, recede to positions of
> comparative unimportance, and I have seen other firms,
> who two and three decades ago were quite unimportant,
> come to the front and become leaders in domestic and inter-
> national finance. . . . The reason is to be sought in the fact

that they have been *more honest* than those who, thirty and twenty years ago, were among the leading banking firms. Not more honest, as construed in the literal sense of the word, but honest in their respect for the moral obligation assumed toward those who entrusted their financial affairs to them, be it in investing in the securities of corporate enterprises which these bankers brought before the public, or otherwise; *more honest* in keeping their own capital from becoming immobile, so that their credit and prestige should not be called into question during times of financial peril and uncertainty; *more honest* in the ways which, not taking alone into account the momentary pecuniary profit, are certain, in the long run, to determine position, credit, and prestige.

Most dishonesty in business is petty and never attracts the law. This level of chicanery, quite commonplace, involves no more than taking simple advantage of customers. A friend of many years has a route business wherein he delivers goods to a variety of outlets. He's always talking about expanding and about big deals that are pending. Nevertheless, his business is at about the same level that it was twenty years ago. Why? He takes sneaky, piddling advantages of his customers. He nicks them just a little. Instead of giving them extra, he gives them a fraction less. He sees his business with blinders on, for it is always perceived in his terms, never his customers'. Thus, he loses his accounts and never grows in line with his hopes and expectations.

You can fool people or get the best of them only one or two times. After that, they invariably catch on. What's worse, hell hath no fury like a person conned. That person will never again do business with that individual or company. So, if people sooner or later always figure out that they've been duped or chiseled and if their reaction is always the same, why would anyone in business follow such a policy? Stupidity! What other label can be affixed to a procedure that guarantees the permanent loss of business and customers?

Bernard H. Kroger, founder of the Kroger Food Chain, commented, "The more I saw of people, the clearer became my realization that they could not be fooled! How I served a customer had something to do with why she bought. Price and appearance had something to do with it. These made a first sale. But what made re-sales was the satisfaction found in the article itself when put to use. If that failed, all failed, and the customer was lost."

If you ever wonder why many small businesses stay small, why they sputter, plug along, and never grow or flourish, you know the reason. The proprietor insists on outfoxing or swindling the customers.

Andrew Carnegie, the wealthiest entrepreneur who ever lived, wrote, "A great business is seldom if ever built up, except on lines of the strictest integrity. A reputation for 'cuteness' and sharp dealing is fatal in great affairs. Not the letter of the law, but the spirit, must be the rule. It is essential to permanent success that a house should obtain a reputation for being governed by what is fair rather than what is merely legal. A rule which we adopted and adhered to has given greater returns than one would believe possible, namely: always give the other party the benefit of the doubt."

In the late 1970s, my company searched for diversification and settled on the numismatic, or rare coin, business. We made remarkable inroads in short order. One reason was the habitual overgrading, overpricing, and promotion of inferior merchandise by our competitors.

On the eve of an impending boom in collectibles, we positioned ourself to take advantage of a market gap you could drive a truck through. Many new investors wanted to buy collector coins, but they wanted quality and accurately described and priced material.

Many competitors peddled shoddy coins at high prices. When the customers checked with another dealer (as they often did), they found out they had been swindled. These dealers destroyed their own customer base, as many good prospective clients quit this sorry game altogether. Others switched sources. The many mischievous dealers simply played into the hands of the few honorable vendors.

In retail businesses that sell uniform products you don't have the problem of price gouging or selling inferior items at high markups. (Aspirin costs about the same everywhere.) In virtually all ventures that lack customer expertise or uniformity (mechanical repairs, tax shelters, art and antiques), pricing becomes arbitrary and problems crop up. Close scrutiny of the highly subjective collectible business discloses this ever-present phenomenon. A tiny minority of dealers (in stamps, coins, antiques, firearms, rare books, folk art, and so on) operate with impeccable integrity. While they flourish, the majority of marginal operators cheat themselves into perpetual mediocrity.

Ross Perot, founder of Electronic Data Systems, attributed to his father this important guiding principle, "He taught me as a small boy that buying cotton from a man once had very little value unless you developed a personal relationship with him, unless you treated him fairly, unless he trusted you. Otherwise he won't come back to you next year."

Business dishonesty takes other forms as well. When my company decided to broaden its line of wood-burning stoves, we took our drawings to a small metals manufacturer. He studied the plans and within a few days we agreed on price, quantity, and delivery dates. He became intensely interested as well as enthusiastic about the wood-stove business.

Much to our chagrin, he failed to deliver our stoves on the targeted date—he had simply lied to get our order. When we finally got the first units, they had been made with cheaper material than our specs had called for. While we hassled with him on this issue, he tried to raise the price on the units to a point well above his bid. Finally, the whole project bogged down in recurring rounds of delayed delivery, faulty product, and incessant bickering over price.

The climax came when our conniving manufacturer decided to bypass us. He made an insignificant design change in our stoves and started selling them himself. He had lied to us, cheated us, and finally wound up stealing from us.

Not that his stove venture ever amounted to anything—it didn't. He managed only to burn off a good customer and further ensure that he would remain a marginal conniver. And so it goes with any firms that follow dishonorable practices. If you make and sell inferior, shoddy, or worthless merchandise, you will eventually fail. If you make bogus claims or false warranties and put out misleading hype for your product or service, the scam you disguise as a business will inevitably collapse.

Not a single company listed in the Fortune 500 (America's largest enterprises) cheats or bamboozles its customers. Companies get big because they practice honesty. Without it, no company can benefit from referrals, one of the truly great wellsprings of business success. This priceless corporate asset cannot be purchased. It can only be earned. It comes to you from "word of mouth."

Before a consumer buys a product for the first time, some unbiased source has generally conveyed satisfaction with the product. Way back in the beginning, Henry Ford captured market share because people told others about the reliability of his cars. Before people go to a movie or out to eat at a new restaurant, they tend to rely on word of mouth. Products, services, and companies alike are judged by these influential verbal verdicts.

My big break came when financial forecaster Howard Ruff mentioned my company in his newsletter. This magnified form of word of mouth led to many thousands of new clients. They, in turn, further spread our name.

People like to be in the know, abreast of trends, and on top of new events. Further, they enjoy dispensing these insights to others. They love to give advice and will always rush to help or aid others with information.

If it seems I am belaboring this simple truth, it is because word of mouth is so critical to start-up ventures. This is especially true for anything new, where every satisfied customer becomes a salesperson. This indispensable asset far exceeds the benefits from any other form of advertising or promotion. When companies mistreat or short customers, they beat themselves out of their most powerful helper. Unless you can unleash an avalanche of positive word of mouth, you will never advance beyond middling success and stagnation.

Stanley Marcus was instructed in the entrepreneurial skills by his father, one of the founders of Neiman-Marcus. The young Marcus built the company into a prominent, high-quality chain based on lessons that extended beyond the realm of conventional customer service and integrity. He recounts,

> Somewhat aghast at a few of the unreasonable complaints and demands which I encountered in my first years in the business, I asked my father, "How can we afford to replace a garment which the customer has clearly abused?" I was referring to a handmade lace ball gown a customer returned after one wearing. "She should have known it was fragile." My father replied, "Yes, she should have, but since this is the first fine garment she's ever bought, she didn't. Explain

to her that we will replace it, and tactfully call her attention to the fact that a delicate handmade lace will wear less well than a coarser machine-made lace. She'll know better next time." Unconvinced, I asked, "How can we afford to take such a loss? The manufacturer won't assume any of the cost." He replied very patiently, "She's not doing business with the manufacturer, she's doing business with us. It costs us over $200 to get a new customer of this woman's buying potential, and I'm not going to lose her for the $175 this dress cost us." And then he added, "When you tell her, do it with a smile." Over the years, this woman spent over $500,000 with us. I had learned one of the most important lessons in my retail career.

Word spread quickly, and within a year of its opening the store had built a clientele of satisfied customers who spread the news of this unique store to all of their friends in the area.

Napoleon Hill tells a similar story of another great merchant.

Marshall Field was probably the leading merchant of his time, and the great Field store, in Chicago, stands today as a monument to his ability. . . .

A customer purchased an expensive lace waist [blouse] at the Field store, but did not wear it. Two years later she gave it to her niece as a wedding present. The niece quietly returned the waist to the Field store and exchanged it for other merchandise, despite the fact that it had been out for more than two years and was then out of style.

Not only did the Field store take back the waist, but what is of more importance it did so without argument!

Of course there was no obligation, moral or legal, on the part of the store to accept the return of the waist at that late date, which makes the transaction all the more significant.

The waist was originally priced at fifty dollars, and of course it had to be thrown on the bargain counter and sold for whatever it would bring, but the keen student of human nature will understand that the Field store not only did not lose anything on the waist, but it actually profited by the transaction to an extent that cannot be measured in mere dollars.

The woman who returned the waist knew that she was not entitled to a rebate; therefore, when the store gave her that to which she was not entitled the transaction won her as a permanent customer. But the effect of the transaction did not end here; it only began; for this woman spread the news of the "fair treatment" she had received at the Field store, far and near. It was the talk of the women of her set for many days, and the Field store received more advertising from the transaction than it could have purchased in any other way with ten times the value of the waist.

Without integrity, no company can have positive word of mouth. Nobody brags about getting cheated. Worthwhile, lasting results come from honest entrepreneurs. The balance are second-raters.

Furthermore, it is far easier to stay straight than not. The wrath of buyers of worthless wares brings ulcers, legal fees, reporters, and painful financial setbacks. Nevertheless, four-flushers and lying promoters abound.

It seems that many in business lack the ability to distinquish clearly between right and wrong. They are so attuned to their own self-interest that the use of unsavory means does not appear wrong to them. What counts is that they get the sale or the order. Their commission or profit justifies exaggerated claims or outright lies. They rationalize that the customer needs or will benefit so greatly from their product or service that the truth can be doctored.

You should make no unwarranted claims, dubious promises, or predictions. You must never publish or speak any misleading information. All facts, good or bad, should be fully disclosed and your positive claims must be offset by any potential negatives.

Typical entrepreneurs starting a new venture have a tendency to embellish the truth about the merits of their products or services but would be astonished were anyone to point an accusatory finger. As we have mentioned, these wrongdoings are rationalized away by self-serving motives.

Understandably, those starting out are under tremendous

pressure. They often have blinders on and can easily compromise ethics for short-term survival.

That's the problem. It is almost impossible to make these particular transgressors see their shortcomings. Suffice it to say that in a new venture you are, at the very least, likely to overstate your case greatly. Unfortunately, one thing leads to another and in time fibs can become felonies.

Whether or not you see yourself as a pillar of virtue, heed the following advice religiously. *Get into the habit of understating your claims and promotions.* Diminish your assertions. Crosscheck all ad copy and sales pitches against the truth. Fastidiously monitor yourself and your employees for anything that smacks of dishonesty. Until you truly understand that the fanatical application of unswerving integrity (which you are not likely to be practicing) gloriously compliments all new ventures, you can never excel.

I have seen too many well-meaning promoters resort to unbecoming tactics and consequently fail. The problem is widespread among start-ups. Many talented and likable people who would otherwise help engineer human progress are snared by some foible that they didn't perceive as wrong. If you are an entrepreneur and you have read this far and are confident that none of this applies to you, you are either a jackass or a jackal.

Those who tamper with truth and trust not only erode their customer base but endanger all their business and professional relationships. A flashy leasing company I became intimate with suffered a small measure of financial adversity and fudged on their financial statement. They planned to slip this misinformation past the bank long enough to finance a pair of super-deals that would make them sound. The transactions flopped, and the bank caught on. An embarrassed board of directors fired the officers and caved in the remnants. What could have been a great public company staffed with a brilliant crew of young turks disintegrated into a hollow shell. Those in charge destroyed valuable business relationships and connections that would have served them for a lifetime.

If you cheat and times get tough, you begin to rely on these shortcuts and forsake remedial measures that can keep you afloat. For many years my company served as wholesaler to a large retail bullion dealer. Although a direct competitor, the dealer placed his orders through my company for a small markup to get better service for his clients.

As our relationship developed, I uncovered a blatant dishonesty about his operation. When his customers sent in money for their gold and silver, he lumped it into one account. He used this account to pay his salary and meet overhead costs. He would use payments on current orders to pay for the old orders. He became further and further behind. Time and again I warned him that this would catch up with him. Finally we broke off our business relationship.

When the boom phase of the gold cycle hit, he built up his overhead. Awash in business, he added staff and squandered profits. When the crunch inevitably came, he ate further and further into his customers' payment money. Soon he found himself months behind, unable to deliver, with customer complaints mounting. Someone invited in the authorities, and the newspaper soon chronicled his scandalous and sorry record.

Through all this he never once considered he might be doing something wrong. He was merely borrowing his customers' money and would eventually get around to returning it. Entrepreneurs must clearly define what is right or wrong in their business, something he never bothered to articulate.

Had he not used his customers' money, he most assuredly would have cut back on overhead, lived within his means, and priced and promoted his product more aggressively. Cheating sows the seeds of failure because the instincts for survival and proper management are lulled to sleep by the false security of unearned funds illegally procured.

Harvey Firestone stated, "The test of a businessman is not whether he can make money in one or two boom years or can make money through the luck of getting into the field first, but whether in a highly competitive field, without having any initial advantage over his competitors, he can outdistance them in a perfectly honorable way and keep the respect of himself and of his community."

Stolen money represents something for nothing. A plague of bitter repercussions accompanies the use of unearned money. You don't have to steal, however, to get unearned dollars. Seductive handouts are available to start-ups from other sources.

The main pusher of this free funding is the government. Through loans and through subsidies or grants, money can be found to bankroll new ventures. Government agencies exist for this very purpose. You're not entitled to this money for two reasons. First, it's generally not earned or deserved, and second, the ultimate source of this money would not give or lend it to you voluntarily. These funds were first harvested from taxpayers who would otherwise have used it for themselves. They surely wouldn't be giving you free dollars to go into business for yourself. You have no right to the earnings of others.

Futhermore, the roster of loans granted by the Small Business Administration (SBA loans) looks like the lineup for bankruptcy court. This agency shows a phenomenal record of funding losers. A venture-capital company they are not. You have a higher chance of failing when you rely on the government for your financing.

It's a neglected cliché, but "You can't get something for nothing." In other words, what seems free costs you dearly. In business unearned money leads to different sets of actions from those you would otherwise take. These actions, or lack of them, lead to failures.

Emerson stated, "everything has its price—and if that price is not paid, not that thing but something else is obtained . . . it is impossible to get anything without its price."

The graveyard of failures financed by government money should convince you not to rely on subsidies. My policy is to take nothing from the government. Develop disdain for the whole sorry process that props up doomed enterprises and promotes failures. Spurn these blandishments for your business. You cannot prosper on the backs of others—nor can you flourish for free.

American agriculture represents a graphic example of the dead end spawned by the "something-for-nothing" ethic. Within our lifetime, this backbone of American commerce has never been truly free. Farmers are served up a blizzard of programs, subsidies, supports, cheap loans, handouts, and welfare. The debt must be paid. Overproduction and falling prices have plunged farmers into economic distress with bleak prospects for escaping. The longer this pipeline of "free" money persists, the greater the debt that must ultimately be paid.

No one escapes these universal laws of compensation. They

are drafted into the proverbs of all nations. Proverbs represent the statement of absolute truth, the law of laws, without qualification. "Measure for measure." "Thou shalt be paid exactly for what thou hast done, no more, no less." "Nothing ventured, nothing gained." "Give and it shall be given you." "As you sow, so shall you reap." "For everything that is given, something is taken."

It is the prod of want and the fear of an empty bank account that forces entrepreneurs to super-perform. Financial dilemmas provoke extra efforts, creative solutions, tenacity, and will. Government doles water down the hardships that teach entrepreneurs the daily acts of monetary magic and financial juggling which give rise to fortune.

For the entrepreneur, unearned money relaxes the adverse circumstances that build self-sufficiency, independence, strength, and confidence. Only by turning your back on handouts will you be forced to take the remedial measures that erase your poverty. Without so doing, you cannot grow and above all you cannot prosper.

Henry Kaiser emphasized, "Men of power, ability and courage do not want a handout. They ask only the opportunity to work, to create, to save, to spend, to be independent of restraints, and to have their greatest energies released for the great business of living."

You are not entitled to the earnings and production of others no matter how far down you are. What is your justification to cut yourself into a slice of someone else's paycheck? Any entrepreneur who can rationalize this subtle form of larceny and make use of a penny of it deserves the moral and financial bankruptcy this weak-kneed philosophy makes inevitable.

True help can be administered only on a voluntary basis. For the truly needy, this is charity for which billions are available. But an entrepreneur needs no good Samaritans. Help yourself. Trade your services. Mortgage a bit of your future. Sell off a part of your new venture. Money can always be found one way or another.

Some start-up entrepreneurs adopt the common practice of collecting unemployment or welfare benefits. They dull the pain of their personal adversity, but in reality practice a small fraud.

There are many hidden penalties working against those

who expect something for nothing. For you, an unwillingness to accept anything for free leads to the character traits necessary for lasting success.

Through self-reliance and integrity, your inevitable business growth gives birth to many opportunities for others in the form of newly created jobs. Of all the by-products of the entrepreneur's search for wealth, new work for others seems the happiest consequence.

In creating jobs, it is hoped you will become a benevolent employer. This new and ongoing relationship has the utmost bearing on the evolution of your enterprise. Happy, fulfilled employees are fundamental to a growing, prosperous venture.

A good rule to keep in mind with your employees is to respect their self-interest. In the long run, loyalty will always be subordinated to salary. You can't expect employees to have the same devotion to company affairs as you do. Present and future compensation motivates employees more than anything else. The way to keep your company upbeat, optimistic, sharp, and attentive is through generous wages.

One day an employee and ad salesman for my magazine venture kidded me about the necessity of starting a union in the company. "That would be great," I replied. "We could get these wages down." Our pay scales were higher than what union demands would have been. Whenever possible, I would propose that entrepreneurial companies follow such a policy. It not only shows concern for your workers, it attracts the best people.

Andrew Carnegie gave this advice,

> The great secret of success in business of all kinds, and especially in manufacturing, where a small saving in each process means fortune, is a liberal division of profits among the men who help to make them, and the wider the distribution the better. Unsuspected powers lie latent in willing men around us which only need appreciation and development to produce surprising results. Money rewards will not, however, insure these, for to the most sensitive and ambitious natures there must be the note of sympathy, appreciation, and friendship. Genius is sensitive in all its forms, and it is unusual, not ordinary, ability that tells even

in practical affairs. You must capture and keep the heart of the original and supremely able man before his brain can do its best. Indeed this law has no limits. Even the mere laborer becomes more efficient as regard for his employer grows. Hand service or head service, it is the heart service that counts.

Generous salaries should be complemented with a solid profit sharing and retirement program, plus insurance benefits and other corporate goodies that compensate workers.

Whenever possible, incentives and commissions that reward superior performance should be put in place. Most companies can't stand to see an employee rack up extraordinary personal income. I had an employee who earned over a million dollars one year. Why be cheap and shortsighted when he made ten times that amount for the company?

Harvey Firestone laid down these four rules in the early part of this century. They still have application:

1. Provide the best possible working conditions.
2. Try to pay a somewhat higher wage than anyone else pays.
3. Provide rewards and facilities over and above what any other company provides.
4. Insist that foremen treat their men as human beings should be treated.

Your hiring policy should be open-minded. No decent company precludes any race, creed, or sex. Nor should you ever spurn the unattractive, the young, the old, the handicapped, or mild deviates. The only worthwhile criterion by which to judge potential employees is merit. They cut the mustard or they don't.

In the best of companies, highly motivated employees experience new challenges, personal growth, and fulfillment. Opportunities for advancement are open to all. Extra effort and excellence find handsome rewards.

Without fulfilled and motivated employees, a company cannot be great. Entrepreneurs set the standards of excellence and performance within their companies. Great entrepreneurs make great companies. Healthy pay scales and splendid opportunities are part of an entrepreneur's formula for excellence. The balance of the recipe for greatness is made up of intangibles that concern the treatment and the familial spirit of people within the organization.

A good entrepreneurial company exudes the spirit of excellence and pride. Concern for the employees, their welfare and their dignity, percolates down from the top. Employees share the high expectations of the entrepreneur. Peer pressure compels high performance. Unity and commitment are commonplace. Under the umbrella of this spirit, productivity flows, suggestions and input abound, harmony blossoms, and the corporate family flourishes.

If your company is such a place, if it is the best place to work, you are in tune with the essential elements of an operating motif we can describe as the "best philosophy." We have dwelled at length on the importance of the best service and the best quality. The "best philosophy" should permeate every facet of your company, from its inauguration to its arrival as an institution. That means the best marketing, the best advertising, the best distribution, the best personnel, the best R & D, the best management, the best controls, the best safeguards, the best computer department, the best operations section, the best mail room, the best telephone service, the best shipping department, and the best security.

David Ogilvy relates how he studied the methods of J. P. Morgan & Company. Morgan had said that his bank must always confine itself to "First Class business and that in a First Class way. This too became my policy at Ogilvy and Mather."

That kind of company can never evolve without integrity. It can never develop by trying to get "something for nothing." It can never happen with disgruntled, undermotivated employees.

Honesty, self-reliance, and generosity underpin the best entrepreneurial performances. These fundamentals are the taproots of quality and service. If you would be a thriving entrepreneur of substance and longevity, you need to practice these three clear and critical tenets.

SUMMARY

No company can prosper for long if it is not scrupulously honest. Don't believe the myth that crooked behavior is a common ingredient in business success. All the great companies have a high level of integrity. You can't give genuine service without it.

Honesty should never be a platitude you mouth without sincerity. When someone talks of honesty most people hear only clichés. Integrity must be an emotionalized, deeply felt aspect of your new company. Nothing is more crucial to your success.

Too many new companies try to get some sort of free financial help from the government. The laws of human nature work to your disadvantage if you embrace this philosophy. Inevitably you will have to earn what you get, and the price comes high. Getting something for nothing will postpone your reward and perhaps nullify it forever.

Once the rewards of your enterprise come in, you should be generous in sharing them with your employees. A highly paid staff is a motivated bunch. You will profit all the more by allowing your workers to reach high levels of compensation. Pass out other corporate rewards as well.

6.
Winning Ways
to Keep You
Going

Within us all there are wells of thought and dynamos of energy which are not suspected until emergencies arise. Then oftentimes we find that it is comparatively simple to double or treble our former capacities and to amaze ourselves by the results achieved.

—THOMAS J. WATSON
IBM

My study of entrepreneurs so far seems to lead to the conclusion that a correlation exists between suffering and success. Entrepreneurs with modest objectives undergo moderate stress and adversity. Those with larger ambitions will, before they succeed, endure painful struggles and overcome long, bitter periods of intense anxiety. The greater the suffering, the greater seem to be the inevitable rewards.

As Edward Acheson, founder of Carborundum Corp., said, "History records few careers which were not marked in their early stages by inordinate, almost superhuman difficulties and trials, calling for immeasurable courage and faith."

The most difficult and momentous step for an entrepreneur is the decision to go ahead and start. It takes a dash of bravery and guts to begin. The newcomer cannot overcome all objections and account for every contingency. There is no assurance of safety, no security—only risk and a host of unknowns. Everything goes on the line.

The entrepreneur stands alone, either doubted, ridiculed, or ignored and believing in self, having faith in an idea, and relying on an intangible dream as an anchor.

The exhilarating emotions that surround the start-up periodically give way to agonizing doubt. The total absence of job, paycheck, and security kindles fear and weakens resolve. Worry and stress plague the entrepreneur. Discomfort and pain start from the very first day.

The daily tasks of founding and running a business often seem insurmountable. Generally, these experiences are bungled the first time through. Nobody does anything well the first time. When Thomas Edison presented his first sizable royalty check ($500) to be cashed, he did not even know enough to endorse it. When asked to do so by the teller, he misunderstood, thought something was wrong, and stumbled out of the bank in awkward embarrassment.

When I delivered my first insurance policy, the policyholder paid me the small premium and asked that I receipt the invoice. After a long, embarrassing silence, I asked him how that was done. He glowered at me, stabbed at the invoice with his finger, and growled in the gruffest tone imaginable, "Put down the date, write 'paid,' and sign it."

One of the most endearing qualities of my partner, Bernie, was his total honesty in handling things he didn't understand. When someone gave us a dissertation on a subject, he would frequently interrupt and ask, "What does that mean?" even if it was something he should have known. This refreshing approach stood out only because so few people were as forthright. The lack of pretense earned him far more respect and insight than bluffing his way through would have. It's a policy I quickly adopted for myself, as should you.

There's no need to be particularly sophisticated or adroit early in your business. Ask for advice or instructions and you'll get them. Only phonies nod their heads as if they know something when they don't.

In any business there comes a time when you have to ask for an order. Consequently, all entrepreneurs suffer serious rejection that they must learn to handle. The initial embarrassment of asking for an order and being rejected terrifies many people. I once had an employee plead with me that he never be expected to talk to customers about ordering or be asked to sell anything. I had no such plans for him. Nevertheless, he was petrified.

Constant bouts of rejection are visited upon entrepreneurs. At first they are excruciating experiences. In time, the skin thickens and rejection can be more easily shrugged off.

One of the first sales presentations for my water machine was to a condominium board in north Miami. The chairman, a wiry little squirt, was most antagonistic to my product even before I started my presentation. Consequently, I froze up during my sales pitch and began to stammer, perspire, and forget my lines. My delivery ended abruptly when he cut me off, turned down my proposal, and verbally kicked me out of the meeting. On the way home, I felt the rejection and humiliation so intensely that I accidentally swung onto the wrong freeway and drove many miles in the wrong direction before my mind switched subjects.

Ten months later, after experiencing a measure of success, I went back to the same condo board. By this time I wanted to prove to myself that I could overcome the prior rejection and show how smooth and confident I had become. The little chairman came in once again and began raising the dickens because I was there. I pleaded for a hearing and he granted me "two minutes." Inexplicably, I blew it again—forgot my lines and looked at my shoes. In moments, he cut off my garbled incantations and again tossed me out. I left totally demoralized.

Rejection can be even more unbearable when it happens in front of a crowd. When I needed equipment financing for my water venture, I called on a former banker who had a small leasing company in Coral Gables. He gave some attention to my request. We had a few cordial meetings, and finally he turned me down. I stopped to see him one last time with a new idea. His waiting room was full. He was busy with people in his office. Eventually he got up from behind his desk, looked into the outer room, and saw me. Suddenly he barged through the door cursing wildly and screamed at me never to bother him again. I jumped up in front of the startled and embarrassed audience and fled. It took me weeks to get over it.

Any new entrepreneur faced with introducing a new service or product will be confronted with excruciating rejection. The cure for the subsequent pain comes from having enough tenacity to keep taking this rejection. Consequently, it ceases to bother, becomes expected, and spurs additional effort. In time, you get tougher, stronger, more persistent, and eminently more persuasive.

Rejection, however, takes a backseat to the worst of all adversities—lack of money. There's no more grievous problem or painful circumstance than running out of cash. The thought of no funds crushes the will and spirit. It gives counsel to fear and leads to a negative mind-set. Nothing else leads so quickly into giving up and quitting. Many would-be entrepreneurs flee this pain and never consider establishing their own venture again. Andrew Carnegie wanted enough capital in his business so he "should never again be called upon to endure such nights and days of racking anxiety." Nothing describes this experience better than Carnegie's phrase, *racking anxiety*.

Some company founders do manage to escape this misery. Smaller ventures can often get by without cash binds. Some larger start-ups are nicely financed by public offerings. Nevertheless, the odds are that most entrepreneurs will have to face this nastiest of all confrontations. At this financial high noon, some will back down and some will fight. Those who plug on inevitably succeed.

In an earlier chapter, I chronicled the perpetual scarcity of dollars that plagued my first venture. When bill-paying time arrived, we sent five dollars on a two-hundred-dollar bill. But at least we paid something. And so our vendors became flexible. We scraped and struggled and made do. Somehow, the money always appeared.

On two subsequent occasions I have gone through similar suffering. Once I limped along for six months with no personal income. Yet I got through. Something always breaks loose to help solve a financial crisis.

Lee De Forest, inventor of the vacuum tube that made modern radio broadcasting possible, advised, "There were times when I felt as if I had gone my limit. Some of my setbacks were stunners. It seemed as if I couldn't get the stamina to start again. But every time, when I had studied things over a little, I would find a way out. No matter how hopeless things look, there is always a way out, if you look for it hard enough."

Monetary deprivation is a time of true testing. It requires a rarefied brand of persistence and courage. My conclusion, based on my own experience and its myriad similarities with that of other successful entrepreneurs, argues that financial affairs inevitably improve. Money always turns up. You hang in there like a stubborn post, suffering in silence, with a blind faith that all will be well and time and again circumstances improve.

If you stick with something long enough, experience will wash over you and in time wear down and eliminate the unpleasant qualities from your personality that impede your success. Rudeness, superiority, and overoptimism vanish. Poor ideas, quackery, and impractical thoughts are replaced with realism.

Failure, in itself, is impossible. You don't fail, you quit. You can't fail if you don't give up, because keeping on precludes failing. No matter how desperate circumstances are, these events cannot force you to quit. Only you can make that decision. There is no such thing as an entrepreneur who failed in business—only one who gave up.

It could be argued that a company forced into bankruptcy takes the decision of quitting out of the entrepreneur's hands. However, many companies survive this debacle and go on to prosper.

Walt Disney suffered through a bankruptcy and a breakdown. Milton Hershey went bankrupt. H. J. Heinz saw his fledgling firm forced into bankruptcy. His misery spilled out into these depressing notes in his diary, jotted down at the time of his failure during Christmas in 1875, "I feel sad, as though I had not a true friend in the world. . . . People care little about you without money . . . friends are seemingly so as long as it costs them nothing. . . . It is hard to lose trade, money, friends and reputation. . . . People talk terribly. I feel sad and constantly worried. It's hard to bear . . . all of us are called rascals." Within a few years, H. J. Heinz had the company that bears his name flourishing.

Even if the entrepreneur is squeezed out of his or her company, with all the attendant humiliation, a fresh start means there was no failure but only temporary defeat. Will C. Durant founded the company that would become General Motors and was subsequently forced out. He started another auto company, Buick, and in time took control of General Motors again.

There are other setbacks that damage every start-up. For some there are canceled orders and broken contracts, for others, dishonest employees or foolish expenditures. Disappointments are endemic to new companies.

Similar sagas color the lives of all entrepreneurs. These frequent bad experiences are shrewd instructors. For, without the rejection and bitter defeat, without financial peril and failure, and without periodic plunges into anxiety and despair, success remains elusive. You don't succeed without a measure of suffering.

Emerson depicted these benefits as follows, "When man . . . is pushed, tormented, defeated, he has a chance to learn something; he has been put on his wits, on his manhood, he has gained facts, learns his ignorance, is cured of the insanity of conceit; has got moderation and real skill."

When I reflect on my business career, I can see that the sharpest defeats taught the greatest lessons. The delays, disappointments, and setbacks led to new plans and greater efforts— all of which paid huge dividends downstream. Each second of pain and struggle for the new entrepreneur adds to a store of gains and benefits to be harvested later. These difficulties are traced and tracked and added to a ledger in your name to be drawn on at some future time.

You may greet your personal pain with aversion or self-pity and let it sap your will. But you should be glad and even rejoice in it, for it is the stuff that clinches your eventual victory.

The best cure for "racking anxiety" is work. As tea company founder Thomas Lipton said, "Work, work, always work, is the only talisman." To banish depression, worry, and fear, go to work. Thomas Edison said, "I have always found, when I was worrying, that the best thing to do was put my mind upon something, work hard and forget what was troubling me."

Like many others, I assumed that simply because I went into business, quick success would follow. I grievously underestimated (and still do) the time necessary for a new project to get into the black. Most of the difficulties I encountered couldn't have been forecast; they managed to catch me by surprise.

When a struggling entrepreneur asked my advice about getting off to a fast start, I gave him the following simple analogy.

Imagine you're pushing a huge ball, larger than yourself, up a mountainside. This heavy ball almost rolls away from you and sometimes nearly rolls back over you. You strain and groan and put your weary shoulder to it. Time and again the incline seems too steep, your muscles too painful to keep pushing. Nevertheless, you stubbornly keep on edging the ball upward. The struggle seems endless and, at times, futile. Near the pinnacle, the incline becomes even steeper, the struggle unbearable. For some reason you push on. Finally, you reach the crest, and the ball is suddenly lighter. You are still striving mightily, blind to the fact that it rolls more easily. Suddenly, the momentum picks up and the ball tumbles free.

One of the crucial elements to ultimate success respects the entrepreneur's reception and response to the word *no*. For various reasons, many people are fond of saying *no*. They have rules and guidelines to follow, but *no* gives them power and often saves them work. In business start-ups, it is a far more universal response than yes. The examples are endless. No, we can't deliver the new furniture this week. No, we can't fix the photocopier until next week. No, you can't get a permit. No, you can't reprint that. No, we don't have a room. No, we can't reinstate that. No, we can't get it placed in time. No, we can't ship today.

You can't do this or you can't do that. Life in business seems often to be an unbroken string of refusals and elaborate reasons why something you want can't be done. Most people seem ready to accept no for an answer, but it should be the starting point in the pursuit of a yes. Most of these rejections can be turned around. You can talk the naysayer into changing his or her mind. You can talk to the supervisor. You can bring the pressure of other people to bear. You can bluster, soft-soap, wheedle, or weep. You can argue, threaten, promise, or beg. When you want something and are met with a no, nine out of ten times you can turn the answer around.

Much of this may seem obvious, but nevertheless, for most people a no means exactly that. They are stopped flat in their tracks. They don't even try to get around this minor obstacle. Accepting no from vendors, service people, bureaucrats, suppliers, shippers, or booking agents, to say nothing of potential customers, cannot be tolerated by any entrepreneur wishing to build a sound and efficient enterprise speedily.

My marketing associate from California, Jay Abraham, taught me an invaluable lesson in turning no into yes in the marketing of his personal services to my company. When Jay called me for the first time several years ago and proposed an affiliation, I was lukewarm at best. He carried a fancy price tag and I quickly lost interest. Thereafter, I was greeted with a daily barrage of phone calls, letters, Mailgrams, wires, and third-party referrals. At the end of the first week I began to budge. By the second week, we were talking fees and compensation. Throughout our dialogue, the bombardment never let up. Far from thinking him a pest, I was impressed with his persistence and expertise. Eventually we made a deal that has lasted virtually unbroken for seven years. As a consequence, my company's sales volume has gone up, and he has earned many hundreds of thousands of dollars.

Sales lore spills over with examples of persistence turning no's into yeses. Good salespeople invariably call and call again. In fact, most sales don't happen until four or five contacts have been made.

This kind of gritty determination proves priceless to entrepreneurs, and it is only part of an ongoing philosophy of total devotion to the cause. The decision to become an entrepreneur means far more than a short-term fling at one's own business. It really means a new way of living, with a dominating and demanding commitment, particularly if you have ambitions to become a superentrepreneur.

A distinction should be drawn here between an entrepreneurial company and a business that has lost that edge. Many one-person start-ups rapidly lose their entrepreneurial aspects. They cease innovating. They reach a satisfactory business level and settle for a comfortable income, reasonably free of stress.

Casualty insurance agents, for example, often quit selling after their business is built up, satisfied to live from renewals. Such a business can no longer be considered entrepreneurial.

Company founders who continue to innovate, to take risks, and to grow remain entrepreneurs. If they keep at it long enough, they become highly successful superentrepreneurs with large regional or national companies.

The balance of this chapter is attuned to those who constitute the latter category. That kind of success requires total involvement. The best word to describe this behavioral state is *intensity*. For example, Willis H. Carrier (Carrier Corp., now part of United Technologies), inventor and developer of air conditioning, was considered dangerous at the wheel of a car when concentrating on the solution to a problem. Once, when he was deep in thought, he boarded a train and completely forgot where he was going.

As a consequence of this kind of intensity, the entrepreneur's business becomes his or her world. Virtually all other considerations are shunted into the background. The company and the task at hand become all-important. The superentrepreneurs funnel their essence into the business. Creativity, labor, inspiration, love, and concern pour into the enterprise. In time this intense application evolves into genius.

Few entrepreneurs start out with a single business concept or organization and follow a straight line to glory. The path is checkered and strewn with an assortment of deals, schemes, pitfalls, and fantasies. An assemblage of wheelers and dealers, wizards and crackpots, peacocks and bullshitters, embroider the journey.

Henry Ford left several auto companies he was instrumental in forming before he went on to raise enough money to start up the Ford Motor Company. Among those investing in the new company were the Dodge brothers, a crusty pair of characters who reaped a fortune from Ford, started their own successful car company, and sued Ford in a monumental and bitter round of litigation.

Thomas Edison, from the initiation of his career, was wrapped up in so many tortuous relationships that it is hard to follow his tangled path. Unquestionably, he went overboard on deals. Naturally optimistic, he accepted help from anyone who might back him or reinforce his efforts. Consequently, he wasted time stalling or extricating himself from innumerable lawsuits.

Although everyone's entrepreneurial experiences are different, they all have a strikingly similar thread. The actors change, the stage differs in time and place, but the play stays the same. It's a delightfully entertaining, brisk, and exciting adventure.

The interminable string of deals and relationships, laced with the inescapable blunders and setbacks of blossoming enterprise, offers priceless experience. The keen insights of the clever innovator and sharp perception of the wise decision maker are thus honed. Only through experience does the subtle mastery of the entrepreneur's craft come about. It is this rich tapestry of events, of partners and problems, of setbacks and survivors, that teaches these powerful and invaluable lessons.

Experience leads directly to higher levels of success. The subconscious and the sixth sense become influential, ever-present directors. The seasoned entrepreneur instinctively comes to feel what is right or wrong. Gut-level bull's-eyes astonish competitors. People and personalities are adroitly employed; weaknesses and strengths assessed and catalogued. The subtle focusing of all experience, crowning achievement of the entrepreneurial mind, brushes the infinite and fosters wisdom.

This art of winning comes through constant application and attention. Neglect and pride whisk it away. Neither will impatience hurry its coming. These talents begin only with proper intervals of time. You will see their presence when you have made your commitment, paid your dues, and proved your merit.

If you last, keep on and maintain your zest for the battle, then ultimately you can become a superentrepreneur. From the earliest days of your entrepreneurial career, your view of the future will help to shape it. I urge you to keep sight of bigger things. Lay down healthy and spectacular ambitions for yourself. Your goal should be centered on a massive amount of wealth you intend to capture. I started out selling an unworkable water purifier, but my goals were articulated in multimillions of dollars.

Later, I crystallized in my mind a strategy that would ensure the volume of wealth I wanted. I began to think in terms of a national, rather than a local, company. Although that thought hardly seems overpowering, it is extremely difficult to adjust your thinking and upgrade the scope of your company.

When I first started in the precious metals business, months would pass when my income rarely covered my expenses. I managed to establish a small beachhead, but I realized that my local business would grant me no fortune. It became clear that I had to switch my idea from a local enterprise to a national concern. Such a change in mental strategy takes concentration and inducement. However, once you make this mental adjustment, your potential rewards become limitless. Whatever your enterprise, bend it and shape it with an eye to national application.

I could have settled for 500 local clients whose transactions would have generated enough commissions for me to live comfortably. But I opted for a national concern and, at last count, my company had 70,000 clients. The rewards for going national are truly great.

The first of several operating philosophies of supreme importance to novice entrepreneurs concerns big versus little. Make a decision for larger size and scope. Define your business and its goals in national terms. Why not? You have the time, you have the ability, you have the exact guidelines that worked for me, and you have Hill's formula to fall back on, which can ensure your success no matter how titanic your struggle.

Those of you with big plans and ambitious goals are needed both at home and in the far-flung corners of the world. You are needed to raise living standards and to help erase poverty. These things entrepreneurs have done—time and again—by creating wealth, by creating work, by creating new technologies and breakthroughs. For two hundred years, entrepreneurs have fed, clothed, housed, transported, and healed us. They have given us our wages and our wealth, our leisure and our labor. They have given us light and heat. They have extended our lives and secured our prosperity as no other civilization before us could hope or dream.

This new wealth supported politicians and clergy, schoolteachers and economists, government employees and professors, many of whom have even seen fit to denounce the source of the largesse. Foundations and charities, libraries and hospitals, science and research centers all found aid and sustenance through the generosity of entrepreneurs. Contrary to popular belief, entrepreneurs have been noteworthy for their generosity. In our country, the bulk of most great fortunes has been donated or distributed away. Our great business pioneers have seldom been stingy.

Unfortunately, an amazingly tiny contingent serves as the wellspring for dispensing the human treasures of comfort, luxury, and fulfillment. That we need more of such men and women goes without saying. They are some of the bravest among us and we are at last recognizing their accomplishments.

For the up-and-coming entrepreneur, these are good times. Society is warming up to its entrepreneurs. Favorable publicity and rewards other than wealth are a bonus. Today entrepreneurs are regarded with new esteem. Truly, it is a time to expand your objectives and build a national enterprise.

SUMMARY

There is a correlation between the misery you experience and the extent of your ultimate success. Initially, you are bombarded with problems. You learn about business as you go through the motions. Don't bluff your way; ask for even the most elementary information if you don't know it.

You can only overcome your sensitivity to rejection by being rejected. As an entrepreneur your skin will get thick in a hurry.

Money problems are resolved through perseverance. Financial setbacks are common to the history of all entrepreneurs. The more adversity you suffer, the more you learn.

The way out of your misery is to go to work. Added efforts bring relief from the business blues.

When someone tells you no, that is just the beginning. The

art of overcoming the word *no* is something you must master.

If you are going to become a major entrepreneur, you need to think about your company as national in scope. Upgrade the perception of your enterprise.

Enough experience will make you wise.

7.
How to Manage Your Up-and-Coming Enterprise

Managing a company is like writing in the snow: You have to go over and over the same words as the snow falls if you want your writing to remain legible.

—HAROLD GENEEN

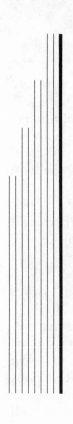

Growth in your enterprise indicates that you have picked the right business and are running it well. The primary mission of your business is to secure customers. The first time someone does business with you is a make-or-break transaction. It's exceedingly difficult to get that first order, but once you've got it in hand, you have a chance to show how good you are.

Customers always tend to return to the same source or establishment for repeat transactions. They lose their fear of the unknown and may even develop a certain loyalty. That is why you must super-perform on initial orders.

A one-time customer is of marginal value, and a business that does but one order or deal with each client is tough to make profitable. If you serve a customer only once, you have to levy a much higher charge or margin.

Profits on a customer usually don't come from preliminary orders. There are high acquisition costs involved with them. When the customer reorders and does business with your company again and again, you will see growth, and with it, the long overdue profits.

Mack Hanan puts it this way, "If you are willing to pay your dues, you can get customers—once. Turning them and returning them to your business is where profit is made. *The faster you bring them back and the more profit they contribute to you on each return, the faster you will grow.*" (Italics added)

As you serve this expanding clientele, you should always search for new quality or service breakthroughs. Anything you can do for customers that improves on your present service will pay off. In my company, for example, we filled our customers' orders, dropped them in the mail, and that was the end of it. We knew our clients were edgy, however, and always a bit anxious until their order arrived.

We began a policy wherein a woman in our office would call to inform our customers politely that their order was in the mail. Have you ever ordered an item from an out-of-state firm that called you to advise it was on the way and thank you once again for your order? Our clients loved us for it.

Once you have secured numerous ongoing customers through outstanding service, you must continue to keep them happy. If they are used to good service from you and there is a lapse into inferior treatment, you are exposed to a curious phenomenon. People get far angrier over bad service on later transactions than they do over equivalent sloppiness on early orders.

Outstanding companies are good at procuring customers and great at keeping them. They consistently please. Only a tiny percentage of their overall transactions go sour. This consistency is the mark of a well-managed company.

As your firm grows and adds new employees, you will be required to understand and implement management techniques that insure the smooth performance of your concern. In a rank start-up, you are the lone entrepreneur, the primary engine of quality. In the beginning, you answer the phone, send out the mail, obtain the orders, pay the bills, and serve the customers. Almost at once, a secretary relieves you of some of these details.

Other new employees lighten your workload or meet the demands of expansion.

Frank W. Woolworth wrote, "As soon as a business grows beyond one's ability to attend to all of the details himself, he must trust to organization and cooperation to carry it forward."

Richard Sears, founder of the company that bears his name, said, "A few notable successes have been made in the industrial world through what is known as the 'one-man organization.' But I believe that in the great majority of cases it is the men you choose as subordinates who make your success.

"Select your men carefully and at the right time—then give them free rein within certain well-defined limits. This attitude toward employees I believe underlies the success of a large number of big businesses."

With up to about ten employees, you are in such close proximity and frequent verbal communication that you manage without being conscious of it. Your mission to procure and keep customers is implanted in your employees' psyches daily by simple exposure to you. If something or someone fails to harmonize with that objective, you can very quickly ferret out the problem. Everyone reports directly to you and is located within earshot.

Back when I had four employees, a customer paid for a ten-thousand-dollar order in cash. One young woman had the job of taking all payments to the bank and putting them in the night depository. She dropped off the checks, but somehow forgot to put in the cash. It wound up in her bedroom dresser drawer. Another woman, verifying the deposits a few days later, called the shortage to my attention. This was a lot of money for us at the time and cause for great alarm. The guilty party quickly broke down and confessed. We rescued the money and terminated her employment. This mishap points out the need for all money matters to be cross-checked by two people and possibly a third outsider—no matter what the size of your company. Also, it indicates the simplicity of keeping track of a small enterprise; a woman merely walked across a one-room office and brought the deficit to my attention. Smallness, by definition, is far easier to manage.

Nevertheless, when a handful of employees are introduced to your embryonic company, you need the rudiments of a management system. Employees bring the need for rules and policies. They, unlike you, do not live the business, work for however long the job takes, or always do by reflex what is best for the enterprise. They need to be told.

Almost from the start, if you have at least five employees, you need a policy manual. These few sheets of paper should spell out work hours, company rules, breaks, vacation time, sick leave, benefits, and health insurance details.

An individual personnel file should be set up on each new employee, which should contain their job application, test score results, and job description. This latter item should point out the approximate tasks they have been hired for. Both you and they should clearly understand what their role in the company will be. A written job description clarifies this matter. It should be reviewed and updated periodically.

You, or someone else, should see that your new employees are trained well enough to begin functioning in their new occupation. Don't expect people to learn their jobs by osmosis. It is a common entrepreneurial shortcoming to expect people to have the same intensity, learning skills, and dedication that you have. They need direction and training. Spell things out.

Right from the early stages of your venture, you should develop some sort of management principles that you want to emphasize. It occurred to me that the most important consideration for my employees and me was to avoid mistakes. A big enough mistake could sink the firm and, at the very least, blunders were costly. The company could prosper without too many errors. I began to repeat aloud many times, *"Mistakes cost money."*

It was one thing to manage for results, in other words, see that the job was done. It was equally important, however, to thwart mistakes that might crop up in all areas of the company. This is especially true in the early growth stages, when a few big blunders could devastate you. A mistake with an order could cost you a customer, but a mistake in your insurance coverage, for example, could finish you.

The average small company pays little attention to major mistake avoidance. An antiques dealer recently had his entire inventory stolen from a truck at a New York show. His insurance coverage did not apply when the goods were in somebody else's truck away from his premises. He lost his business as a result.

Never allow your major company assets to be exposed. Always maintain tight security, keep hedged, don't trust anyone else's insurance coverage (it never covers you).

Never count on anyone else's promises or commitments if their failure to come through will damage you. Don't pay for anything up front. Get the goods before you remit. Employ all kinds of safeguards, cross-checks, insurance, and fail-safe measures. Think defensively. Always examine how you might be hurt in a situation. Don't set yourself up to be cheated or swindled. Don't be too trusting. Get advice from accountants, attorneys, and insurance agents on any new contingency you are faced with. You should always be trying to checkmate exposures, loopholes, mistakes, and unexpected circumstances that could harm or destroy your company.

My late partner, Bernie, taught me the value of a slight dose of paranoia. He never totally believed anyone's promises or assurances when it came to major monetary affairs. He remained somewhat skeptical, didn't trust anyone with our assets, and always limited his exposure. He converted my gullible and somewhat naive perceptions into a far more realistic interpretation of the world. A little paranoia in business is good.

By the time you've hired ten or twelve employees, one of them should emerge as a managerial type. In addition to his or her other duties, you should make this person your management assistant. This will relieve you of preliminary screening of new employees, personnel requests for time off, and other similar demands on your time. This person can supervise the results of your workers and review salaries and raises with you. If you are likely to keep on growing, plan to groom this person as your chief manager. Send him or her to a few management seminars, with instructions to take notes and review the seminar for you.

There are two types of employees in the start-up company —those who produce the business and those who support that initiative, the operational people. Initially, you—the founder— are probably a producer. Much later you will become a third classification—top management.

Operational or management problems (how to do things right consistently) begin to unsettle you and your enterprise from early in its development. Growth compounds these irritations by presenting new snafus that demand your attention. In the early stages of growth, anything unexpected should be confronted and resolved by you. Procedures and operations that have been mastered by you can be passed on to others.

The responsibilities you turn over to others can immediately become Achilles' heels, however. In my company's early days, we were an investment company and, as I have mentioned, we also made and marketed wood-burning stoves. In time I turned responsibility for the wood-stove division over to a semi-experienced thirty-year-old who seemed to master the operation quickly. I gave him a small commission on all stove sales.

In less than a year, he managed to get me into a ticklish mess. In addition to selling stoves, we licensed other manufacturers to make and sell our line of wood burners. We controlled the royalties owed us from the cast-iron door on the stove. Licensees had to order doors from us for any stoves they made.

It looked as though a big year was coming up in wood stoves. With energy costs soaring, demand appeared high. We were going to go with a new, attractively enameled stove door. My manager had been negotiating with an out-of-state firm that would cast the doors and add the enameling. We would pay them on completion of the project.

An invoice rolled in a few weeks later, and an incredulous clerical staffer approached me. "Did we order sixty thousand stove doors?" "Sixty thousand stove doors," I blurted, "Are you mad?" I grabbed the bill from her hand and scanned it. Sixty thousand stove doors at fifteen dollars each came to an amount so huge it momentarily paralyzed me with terror. I ordered the manager over to my desk and he verified that he had placed the order. In those days, adversity had yet to mellow my temperament. I threw a tantrum of rare intensity.

Fortunately, the stove door company had just begun their work on our behalf. I was able to kill the mammoth order and negotiate our way out of the agreement. Within a few more months, I spun off the business. Gone unheeded for a few more weeks, the order for stove doors would have generated a liability we could not have met. Furthermore, the stove business hit a downdraft, and most companies producing them choked on their inventory.

In a new company, many inexperienced people are doing jobs for the first time. My stove manager was seemingly adept but turned out to have little common sense. You can never be sure initially about anyone, so you must safeguard yourself against their irresponsible actions. Unfortunately, there is a tendency for them to hide these bad decisions and blunders from you. This chapter will tell you how to concentrate on establishing reporting systems that will get you the information you need to spot these problems.

Your employees will likely make a number of bad decisions, but you can exert a measure of control in prohibiting the big, important decisions from being bad ones. Employee experience and training will take care of the small decisions. You must set up a control or system that enables you to change or intervene before bad decisions are acted upon.

Invariably, the big areas that can hurt you involve spending money. Normally, you are in touch with these expenditures. However, when you put someone else in charge of a project, that person may have the power to obligate you financially. My company has consistently failed to police this responsibility adequately, a failure that has on more than one occasion proved costly and embarrassing.

This problem afflicts companies who diversify more than those that don't. The appointment of a project manager sets the stage for the eventual problem. However, anybody with the power to order or buy for you can harm you. A few years ago one of my buyers spent an extra million dollars while buying inventory for our jewelry division. It caused no end of problems and the eventual loss of a sum almost that large.

You must devise a system that necessitates that all expenditures over a certain amount be passed by you for your initials or signature. You set the amount and revise it upward as you grow.

Then establish a purchase order system. Every item your company buys or orders must be written up on a purchase order. If it's over a certain amount, it requires your initials. Plant this mandatory requirement in all your operations. Write it out and put it in your new policy manual. It will be much easier for your employees to follow your directives if they are clearly spelled out. Furthermore, your policies will work far better if universally applied. Company policy must be uniformly and consistently followed and acted on. For that task, you rely on your managers.

Mack Hanan offers these insights: "Policy must be nailed because it is the hallmark of leadership. . . . Policy must be unequivocal. Objectives must be crystal clear. . . . No organization can survive, let alone grow, if its policies are subject to frequent change or are fuzzy or are communicated so vaguely that they appear to be altered from one expression to another. For this reason, you must be the single professor of policy: its one source and its final interpreter."

My stove door buyer had no specific written rules and controls. I assumed he got the drift about my hopes and intentions for the stove division through our frequent conversations. I lacked the experience to see how inordinately affected he was by his override and commission. He was doing a measure of wishful thinking that we would sell an incredibly huge amount of stoves. He would rack up a fat commission. That is one way in which incentives can work against your interest.

You will notice that employees with commissions or over-rides tend to grow blinders. They concentrate solely on their financial rewards and sometimes lose sight of the bigger picture, the success of the company as a whole. While incentives tend to improve performance, they have an unattractive side of which you should be aware. Keep this in mind and convey it to your managers so that unwise decisions are never made in order to preserve or enhance someone's commission.

A far more distasteful aspect of my stove manager's behavior was the "big man" syndrome. A high percentage of men tend to render decisions based on what makes them look important. I call them "ego decisions." They are the direct opposite of bottom-line decisions. They are made not to maximize profits but to make the decision maker look important. As such, they court disaster.

At the risk of sounding prejudicial, I must admit that in my experience males under the age of thirty-five are far more likely to make foolish, ego-centered decisions than any other age group or gender. You have to be more careful when handing out responsibility to them. When I read recently about a wild, young bank vice-president throwing food around in a restaurant, it fit with the fact that he had also buried his bank in a portfolio of bad oil loans that forced them to close their doors. Young, unseasoned men with big egos and big responsibilities can often be a volatile mixture.

You run similar risks with your own behavior in the major decisions and directions of your enterprise. With profits and success, you become less bottom-line oriented. Your ego swells. You must learn to invoke a fail-safe in all your decisions and be able to sense whether you are feeling self-important over a decision. Ask yourself whether you are making this decision to maximize your profits or to make yourself look good.

Ego decisions are always bad decisions. They come back to haunt you. Unfortunately, more than a few decisions by entrepreneurs or managers are predicated on at least a measure of self-importance. When you catch yourself saying or doing things to look good, to be a big shot, you are on the threshold of a nasty lesson. You must learn to control any hint of egomania and base your decisions solely on business considerations.

Mack Hanan spells out an excellent personal management technique,

> manage yourself as if you are an investment banker to your business. . . . If you take the position of principally having a fiduciary relationship with your business, you will have a singular advantage. You will be better able to resist the tender traps of becoming romantically involved with its products to the point where you may try to maximize their technical inputs or their market share instead of their contribution to profit.
>
> The return-on-investment thinking that this mind set fosters will aid you in making and revising appropriations, setting and enforcing policy, and conducting yourself in proper growth business style. To be growth-minded, in this sense, means that you quite literally mind your business: that is, you become a bottom-liner who runs a tight shop that brings in the bucks.

By the time you have twenty or more employees, you need to invoke additional management programs and techniques. Every company should have a corporate philosophy centered on quality, service, honesty, and whatever else fits that particular company's role. It should be written out and placed in the policy manual.

All newcomers should be indoctrinated with this philosophy and old employees constantly reminded. This upbeat philosophy should be conveyed to employees verbally and in frequent memos and meetings. Our company message stated that we were a highly ethical firm, concerned first and foremost with our customers' interests. It was made clear that we would not tolerate lying, rudeness, low-quality goods, or poor service. In time, our employees were so permeated with our corporate philosophy that tremendous peer pressure arose to ensure everyone's compliance.

This message and others important to your company must be repeated endlessly. An ongoing process that keeps the message in front of every employee should begin with you and be reinforced by your managers.

Your corporate philosophy should be included in all training programs, classes, and meetings your company conducts. This message serves as the foundation to all instruction and training. Thus included, it becomes permanently interwoven in all company doctrine.

"[Y]ou must gain your people's commitment to a similar allegiance," says Mack Hanan. "One way is to charge your staff to implement policy. This will require you to communicate policy. It will also cause you to politic inside your business to urge your team's adherence to it, assure yourself that they understand it, and monitor their compliance with it."

Encourage training and instruction sessions in your company. Supervisors become more adept through the act of teaching. Employees need to be taught over and over again. Simply because they have been told something a time or two, it doesn't mean they have grasped the message. Human nature dictates that learning be reinforced. Information needs to be presented time and again before it's absorbed and mastered. Make sure that training is a continuous, permanent activity in your company.

Along the way, you must also develop an organizational chart. In a young company, the hierarchy and pecking order are often not clearly delineated. If there is any confusion over who an employee works for or reports to, you have the likelihood of bickering and disgruntled personnel. Everyone should know his or her exact place and relationship to everyone else. Put your chief manager in charge of this project and see that this document is published and maintained. It should then be initialed by you and placed in your policy manual.

There will be times when valued employees terminate their jobs with your firm. Replacement people will lack similar experience and be unable to perform as well. Certain aspects of the jobs will be overlooked, and severe errors are likely to crop up. For all crucial jobs or departments, a procedures manual should be established. This information pinpoints the precise method of performing that task. All the subtleties of the job and procedures should be covered. This manual will not only help ensure the smooth, consistent performance of a specific operation by experienced employees, but it will pass on to replacement personnel the precise fashion in which the job should be carried out.

Maintenance of policy and procedure manuals seems to be a chore that most people neglect. In a growing company, manuals quickly become obsolete and those that cover new circumstances never seem to get off the ground. Your management assistant should be in charge of these projects. A brief monthly review and update program can be monitored by this assistant.

Perhaps the preceding advice seems extraneous and merely boilerplate. But if you want to grow fast, keep yourself insulated from a batch of unnecessary problems, make a lot of money, and hold onto that money, *you need to read, reread, and implement* the devices explained here. There are infinite ways your organization can falter from loose procedures, miscommunication, mistakes, and sloppy implementation.

Rapid growth requires careful and intense monitoring. You will have no choice but to be totally absorbed by it. You can't be away for long vacations or trips. So much of what happens will be new and unprecedented, you will be making decisions and choices with limited experience, some intuition, and, I hope, a generous measure of common sense.

One of the best ways to manage during these hectic periods is to participate in the work at various levels of your organization. If a particular department is behind or doing poorly, you can learn a lot by joining them and helping for a few hours. On one occasion, I worked a half-day in the shipping department to help it catch up. Another time a telephone operator couldn't get the proper lilt to her voice. I sat down beside her and answered the phone in exaggerated politeness until she could imitate me perfectly. Not only do you learn about your company this way, you inspire your employees.

You should always circulate through your company, no matter whether business is growing, stable, or shrinking. Visit each profit center. Walk through every department at least once a week. Talk to your people. Ask questions. Encourage suggestions. Let them know you are on top of things. Make sure they know you're aware of their role and their performance. Pass out compliments. Inspect the housekeeping and point out any mess, disorderliness, or sloppy-looking work areas. Insist on neatness. Tear down handwritten signs and pick up scraps from the floor yourself. Frown on any goldbricking you might see.

Hotel-chain founder E. M. Statler knew how to get maximum results from periodic visits to his hotels. He turned them into inspections. Floyd Miller writes in his biography, *Statler*:

> As with all things in life, a business empire cannot stand still—it either grows or diminishes. Statler was determined that his organization would continue to grow, not just in numbers of buildings but in efficiency and quality of service to the public.
>
> Every aspect of hotel work, from the duties of bus boy to manager, had been analyzed and formalized. In theory, the traveler checking into a Statler Hotel would receive perfect service. There was one flaw, however; the work had to be performed by human beings who were subjected to fatigue and boredom and frustration and jealousy and hangover.
>
> To combat these, Statler devised a thing he called "indoor golf." It was nothing more or less than frequent and unannounced inspections. The name came out of an experience he had at the Pennsylvania. One day he and a friend planned a golf game and they left Statler's suite on the top floor and punched the elevator bell. By habit, Statler clicked a stopwatch. There was an unusually long wait for service that morning and when they were finally delivered to the lobby Statler clicked his watch again and frowned at it. John Woelfle was in charge of the elevator service and when

he saw the frown on the boss's face he knew he was in trouble.

Statler walked up to him and shook the stopwatch under his nose. "Do you know how long it took us to get service to the lobby?"

Woelfle made a tactical error: he gave an alibi. "This is a rush hour, Mr. Statler."

"Damn it, that is all the more reason to give good service. By God, I'll show you how it's done." He threw his golf clubs on the floor (they didn't make too much noise because he carried only three clubs—brassie, mashie and putter), stepped before the bank of elevators and took over the starter's job. There was an immediate and dramatic improvement in service.

After some ten minutes of this, his friend became impatient and said, "Stat, we gonna play golf or not?"

Statler grinned at him. "I'm playing indoor golf. It's almost as much fun."

When Statler set out on an inspection tour he took great precautions to keep the fact a secret but invariably there were leaks. The various managers tried to protect each other and frequently wired two little words: "He's coming."

On one of his first inspection visits to Cleveland, the manager met him at the front entrance and said, "It's wonderful to have you here, Mr. Statler. Everything is in tiptop condition and I'm sure you're going to be pleased. We have a room all ready for you, here's the key."

Statler looked at the key as if it was about to bite him. "To hell with that," he said. Then he walked behind the desk and picked a key at random off the rack. "This is the room I'll take," he announced.

In the room that had not been prepared for him, he found a number of things wrong. He lay on the bed to look at the ceiling and discovered a stain. He said to the manager, "The guest's view of the room is often the ceiling. Keep it clean."

When he moved off the bed it squeaked. "Have the carpenter brace that bed with an iron bar through the spring," he ordered.

He inspected the supply of stationery in the desk, the

pins and needles and thread on the dresser, the cleanliness
of the bathroom. From there he went to the public rooms,
the kitchens, the basements. When he left after twenty-four
hours, the staff's nerves were shot.

The larger your company becomes, the further out of touch
you get with your front-line troops. Initially an entrepreneur
with a small company has extensive worker input. These are
often valuable suggestions or justified grievances. Establish a
committee of lower-echelon workers who meet at least quarterly for the purpose of giving you feedback. Change the
makeup of this group periodically to catch a wider sampling of
viewpoints.

You should never neglect the opportunity to talk with a
client. No matter how big you become, always take time to chat
with your customers. In that way, you will uncover many
needed improvements, problem areas, and significant opportunities to serve. In these ways, you will maintain the impetus
and momentum of your growth. Customers will tell you a lot.

In the modern company, you will generally start out with
a sales department. In some companies, you will have to manufacture or make your product. You begin alone or with a tiny
cadre of workers and helpers. You add secretaries and clerical
help. Then you bring on a bookkeeper who in time you hope
to make a controller. You promote someone to be your
managerial assistant. Over the years a personnel department
arises. With volume comes the need for computers and eventually a computer department. The clerical end evolves into an
operations department. You set up a receptionist, a phone
room, and a mail department. You may add art, shipping, or
security departments and sundry other units that fit your company's specific needs. You create more and more department
heads and managers.

Ernest Henderson, the founder of Sheraton Corporation in
Boston, gave valuable advice on making the transition from a
small company into a more sizable entity: "The small operator
excels by personally supervising all minute details. In large
hotels, however, the ability to delegate authority is often the
principal requisite. Success depends more on talent for selecting, training, and inspiring department heads."

Entrepreneurs who make it big, such as Henderson, must

become good managers. There is a great deal of confusion over the roles of managers and entrepreneurs. My company is, without question, the best-managed company in the hard-money business. It has been widely copied. These management talents overlap into a smooth-functioning securities, mutual fund, and money management business. Yet several years ago, when my company encountered tough financial sledding, my attorney and others claimed we were poorly managed. I was a bad manager.

Manage, manager, management—what exactly do they mean and what functions do they encompass? From my frame of reference (that of the entrepreneur) they mean effectively executing my innovations, directions, and decisions.

The genius of Austrian economics, Ludwig von Mises, saw managers as follows: "The managerial function is different from the entrepreneurial function. It is a serious mistake to identify entrepreneurship with management. The management function is always subservient to the entrepreneurial function.

"The entrepreneur determines alone, without any managerial interference, in what lines of business to employ capital and how much to employ. He determines the expansion and contraction of the size of the total business and its main sections. He determines the enterprise's financial structure. These are the essential decisions which are instrumental in the conduct of business. . . . The execution of the details of his projects may then be entrusted to managers."

Entrepreneurs are founders of companies and innovators of new concepts. At the same time, they make important financial decisions, such as where the money is going to be spent. They determine expansion and diversification. They set the tenor and spirit of their organization and they establish and maintain significant outside relationships (banking, legal, and so on). They also know how to make use of good managers.

The concept of management, as popularly practiced and defined today, sometimes includes all the foregoing definitions. A good manager is often thought to possess the skills and responsibilities of the entrepreneur.

At the same time, when most of us think of managers, we visualize people practicing the systematic application of methods that produce and measure results—a noninnovative, but important, function. A good manager of this type may have little promise as a skilled entrepreneur. Thus, we have confusion. *Management,* in the contemporary management vernacular, means two things: innovative leadership and at the same time steadfast supervision.

Problems can arise from these definitions. It could be a blunder to place a supervisory type of manager in charge of a company and expect entrepreneurial results. Furthermore, communication is often obtuse. What is really needed at the head of any established business organization is an entrepreneurial manager. This person should be not only a good entrepreneur, but a good top manager as well. Rather than adopt the cumbersome terminology, "entrepreneurial manager," to define this individual, I suggest a new and easier term, *manageur.* In this fashion, we can denote those managers with entrepreneurial skills and end confusion.

Pierre du Pont, who created du Pont, and Alfred Sloan, president of General Motors for many years, are thought to be the fathers of modern management. More than anything, however, they were innovative and entrepreneurial. Pierre du Pont rescued a minor, struggling gunpowder maker and turned it into a massive multinational. Alfred Sloan struggled to start up a successful auto parts manufacturing company, which he eventually sold to GM. The fact that he steered a floundering General Motors into a dominant world position is rooted in the entrepreneurial talents he developed while founding his own enterprise. Both men were *manageurs* before they were managers. Manageurs run many of the great corporations in the world.

I once asked my friend and business associate, Swiss designer Eduard Schweizer, what key ingredient he found in the many successful companies he had dealt with over the years. "One person," he replied. "Always, there is one strong person."

David Ogilvy wrote, "I have observed that no creative organization whether it is a research laboratory, a magazine, a Paris kitchen, or an advertising agency will produce a great body of work unless it is led by a formidable individual." Harvey Firestone put it this way: "A company must have one head and only one, and he must be the real executive head. The board of directors can advise on policies, but it cannot run the business."

In their best-seller, *In Search of Excellence,* Peters and Waterman, Jr., assess America's greatest companies and ask:

How did these companies get the way they are? Is it always a case of a strong leader at the helm? We must admit that our bias at the beginning was to discount the role of leadership heavily, if for no other reason than that everybody's answer to what's wrong (or right) with whatever organization is its leader. Our strong belief was that the excellent companies had gotten to be the way they are because of a unique set of cultural attributes that distinguish them from the rest, and if we understood those attributes well enough, we could do more than just mutter "leadership" in response to questions like, "Why is J&J so good?" Unfortunately, what we found was that associated with almost every excellent company was a strong leader (or two) who seemed to have had a lot to do with making the company excellent in the first place. Many of these companies—for instance, IBM, P&G, Emerson, J&J, and Dana—seem to have taken on their basic character under the tutelage of a very special person. Moreover, they did it at a fairly early stage of their development.

Why the authors consider this finding unfortunate, I don't know. Perhaps the cult of management harbors some less-than-noble sentiments toward entrepreneurs.

If so, it's well to remember that virtually every major multinational on earth was at one time an embryonic dream of a single person. Conglomerates are a cluster of companies, each emanating from the efforts of one dedicated soul. There would be no Fortune 500 without five hundred hard-charging founders.

Once established, the great corporations are huge and powerful forces in the market that make an ongoing contribution to human advancement. They are well financed and entrenched. Once it has a giant slice of a market, perhaps some favorable legislation, gargantuan R & D budgets, and the ability to get all the financing they need, then a large company will tend to prevail. Unless they become unresponsive or careless, such corporations persist with far greater ease than their upstart challengers.

Many such companies maintain themselves by constantly acquiring new and prospering enterprises. These new divisions carry the entrepreneurial fire and innovation of their founder and contribute generously to earnings. Other companies have the good fortune to corral innovative talent that allows the development of breakthroughs from within.

No matter how large or great a company, it must have more than ordinary managers to survive and prosper over a lengthy period. When Sears, Roebuck made the revolutionary change from mail-order to retail stores, it implemented a policy that enabled it to prosper for the balance of a century. Robert E. Wood foresaw the impact of the population shift from rural areas to the cities. When he conveyed his views to Julius Rosenwald, the architect of Sears' great mail-order success, he was offered a position with the company. A few years after Wood became president of Sears in 1928, the retail outlets sold more than mail order. Sears was blessed with two innovative business giants at its helm for sixty years. Each pioneered breakthroughs in marketing, sources of supply, and employee compensation.

It's simply not enough to call these men good managers. They introduced new concepts and took calculated risks. They were decisive, powerful individuals who parlayed a continuation of innovative and supervisory skills into legendary success.

While neither was a founder of Sears (Richard Sears was a clever mail-order liquidator of distressed merchandise), they lent to the venture the same skills possessed by entrepreneurs of prodigious accomplishment. Innovation is the common ground that links great entrepreneurs. They create and conceptualize outside the bounds of what has been done before and back it with all their energy and will. They push and advance their beliefs with fierce determination and a refusal to bend to what others consider impossible or unworkable.

Henry Ford insisted that an automobile affordable for every American was possible when the wisest of men wrote it off as an impractical contraption. When Adolph Ochs borrowed money to buy the moribund *New York Times*, his mother talked about legally restraining him. When Walt Disney proclaimed, "I'm confident we can create right here in Disney World a showcase to the world of the American free enterprise system," who among us could fathom a glimmering of what this entrepreneurial genius had in mind? The incredible vision that inspired his theme parks was outside the realm of other imaginations.

Since entrepreneur Eli Whitney first engineered vast economic changes up until the technological wizardry of the silicon superstars, entrepreneurs have formed the cutting edge of human advancement. (In addition to inventing the cotton gin, Whitney was the first to mass-produce interchangeable parts, and this revolutionary principle became the bedrock of industrial progress. He was also the pioneer of mass factory production, which made slavery obsolete.)

With all of their accomplishments, many of these innovators suffered major setbacks along the way. All ventures go through cycles. No company experiences uninterrupted growth and profits. Sooner or later, it is visited by a decline, shrinking profits, and internal unrest. When this happens, the founder or chief executive comes under fire. Those who lack majority interest are often dismissed. A number of our most prominent companies bear the name of an entrepreneur who was ultimately pushed out.

Perhaps those companies would have been far better off to keep their founder. We cannot know how many entrepreneurs who were removed from companies they founded would ultimately have turned things around. There are few more unsettling struggles for a company than to terminate its founder. There are few more humiliating experiences for an entrepreneur than to be terminated. You will be wise to think long and hard before relinquishing shares in your company. Declines are inevitable, and human reactions to them are only too predictable.

When a highly visible entrepreneur is evicted from the executive suite, it reinforces the mythology that entrepreneurs can't run a company. The facts argue otherwise. In addition to their flair for innovation, many entrepreneurs build huge and efficient organizations—such as those behind Disney, McDonald's, Hewlett-Packard, Polaroid, and IBM.

Another commonly heard criticism of entrepreneurs suggests they won't relinquish decision making to their underlings. This supposedly inhibits the realization of a company's full potential. In reality, nobody comprehends the fundamentals of the business better than the entrepreneur. You should make as many significant decisions as is humanly possible.

Joyce Hall, the founder of Hallmark, always took part in minute decisions affecting his company. Almost nothing went into production without his initials "OK, J.H." On his judgment of the potential of cards, Hall said he relied on hunches, "the vapor of past experience," and he was virtually never wrong. "They'll show me a card and I'll say, 'No, I don't want it,' and then I'll have a hard time explaining why. But I know I know, and I know I'm right—there's something in the past 48 years that's telling me."

However, making the transition from small to large does require passing out certain responsibility to others. How an entrepreneur negotiates growth and broadens the responsibilities of managers will have an important bearing on future results. Once someone has handled an assigned task flawlessly, you can begin to rely on that person to do it in the future. Then you need to monitor performance and results.

Rapid growth in the early stages requires close attention and the total involvement of the entrepreneur. You may not have the time to attend to management details. I advocate a strong management personality to coordinate with you daily. As your company stabilizes and you are up to one hundred employees or more, the various heads of departments and others with responsibility should be knitted together into a management team. This group should meet weekly, more often if necessary. You should preside over this meeting. Someone should keep track of the topics, record them, and publish a memorandum for later perusal. These meetings give your staffers insights into what you are thinking and where you are heading. In smaller growth companies, many supervisors don't have a clue to where the firm is going. As a consequence, the company is always reacting to situations rather than anticipating them.

Managers need to know what the others are planning and thinking as well. They critique, make suggestions, and coordinate with other departments. Inadequacies and problem areas are scrutinized. Solutions and suggestions are offered to improve shortcomings. Everyone gets a better feel for the company and its personnel.

As the chief executive, you need a steady flow of information. You get it from your management meetings and individual conversations. However, the most important data come through written reports and statistical breakdowns of the numbers. You need to know exactly what's going on in your company. Daily reports should bring you information on sales, purchasing, inventories, shipping, backlogs, orders, production, and so on. You need a weekly financial summary pointing out how much in cash or cash equivalents you have, your *net quick assets.* Weekly reports on personnel, work output, and other matters especially tailored to your operation should be forthcoming.

A brief written breakdown from the chief individual in every department should also cross your desk each month. This should disclose positive results and also point out problems. Managers who are required to write up their accomplishments on a regular basis are inclined to pay closer attention to detail, to be more thorough in the execution of their responsibilities.

You need to examine all these reports fastidiously. Not only are they of great value to your decision making, but they improve efficiency.

Harold Geneen, main architect of ITT, writes in his book, *Managing,* "Paying attention to the numbers is a dull, tiresome routine, a drudgery. The more you want to know about your business, the more detail you want to have, the more numbers there will be. They cannot be skimmed. They must be read, understood, and thought about and compared with other sets of numbers which you have read that day, that week or earlier that year. And you have to do it alone, all by yourself, even when you know that it would be far more stimulating to be doing almost anything else."

Always insist that reports be presented on time. There is an ongoing tendency to slough off this task. Unless you pointedly insist on timely reporting, these memorandums will quickly fall into disuse. Neglect this requirement once or twice, and the vital information flow will stop. Come down hard on those who procrastinate and, in time, consistent reports will be routine.

Each section of your company should have written operational procedures and policy manuals. These are part of the controls on your organization. The reports you receive should measure the results of your company's performance within the framework of your procedures. Your reports should deliver the key facts simply and be timely and pertinent.

The purpose of all this is to spot problems before they hurt you, to pinpoint financial erosion before it damages you, and to discover better methods and procedures before your competitors outpace you. This is what managing is all about.

The key to good management of your company lies first

with obtaining solid data. You need always to be in touch with the important matters surrounding the firm's operation. You must have a grasp of the big picture. Your controls come through regular reports and frequent verbal and written communication reinforced with thorough policies and procedures and constant instruction and training.

Alfred Sloan thought proper accounting to be the essential element in establishing a well-run company. He said,

> Many of our dealers, and the same thing applies to dealers of other organizations, have good accounting systems. Many of them have indifferent ones and I regret to say that too large a percentage of them have practically no accounting system at all.
>
> Many of those who have accounting systems, through lack of their being properly developed, are not able to effectively use them. In other words, they are not so developed that they give the dealer the facts about his business; where the leaks are; what he should do to improve his position.
>
> As I said before, uncertainty must be eliminated. Uncertainty and efficiency are as far apart as the North Pole is from the South. If I could wave a magic wand over our dealer organization, with the result that every dealer could have a proper accounting system, could know the facts about his business and could intelligently deal with the many details incident to his business in an intelligent manner as a result thereof, I would be willing to pay for the accomplishment an enormous sum and I would be fully justified in doing so. It would be the best investment General Motors ever made.

As you grow, you may relinquish certain decisions to your staff. But you should always keep for yourself the major decisions on company direction and policy and have effective control over anyone making spending decisions over a specified amount. It's so much poppycock to suggest that the leader of a company is remiss for not turning over major decisions to others. That is what you are there for. The bigger you get, the larger the decision you concentrate on. Obviously you won't be involved in determining how many paper clips the company buys. But you certainly need to know about the cost and capabilities of your next computer. Perhaps in time, with far-flung branch offices and a thousand employees, those matters will be left to others.

The scope of your decisions will parallel the size of your organization. If you have implemented the management tools outlined here, the appropriate level of your involvement will evolve, fortified by experience and common sense.

"Mr. Sheraton," Ernest Henderson, talks about the entrepreneur's need to avoid making the wrong kinds of decisions concerning corporate directions:

> In the operation of a business enterprise, errors of omission are often more costly than those actually made. An important responsibility of a president is to hold down, when possible, losses which arise from neglected opportunities. Once during the depths of the depression we were offered the Empire State Building for five million dollars, only a half million of this to be in cash. Timidity discouraged us from asking our Boston bank for the needed loan, though in retrospect I am sure the money was available. Today [1960] such a half-million-dollar "equity" in the Empire State Building would be worth thirty millions or more, sixty times the cash requirement once indicated, in illustration of the miracle of leverage as well as the magnitude of possible errors of omission.
>
> I believe it was H. L. Mencken who once shrewdly observed that it is not the things we do but rather what we don't do that we eventually regret. I confess a profound admiration for the controversial Mencken, particularly when casting long glances at the majestic dimensions of the Empire State Building.

As your company grows and stabilizes, you must pay some attention to return on investment (ROI). Alfred Sloan reminds us that "even the least sophisticated investor measures his profits from stocks, bonds, or savings accounts in terms of what he puts into them. So, too, I imagine every businessman evaluates profits in terms of his total investment. It is a rule of the game, so to speak."

Return on investment is a different concept for an entrepreneur to concentrate on. Early on, it may not make much sense.

We raised $62,000 to start Investment Rarities. A fabulous return on that would have been $15,000. We returned nothing. After two years in business, I was operating alone with my two secretaries. We were $25,000 in the hole, and I couldn't take a paycheck for several months. I talked my major creditors into letting a few payments slide. I borrowed a few thousand from a friend. Standard Oil and American Express closed me out.

Four years later we made fifteen million dollars. ROI yardsticks simply don't apply to these types of situations. Alfred Sloan readily points this out,

> A word on rate of return as a strategic principle of business. I am not going to say that rate of return is a magic wand for every occasion in business. There are times when you have to spend money just to stay in business, regardless of the visible rate of return. Competition is the final price determinant and competitive prices may result in profits which force you to accept a rate of return less than you hoped for, or for that matter to accept temporary losses. And, in times of inflation, the rate-of-return concept comes up against the problem of assets undervalued in terms of replacement. Nevertheless, no other financial principle with which I am acquainted serves better than rate of return as an objective aid to business judgment.
>
> Rate of return is affected by all the factors in the business; hence if one can see how these factors individually bear upon a rate of return, one has a penetrating look into the business.

Finally, with breathtaking clarity, Mr. Sloan sums up this sophisticated and complex management tool: *"Essentially it was a matter of making things visible."*

One of the knottiest problems of business growth involves management of inventories. In product businesses, optimistic entrepreneurs usually forecast far higher sales in a given year than they ever reach. As a consequence, they pile up finished goods or raw materials that become a financial burden.

When my company launched our marketing scheme for the Fotoshow, a photo storage device, I ordered the manufacture of well over 100,000 units. The product sold lackadaisically in the

Midwest market where we introduced it. Consequently, it took several years to chew through that large inventory. I could have used some of that locked-up capital elsewhere.

You need to think long and hard about sales forecasts and necessary inventories. You must avoid getting trapped by the CB phenomenon. When demand for these popular radios was soaring, most manufacturers were whipped into runaway enthusiasm and cranked them out in huge quantities. Soon the market was glutted, consumer demand dried up, price reductions and cutthroat competition broke out. Losses piled up.

Your basic operating rule for inventories should be that *it is far better to run out than to overstock.*

Don't make the same old mistakes by allowing unbridled enthusiasm to sweep away your good judgment. This is especially true when market demand for your product is hot. When sales are soaring you are close to the peak, the edge, and the abyss.

When Alfred Sloan became the new president of General Motors in 1921, he was faced with these very same problems.

> The new administration in 1921 had very little data on which to base a production schedule, but we had to proceed anyway. . . .
>
> The big gap in our information system at headquarters and in the divisions was at the retail level. We knew how many cars and trucks our divisions were selling to our dealers, but we did not know the current rate at which those vehicles were being resold to the public. We were not in touch with the actual retail market. . . .
>
> The year 1923 had been so good that some of our car divisions, particularly Chevrolet, had lost potential sales because they were unable to supply the ultimate consumer with cars when required. Most of the division managers projected this experience onto the prospects for 1924 and resolved not to miss any more sales because of underproduction. . . .
>
> Although I thus shared the belief that an increase in sales was to be expected, I also held the view that some of the divisions were planning to build more cars than a moderate improvement in sales would justify. I asked several of the divisions' managers to reconsider their production

schedules. In each case, the reply was that in their opinion the schedule was justified.

Signs of distress began to appear early in 1924. In a report to the Finance and Executive Committees dated March 14, 1924, I pointed out that the corporation and the industry as a whole had what was probably a larger number of unsold cars in the hands of dealers, distributors, and branches than at any previous time. . . .

I warned the managers of the divisions of the growing danger, and at Chevrolet and Oakland I insisted upon immediate and drastic curtailment of production schedules. . . . I made a trip into the field to discuss distribution problems with the dealers in their places of business, and on that trip I came to know beyond doubt that the March cutbacks had been inadequate and that overproduction was not just a possibility for July but already a certainty. It is not often that the chief executive of a large corporation himself discovers visible overproduction by a physical check of the inventory. But automobiles are big units easy to count. In St. Louis, my first stop, in Kansas City, and again in Los Angeles, I stood in the dealers' lots and saw the inventories parked in rows.

I then issued one of the few flat orders I ever gave to the division managers during the time I served as chief executive officer of General Motors. This order directed all division managers to curtail production schedules immediately. . . .

I have recounted this episode of 1924 because of its consequences, for it marked the beginning of reasonably effective production control in General Motors. In a certain very important sense, this involved the reconciliation of the work of two kinds of persons in General Motors—essential, I should think, in any corporation with a nationally distributed consumer product. One kind is the sales manager with his natural enthusiasm, optimism, and belief that he can, by his efforts, influence total sales. The other is the statistical person who makes his analyses objectively on broad general evidence on demand. . . .

Two things were involved: First, the art of forecasting, and second, shortening the reaction time when a forecast proved wrong. . . .

The information, as I have said, was weak and late. The information was weak because it was neither accurate nor comprehensive enough. It was arrived at by inference from dealer stocks and unfilled orders. This was good enough over a period of time, but the critical trouble was precisely the length of the period.

Sloan implemented remedial measures. "We worked out in 1924 and 1925 a system of statistical reports to be sent by the dealers to the divisions every ten days. With this information in hand each ten days, the divisions thereafter had an up-to-date, comprehensive picture of the situation in the field."

As he points out, the key to inventory forecasting is rapid and accurate transmission of pertinent data. You need the facts and you need them fast. Then you must react.

How did such a system work for General Motors and Alfred Sloan in later years?

With the big depression—from 1930 to 1934—there was contraction in General Motors. But this time, unlike 1920–21, and despite its greater severity, the contraction was orderly. Of necessity, dividend payments were lower in some of these years than in others, but in no year did the corporation fail to earn a profit or pay a dividend. . . . What accounts for this exceptional record in a period in which many durable-goods producers failed or came close to bankruptcy? It would be unfair to claim any particular prescience on our part; no more than anyone else did we see the depression coming. *I think the story I have told shows that we had simply learned how to react quickly. This was perhaps the greatest payoff of our system of financial and operating controls.* (Italics added)

You may need help putting the management procedures I've explained into place. In every city, there are management consultants you may wish to employ for a while. They will advise and assist in setting up the controls you need. Tell them what information you want and let them work up the reporting system. Timely dialogue with these consultants can prove worthwhile. The internal management systems you need are not something you instinctively toss out at the necessary moment. They are a science of their own. The busy entrepreneur may be focused on sales and marketing or product development and manufacturing, rather than the subtleties of management. An outsider can teach you the rudiments, vastly improve the skills of your managers, and put the systems you need in place. The best of them can get inside your operation, understand it, and direct you toward sound procedures.

You may very well be visited by a sales representative of an out-of-town management firm. They do an analysis of your company by interviewing all the employees. Someone once joked that they borrow your watch to tell you what time it is. Then they tabulate the results and come into your office to convey the sentiments of your people and close you on a management contract for a month or more. You will be shocked to find that many of your employees think you are an SOB. You will hear a broad array of gripes, malfunctions, and most of all wails about low compensation. This rude knock to your self-image as a benefactor is good for you. It gives you a better perspective in dealing with your employees.

A substantial element among the people who work for you invariably feels undercompensated. I frequently ask managers what they think their salaries should be (they usually want more than I expected) and give them exactly what they ask for. I have found this to be a rarely abused technique and highly satisfactory to my employees. No matter how well people are compensated, however, they eventually get around to wanting more. You may think you are terribly generous, but there will always be some bitching about pay. Don't let these complaints hurt your feelings; it's the nature of the beast.

Occasionally, you may have to reduce pay levels, scratch bonuses, or eliminate certain commissions. Expect plenty of argument from employees. A howl always arises when you take something away. Worse, however, is a perceived inequity. When someone appears to make more than others with a similar job, dissension ripples through the organization. Always try to avoid extra benefits, more favorable conditions, or better pay for one person in an identical group, unless reasons of obvious merit dictate such rewards.

Some people are never satisfied. Your supervisors should be able to select out these chronic complainers and rid you of them. Negativism is catching. Those who squawk the loudest generally do the least work. They are quick to support any outside organizers or company cliques who want to dictate terms and policy to you. These people always think they know more than you do.

Since people will be demanding of you, quick to criticize, and insatiable in their salary requests, you can feel comfortable in expecting more than a little from them. Get rid of subpar workers. The tendency is always to stretch to the limit with marginal producers. You may feel sorry for them, but you should maintain high standards of productivity and fire these shirkers.

You're not running a social welfare agency either. It's one thing to offer alcohol and drug treatment programs for those so afflicted, but one time through is the limit. I once had a broker come to work full of morphine and booze and proceed to dance on his desk. We put him in treatment for a few weeks, but he came back to us hopped up again. It was time to say good-bye. This disturbed personality continued calling people and using our name after he'd been let go. You can't make winners out of losers, reshape flawed personalities, make the lazy ambitious, or instill character in liars and cheats. Give it one try and then part ways.

Alfred Sloan summed up the typical lack of resolve and ineptitude when it comes to firing someone: "I think we have lacked and perhaps still lack courage in dealing with weaknesses in personnel. We know weaknesses exist, we tolerate them and finally after tolerating them an abnormal length of time, we make the change and then regret that we have not acted before."

My marketing associate, Jay Abraham, says, "A little attrition is healthy." The firing of a poor performer does indeed get everyone's attention. Productivity seems to rise for a few days following a termination.

Firing should be done in a crisp and straightforward manner. The fired person should depart the premises at once. After he or she has been gone a few days you usually find out about other problems the person created, which you had overlooked. Then you feel good about the firing. You know you did the right thing.

I fired a young, hardworking broker one day and immediately began to have second thoughts. By evening I was so uncomfortable, I called the sales manager at home. He invited the young fellow back the next day, and I was relieved. I had made a mistake. If a marginal performer is working hard, that person should be given as much time as possible to perform.

If you make a mistake, you can rehire a worker. However, it's generally an error to talk someone out of quitting. On occasion I have convinced people who were bored or dissatisfied or who believed themselves underpaid to stick around. I should have let them go. They seldom, if ever, work out.

One of my best managers confronted me with a big offer he had received from another company. He complained about his circumstances and suggested he might have to leave if he didn't get a raise. I didn't want to lose him, but I would not match the other salary. I suspected he was bluffing somewhat and that the other offer probably had some strings attached. I held firm . . . he stayed. Later he came in to apologize for the unbecoming nature of his request for a raise.

Often before quitting, a person will become hypercritical of you and the company. Apparently this bitterness serves to rationalize the move. Any unusual outbreak of vitriol serves to warn you of a pending break.

Once you have assembled a large staff of managers, department heads, officers, and project directors, you are likely to see patterns of behavior that are less than flattering. Among your group there may be jostling for power and dominance, undermining manipulations, and unsettling outbreaks against certain individuals. Some people can become entirely too aggressive in assuming power. They may even decide to make a run at you. Once again, this is where control helps beat back any challenge.

Peter F. Drucker, in his entertaining semiautobiographical account, *Adventures of a Bystander*, writes about Henry Luce, founder of *Time*, *Life*, and *Fortune* magazines, and his modus operandi to assure his control.

> I don't think Henry Luce ever thought out his way of handling people. He applied what has been the age-old Chinese way of running any organization [Luce was born and raised in China] from the Han Emperor of olden times on. Mao Tse-tung ran his government and party exactly the way Henry Luce ran his magazines: by creative factions; by working around people who had the title, office and responsibility; by encouraging juniors to come to him but enjoin-

ing them not to tell their bosses; and by keeping alive feuds, mutual distrusts, and opposing cliques.

By having people work for him in each enterprise around their official boss; by working around the people who had the title and directly with subordinates of theirs; by seeing editors, writers or correspondents more or less behind their superior's back—though often quite openly— Luce made sure no editor or publisher of his would ever be in control.

Naturally, Peter Drucker found this technique distasteful. These shenanigans are used to some degree in many companies, often by those whose control may be threatened by upstarts. When a founder, such as Luce, knocks off a pretender with Machiavellian malice, it may be rash to criticize too vehemently. In all likelihood, most people in similar straits would resort to identical tactics.

I don't advocate his strategy. However, even in companies where the founder owns control, it may be necessary to beat back certain brash individuals. Although the direct threat of firing works far better on overly bold employees, manipulative undermining may rarely have its place.

A measure of factionalism and rug pulling goes on within the hierarchy of any organization. People are always interested in nudging others aside. You need to be aware of this when making judgments. Bias against other employees may color or poison the opinions and reports you get. Behind all such manipulations, whether ruthless or bland, the seed of self-interest lurks. There's a little of this Chinese strategy in all of us.

SUMMARY

Profits come from repeat customers. One-time customers are expensive to acquire. Do the little things that make your customers love you. Whatever it takes, keep your customers happy on repeat orders. Consistency is the hallmark of a well-managed company.

Employees bring the need for rules and policies. With your first employees, you need things like policy manuals and personnel files. They must also be trained; osmosis is a poor training technique. Practice mistake avoidance. Employ safeguards. Become slightly paranoid.

Keep the important decisions from going sour. Set up controls on spending decisions. Establish a purchase order system.

Rely on your managers to apply policy consistently. Watch for ego-based decisions by your employees and yourself.

An upbeat corporate philosophy will be reinforced by peer pressure. Repeat this and other crucial messages on an ongoing basis. Encourage frequent training and instruction sessions.

Inspect your company at least once a week. Set up a worker committee to gain feedback.

Make as many decisions as you can, but learn also to delegate responsibilities. Pick your trusted managers by measuring performance.

As you grow, develop a thorough reporting system, obtain solid data on a timely basis. Manage inventories conservatively.

Give particular care to avoid inequities among employees. Weed out the poor performers. A little attrition may be healthy.

8.
How Taxes and the IRS Affect Your Business

The key to growth is quite simple: creative men with money. The cause of stagnation is similarly clear: depriving creative individuals of financial power.

—GEORGE GILDER

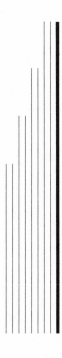

As a novice entrepreneur, it's never too soon to begin assessing one of the largest impediments to your success—the Internal Revenue Service. From the first day you begin to make money, your attitudes and views toward the IRS will be dramatically restructured. You will see the government's demands on your profits in a totally different and threatening perspective. As you see your reserves against calamity stripped away, your attempts to thwart the IRS will become an obsession.

Approximately half the profits from your enterprise are funneled into IRS or state coffers. They take the cash off the top. You get to pay for desks, calculators, and typewriters with the half they leave you. This huge tax bite punishes companies that grow rapidly. The most exciting and glamorous growth companies are left terribly exposed to a business decline.

As this is being written a number of tax reforms are being proposed that will alter many of the things dealt with in this chapter. Even with reduced levels of taxation, however, start-up companies will remain highly vulnerable. The entrepreneur will still have to remain nimble in attempting to hang on to earnings.

Suppose your new company suddenly breaks out with a year or two of huge sales. Profits mount. You look at this fresh capital as a reserve to carry you through any possible setbacks. Your tax bill, however, eats away half your pile, while capital expenses that are not deductible reduce it further. Suddenly the economy sours and orders dry up. Profits evaporate. Your overhead, once manageable, generates heavy losses. You cut and slash, painfully dismantling your organization. Cash flow dries up, working capital disappears. Business falls further. Suddenly you're in trouble. The huge outlay made to the IRS can't be recaptured for another year, when current losses offset the prior year's profits. By then it may be too late. If only you could have kept some of this money paid out to the IRS, you could manage to get by.

Most entrepreneurs, however, don't relinquish the IRS's share without a struggle. They anticipate these potential business problems ahead of time and through all available means attempt to forestall paying at least a portion of their taxes. Once you make money, you will see how compelling this goal becomes. The ability to defer taxes becomes a primary managerial skill. In fact, it may be mandatory to your eventual success and longevity.

Rather than pay out the top half of their earnings, entrepreneurs are forced to manage for tax savings and deferrals. The obsession to avoid taxation leads some to make bad business decisions. Concentration on tax avoidance leads to economic policies that could backfire. Resources are frequently wasted or poorly deployed. Money that should be used to build the company's health may be frittered away. This is to say nothing about the huge investment in wasted time and outlandish legal expenses.

The first year my company made a profit, I began to worry about the impending tax bite. I needed my precious capital to

handle a growing flow of business. After several years of impov-
erishment, I was terribly reluctant to use my gains for anything
other than a reserve against future slumps. I perceived my tax
bill as a direct threat to my survival.

Consequently I began to investigate a host of tax shelters.
I finally settled on a Colombian gold-dredging scheme. This
complicated investment allowed me to write off approximately
four times my contribution. I cut almost $20,000 off my bill,
which at the time represented a hefty chunk of working capital.

The promoters of the scheme wasted the money. In fact, as
with many such shelters, they may have perpetrated fraud. We
never got anything back on the investment. The IRS later challenged the favorable tax ramification. For six years the case was
tied up in legal questions. Recently we were required to pay this
tax bill plus interest. Nevertheless, throughout the interim and
especially during the critical years following employment of
this tax device, we saved and used the money.

A critic might level charges of unpatriotic behavior on our
part. The name of the game, however, is to employ legal means
to thwart tax collection. Judge Learned Hand expressed the
following dictum, which justifies our methods: "There is nothing sinister in so arranging one's affairs to keep taxes as low as
possible. Everybody does so, rich and poor; and all do right, for
nobody owes any public duty to pay more than the law demands: Taxes are enforced exactions, not voluntary contributions."

The government has moved to put an end to these exotic
shelters. But there will be new, provocative wrinkles in the tax
laws.

Unfortunately, many tax deferral devices are not clearly spelled
out as legal. Tax laws are constantly changing and being updated to checkmate new loopholes and tax-saving strategies. At
the same time, a veritable army of attorneys, promoters, and
manipulators is formulating new tax-saving schemes. Many of
them are brilliant, well-conceived ploys, others are dubious and
hard to judge. Some are shams and outright frauds.

The entrepreneur's objective to shepherd and husband capital becomes exceedingly difficult when sorting through the vast
array of schemes available for tax management. Attractive shelters, though desirable, may leave the entrepreneur open to at-

tack by the IRS. Some shelters can lead to charges of fraud. The wrong decision can bring worry and aggravation. You may even be subject to prosecution. The next round of changes in the tax laws may eliminate these shelters. In exchange for a reduced tax level, there will be few complaints.

The present Byzantine welter of tax rules encourages scams, many of which though innocently employed can trip you up. If you are a highly visible entrepreneur, you are much more likely to be persecuted. The IRS practices selective prosecution. If you are a community leader, celebrity, or successful entrepreneur, you will be chosen over an unknown personality. Success is a primary criterion for prosecution. Your conviction supposedly frightens other taxpayers into full compliance.

Since outside tax shelters will continue to incur the wrath of the IRS, their attractiveness has been greatly diminished. You must, therefore, look inward for tax deferral opportunities. That means you need to divert profits within your organization by adding expenses. This means diversifying or broadening the thrust of your business. It may mean adding to your R & D budget or other similar expenses. In other words, you must invest now in ventures that you hope will bear fruit later. You need to divert profits into areas that will bring income in future years.

You will always be balancing the capital necessary to lubricate current business expansion against the funding of future projects and your current tax liability. No other circumstance tests your judgment, business acumen, and financial skills as much or strains you more.

It is the entrepreneur with the most talent and ability who bears the greatest brunt of the burden of the corporate tax. Those who engender growth, who enjoy success with breakthrough products, who create the most new jobs and public wealth are punished more so than the mediocre performer. A new company's assets are skinny, but large firms with favorable banking and financial arrangements, with well-entrenched markets, and with unjustified regulatory protection can far more easily withstand the tax bite.

Some economists suggest that large, stable companies have tax liabilities built into their pricing which are really paid for by the consumer. The entrepreneur struggling alone in uncharted waters with new products and services enjoys no such padding. They, who need every penny of capital to build up, nurture, and protect their enterprises, are stripped of their financial lifeblood.

Old, established firms are privileged by the current tax system. The threatening new competitor is prevented from adding critical new capital. This insulates old-line firms from the challenges of underfinanced entrepreneurs.

Seldom, if ever, will you hear the voice of business vigorously raised against the IRS. Many who are bitter and disenchanted refrain from criticism. Corporate leaders seldom speak out against certain unjust devices employed by the IRS. Why is that? Probably every corporation in America today fudges on their taxes. Some don't even realize they do. Somewhere in that tax filing lies an error, a misrepresentation, a stretching of what is allowable. Frighteningly enough, there are uncertainties over what the company can write off or get by with. "Frightening" because these gray areas can be uncovered and charged for, meaning punishment and even prosecution. Businesspeople are afraid to speak up. They fear the IRS.

If you set out to devise a prehistoric system, you could promulgate nothing more dismal than the IRS corporate tax code. It is not clear-cut; it's open to misinterpretation and is often highly subjective. Thus, it encourages cheating and promotes misunderstanding.

The enforcement of this tax law through arbitrary and selective procedures, haphazard audits, subjective evaluations, and inevitable oversights leads to further skulduggery. The whole process brings out the worst, not the best, in people. Borderline cheating is sometimes allowed, sometimes not. Friendly agents skim the books, while unfriendly agents dig deeper. There is an unwritten law that you can get away with this or that if you agree to come clean on some other issue. It's called "swapping adjustments."

Accountants negotiate deals while their clients tiptoe through the hallways smiling broadly at the auditing agents and praying to be left alone. A tinge of fear hangs in the air.

If you have tripped up badly or violated a major tenet of the tax code, you will really be turned upside down. Special agents, whose task is to comb through every circumstance of your life in order to ferret out facts necessary for your public execution, will humiliate you. They are masters of fear and relish hounding their quarry. If you experience this contemporary sequel to *Les Misérables*, you will understand the deep-seated philosophical questions raised about the coexistence of taxation and liberty.

If Thomas Edison were alive today, I doubt he would have much time for inventing. Always careless about recordkeeping and cavalier with money, the IRS would tie him up in knots. This intense genius would probably have invented far less in today's tax environment.

Because an entrepreneur sometimes exists in the financial twilight between bankruptcy and survival, he or she, above all, is subject to a particularly insidious IRS power when an amount is owed the IRS and that agency believes the entrepreneur is going broke. For example, it may audit your tax return for a given year and find you owe more. If it decides that your financial future is bleak or that your business won't fly, the IRS is empowered to come in and seize your assets and shut you down. On paper a company may appear to be broke, but in will, spirit, and ingenuity it may be far from it.

At one time my tax attorney and accountant raised the specter of this ugly event happening to me. No more paralyzing fear ever fostered my insomnia. Neither the IRS nor anyone else can ever judge when an entrepreneur will fail. They can never determine the merits of an enterprise. The greatest economic breakthroughs are often accompanied by public scorn and ridicule. The thought of some faraway bureaucrat dictating the ruination of a struggling entrepreneur seems foreign to our idea of democracy.

Entrepreneurs often have tax problems and endure frequent inspection by the IRS. Your object should be to diminish this attention, to get by without audits, and to lessen your tax bill to the limits of the law.

One matter that you should never trifle with is the collection and payment of your employees' withholding taxes. A start-up company I knew of once found itself in dire straits and dipped into the employee withholding tax account. The IRS does not fool around with this monumental business no-no. They nailed a notice up on his office door before he could repay them. No matter how desperate you may get, doing something stupid won't help.

You have a responsibility to set up a program of accurate and timely payments. On one occasion an IRS agent visited our office and claimed we had been delinquent in our monthly withholding payment and had failed to pay for several months. He and I immediately clashed. I was hopping mad and led him to my bookkeeper's office. She was busy entertaining three insurance agents whom I immediately dismissed. After a rigorous grilling, we discovered that she had indeed been late in sending the payments. Worse, we found a check several months old stapled to the payment material in one of her drawers. She had carelessly failed to mail it in. I fired her on the spot. The IRS agent mentioned penalties and threatened me with a special monitoring program. We had another blustering confrontation, and I shouted my refusal to go along with his plan (although I would have had no choice). We paid the taxes and penalties, kept ourselves current, and heard no more.

It generally doesn't pay to holler at an IRS agent. When you are visited by an agent conducting an audit, you should give him or her your Dale Carnegie best. Human relations are such that you may influence the severity and rigors of an audit. Often, an IRS auditor will make a superficial check, find a few inconsistencies, agree on charging you some additional tax, and move on. Let's face it—the deeper agents dig, the more they're going to find. There's always a chance that if they like you they will quit searching after digging up the first few skeletons.

My late partner, Bernie, was always in some sort of tax trouble. When the agent visited him, Bernie would invariably move the discussion away from his tax problem. He was a great conversationalist, and he and the agent would soon be exploring some exotic subject for hours. The agent really enjoyed Bernie and must have looked forward to the dialogue.

For as long as Bernie and I were together, the agent came three or four times a year. He would call for an appointment, and Bernie would gladly oblige. The meetings were held at our office, always about midafternoon. Bernie never had the requested data or tax information for him, but it hardly seemed to matter. At about five o'clock they'd wind down and the agent would leave.

Finally the agent retired, and a new person was assigned. She was most irritated with Bernie's delays. Bernie always regretted that his agent had retired. Not only did his tax problem worsen, but I am sure that as much as anything he missed the chance to have a good talk.

Whether IRS agents truly respond to blandishments and pleasantries, nobody can be sure. Each individual is different. I think they do. More important, so do businesspeople, lawyers, and accountants. They do their best to avoid alienating the agent.

My audits have been thoroughgoing and detailed. No stone seems to go unturned. My accountant separates me from the auditing agent after a cursory introduction. They don't want us to ruffle one another. I suggest you follow the same pattern. Let someone else be your buffer and fulfill the auditor's requests for data and information.

IRS auditors or agents are just people doing their jobs. My tax attorney in St. Paul, Mark Arth, quotes from some unknown source, "To tax and to please and love and be wise are two impossible things."

Some agents are skilled professionals and others are bunglers. It's pointless to hate them, mandatory to make their job easier. It is certainly to the credit of the IRS that few, if any, agents ever take bribes or shake down businesses. They are in a position to make unethical requests and, to my knowledge, never do so.

The IRS possesses broad powers. It can sweep aside your legal roadblocks. It can ferret out banking and contractual information. You can't hide anything from it. It will hold your feet to the fire and, if necessary, those of everyone who knows you or ever did business with you. It can be an implacable foe who will bully you into submission. The law grants it the right to coerce you. For, in the final analysis, if you fail to pay them part of what you earned, someone will come to get you with a gun.

Therefore, it makes little sense to cheat. Deliberately defrauding the IRS can lead to severe repercussions. The major problem with seemingly foolproof tax cheating is that someone besides you generally knows about it. Business associates, friends, or relatives could hold knowledge that leaves you exposed. It just isn't worth the worry. They might be caught doing something illegally and squeal on you to save themselves. Not only that, the IRS pays a reward to anyone who informs on others (a truly ennobling process).

Once again, the way to diminish taxes lies with the accentuation and full use of write-offs and tax diversion. These procedures are full of gray areas. Your accountant can help you with advice on many of these tactics.

Avoidance or deferral techniques may be employed that, although risky, are gray enough to let you get by. New techniques pop up from time to time. The best of these has yet to be ruled on by the IRS or by tax courts. If you get in on a tax deferral device before it is rejected by the IRS, you probably won't get into trouble with it.

At the peak of the inflation cycle my precious metals business delivered a one-time profit into the millions. Rather than pay half of this in taxes, I gave the IRS a few million and deferred the balance by using silver commodity straddles. This device was advocated by no less than one of America's largest brokerage firms. I knew from this information that I wasn't in quicksand.

The following year I used the money to expand my company in the financial business. We funded the invention of the Cob Camshaft. We also started an oil company and began to find gas and oil. Then we funded the development of the S-Box, a revolutionary packaging concept by Swiss designer Eduard Schweizer. We also poured a little into charitable pursuits and secured some wildlife areas and wetlands for conservation purposes. Ironically, the government would have thwarted all of this with burdensome taxes. At least to me, my alternative seemed like a healthier option both for us and for society.

We laid the foundations for innumerable new jobs, new wealth, enhanced prosperity, and our own security and well-being. We kept money away from the IRS and spent it on many new projects. This policy translated into millions of dollars in losses for us in the twelve months following our big profit year. When the IRS rushed in and uncovered our straddles and the millions due them, we countered with our current year's losses as an offset.

Naturally, when you maneuver in this fashion you can self-destruct. The secret of these manipulations lies in an understanding of what you are likely to get away with.

As an entrepreneur climbs the ladder of profitability, an intense focus on tax matters evolves. You will read everything about taxes, consult attorneys and accountants, observe the torment of others, gather your own experience, and over time sense what will work and what won't.

If problems arise, you will need the assistance of wise tax counsel. Former IRS attorneys make the best choice. They know their way around the service, understand procedural nuances, and are often well connected. Try to pin down their charges in advance. As with any legal counsel, the one-time use of their services will generally cost far more. If you are in trouble, they have little mercy when billing you. You should encourage all counselors to visualize themselves in a long-term relationship with you. It's far cheaper.

If you have done something wrong, never discuss anything directly with an IRS agent. These agents are not your friends. Don't give them any information. *Let your attorney handle everything.* Many people who have slipped up on their tax payments are prone to invite IRS agents into their confidence and try to win them over. There's no way. It's like helping the hangman tie the knot. You are only ensuring that your problem will get bigger. This advice is so often ignored that it would pay you to read it again.

The corporate tax system needs to be revised. Favorable capital gains taxes only help entrepreneurs if they sell out their stock interests. They should be encouraged to hold rather than sell. They should continue to be at the cutting edge of economic development. A far more favorable corporate tax rate would unleash their talents all the more. The simplification of the corporate tax structure would free entrepreneurs from ongoing concentration on tax deferment and avoidance. No longer would the knock of the tax auditor paralyze innovation and strip the entrepreneur of precious capital.

Furthermore, the sources of capital for start-ups, personal wealth, and savings need to remain untouched by the tax collector. At the very least, seed money for new enterprise should enjoy special considerations, such as tax credits or write-offs.

The tax system currently enables the IRS to prosecute selectively. Harassment and vendettas against enemies of the IRS may be promoted. Worst of all, since every corporation is encouraged by the system to get by with all it can, almost any business can be singled out for prosecution. After writing all this, I worry about myself.

A recent article in a business magazine disclosed how the IRS was trying to nail a well-known corporate takeover specialist. This prominent personality had possibly used the corporate aircraft for personal trips. The IRS was on his trail. Virtually every plane and auto used by all companies in this country is employed at times for personal use. The IRS could snare every executive and small businessman in America for this minor abuse, but only those currently in social disfavor or unpopular with government agencies are usually picked on.

It is worth mentioning several additional tax provisions that penalize initiative and hinder human progress. One is known as the accumulated earnings tax. If a corporation builds up cash reserves to a level unacceptable to the IRS, it is taxed at a 70-percent rate. When my company first began to make money, the accountants worried about this possibility. I was shocked. After years of struggle, we were finally building enough assets to survive for a few years and now we had to worry about the government arbitrarily ripping us off.

I was even more incredulous another year when the auditing agent suggested I had received too much income. Rather than tax all my salary at the regular tax rate, he wanted to call a chunk of it a dividend so that it would be taxed twice. I was flabbergasted. A portion of my salary was deemed "unreasonable compensation," and I was forced to pay this added and onerous tax burden. After a decade of little or no income, this seemed horribly unjust.

Sometimes it seems that our tax system purposely sets out to discourage entrepreneurs and depress innovation. The complex and subjective tax code is full of traps and outright invitations to transgress. An abundance of punitive, high-handed, and capital-destructive measures constantly thwart the entrepreneur's progress. It is a faulty system that prohibits the accumulation of wealth by those who try to please the public. It is a perverse phenomenon, indeed, that strips the entrepreneurial company of its rewards.

What happens with these so-called profits, these earnings left over after transactions are completed? Are they grabbed up by business villains suited to duels with James Bond? Are they used for treacherous corporate dealings aimed at the subversion of society? Are they employed to grab power and corrupt? Should they be taxed off by the government before they generate mischief?

Henry Ford gave us the answer.

> Suppose you buy a Ford car. Part of the money you pay the dealer goes to the dealer for his service. Part of it goes to pay the workmen who helped build the car. Another part goes to pay for the material in the car, and there are incidentals to be paid, such as freight and taxes. These are just charges. After they are paid, what is left of your money goes into the business. It is plowed back into the business.
>
> This money may buy some bricks for a new building; it may build a new power unit; it may be spent in experimental work on a new model car.
>
> If possible, we want you to pay less for your next car than you did for this one. At the same time, we want your next car to be a better car than this one. We want the money you have spent with us to come back to you in a definite, tangible way. Furthermore, it should come back to you in a way not so tangible but just as definite, because you've done more than merely buy an automobile. You've helped give work to other men; perhaps you have helped to raise wages; perhaps you have shared in a new discovery in the laboratory.

It is this partnership of consumer and entrepreneur that fuels the advancement of a free society. In the brief span of years that covers a business career, the entrepreneur guides this relationship of mutual benefit. Nothing before or since has ever worked as well. The debate is over, the results are in.

The greater the capital that accrues to profit-making companies, the greater will be the rate and quality of human progress. Profits mean new products, new ventures, and new services. Entrepreneurs should be allowed to keep and reinvest as much as possible. *The taxes entrepreneurs pay are a penalty on progress.* They punish every citizen because they deprive them of goods and services, of jobs and prosperity.

For specific advice on tax strategies that affect your business, you must work closely with your accountant. I have at least one monthly sitdown discussion with my accountant, Everett

Ostermann, of Faribault, Minnesota, wherein we discuss a wide range of tax topics. We assess our probable current tax bill from the vantage point of each passing month. We plan our strategies to reduce this load and reckon how much cash we will need at payment time.

As I have mentioned, you need to strike up a relationship with a competent accounting firm, and you must get its advice before you start. You need to file certain tax forms early in your new enterprise. Although you may have no employees and make no taxable income, reports, filings, and tax returns may still be necessary.

One of the surest ways to get the IRS snooping through your financial records is to be late, sloppy, or in violation of the codes. File on time, comply with the tax code, and be reasonably honest and you will be spared much grief.

When you begin to make money, keep a low profile. Bernie and I used to chuckle about how we could always tell when a struggling entrepreneur's fortunes were turning up; the first thing he did would be to buy a few new suits and get his teeth fixed. Just as predictable is the super-successful entrepreneur, who seems obliged to buy an expensive auto and then tip the whole world off by going overboard on a big house. A former IRS employee told me that revenue agents sometimes cruise the countryside until they spot a fancy house surrounded by toys— motor homes, boats, four-wheel vehicles—and then target the owner for an audit.

Once your company reaches a certain size, annual audits will be routine. Keeping a low profile will do little good. However, you still may wish to keep your financial affairs private for numerous reasons, including security. Unfortunately, busy tongues generally ascribe to you a fortune far in excess of your true net worth.

I have been audited for over ten consecutive years. I foolishly drew attention to myself in my start-up days by filing late. Consequently, I have had a lifetime of experience in dealing with the IRS. When you are struggling against all odds to make your deal work, when you are in pain, when so much is at stake, when your plans are beneficial to others, when your task is formidable—nobody at the IRS cares! Some struggling entrepreneurs develop a mind-set that their particular strife somehow excuses them from other responsibilities. That's a dangerous and false conclusion. Your war stories won't sway the government at all. You either follow the rules or you don't. If not, they are going to muss you up.

I have one last piece of tax advice, not so much for start-ups but for those business owners who have been established for a while. There are things that I have never done, which I know from experience are done by some business people. If you have your company pay for significant personal bills; if you make extensive use of company assets for your personal use; if you fail to report outside income over a few hundred dollars; if you make sweetheart deals or take anything from those you do business with, then you had better throttle down. You need first-rate tax advice on how to rid yourself of these illegalities.

If any of these abuses are ever caught, you will be put under a microscope. What happens to you when the IRS analyzes each and every check you have written; when they make you account for every deposit; when they personally question the recipients of your checks and the individual sources of your deposits; when they question nervous friends, associates, employees, and those you do business with? They will track and trace and learn more about you than your mate knows or that you can even recall. One endorsement on one check—that's all they need to pry it open, one little slip.

Any new entrepreneur should conclude from these comments that prudence dictates a policy of no tax cheating. Don't abuse your control over the corporate purse strings. Don't try to slide any significant income by without a tax bite. Believe it or not, you can do time in prison for a few of these self-serving little oversights. The psychic punishment alone makes it a poor policy.

SUMMARY

From the moment you begin to make a profit, you will see the IRS in an entirely different light. The money you need as a reserve for bad times will be siphoned off by the tax collector.

The best tax shelter may be plowing money back into your own company.

There will be gray areas in your tax filing as well as in the tax code. Most companies make tax mistakes and are vulnerable. The IRS possesses broad powers, and you will be virtually powerless against them.

Be sure that you make the proper tax filings and necessary reports from the first day of your enterprise.

Various methods of tax cheating can tempt businesspeople. However, the punishment and the worry make it unwise.

9.
How to Diversify Your Growing Enterprise

The universal genius who can manage all himself has yet to appear. Only one with the genius to recognize others of different genius and harness them to his own car can approach the "universal."

—ANDREW CARNEGIE

Once your company is nicely in the black and running smoothly, you need to give some thought to diversifying. There are a number of reasons to spread out your business activities:

1. Your basic business may experience a cyclical downturn.
2. Competition may retard your business.
3. All businesses take periodic nosedives.
4. Diversification is insurance against all the above events.

Washington National Corporation once ran an ad in several publications titled, "The Hider and the Seeker." The Hider was a tortoise with his head pulled in; the Seeker, an eagle soaring overhead. The copy read:

> Once upon a time there were two companies. One was a hider and one was a seeker.
>
> The Hider produced only one product. Refusing to look into new fields, he relied solely upon the continued success of this single pursuit for his prosperity.
>
> The Seeker offered the same product as the Hider. But, using his hard-earned profits, he branched out into many other productive areas, constantly seeking innovative ways to grow.
>
> Both prospered for a time, but by and by a change occurred in the marketplace and suddenly their original product became obsolete. Overnight, the Hider found himself out of business. He retreated into his shell and remains there to this day. Whereas the Seeker, having so many other business interests, can still be seen soaring high and wide.
> Moral: Diversity is the best insurance against adversity.

While successful diversification offers security, it also represents significant peril. We need to differentiate between two types of diversification, one of which works far better than the other. The best kind of diversification moves the company into an associated business. The most dangerous diversity lies in the direction of a totally unrelated venture.

George Eastman, founder of Kodak, initially made dry plates for the growing photographic business. He was eventually faced with a decision either to perfect dry plates or to plunge ahead in the entire broadening photographic field. "Some such choice comes to nearly everyone in business. There is always a forked road of policy. One may make a thing and make it well and consider his business as primarily a making of things. Or, one may set up an ideal and consider those things which he makes only as steps toward that ideal. The first method held no attraction for me; it is a journey with but money as a destination. I adopted the second because, with an ideal, the journey's end is never reached: there is always the experiment, the hazard of going beyond where anyone else had gone. It holds as great a measure of fascinating adventure as did the search for the poles."

My company started out selling gold and silver that we delivered to investors. Then we diversified into collector coins. This move broadened our profit base. Our customers were interested in both products. The key to this kind of diversification is the enthusiasm with which it is greeted by the company's clients. A natural, smooth-fitting diversification offers the same customers an additional service they need.

As previously mentioned, we established an insurance company to provide coverage for contents of safe deposit boxes. We published a price guide for some of the collectibles the company sold. These latter two start-ups were market gaps that were related to our business.

Since we saw ourselves as offering a financial service, it was easy to expand the number of financial services we offered. Our next move was to start a stock and bond brokerage firm. Then we began a money management company and next our own mutual fund. All these diversifications were in harmony with our basic business. Our major aim was to serve our clients' financial and investment needs in every way we could. We had a measure of prior experience in these areas. We weren't too far out of our own field and our present customers were the candidates for our new services. Those three ingredients make for the best and safest diversifications.

Although our move into securities offered no particular market gap, we had a large and loyal customer base. This factor offset our lack of any unique attribute.

A second style of diversification centers on starting up, investing in, or acquiring an entirely unrelated venture. Business lore insists that this represents a grave risk and is likely to end in disaster. This is the kind of diversification steel magnate Charles Schwab was referring to when he said,

> My experience teaches me that men fail by going outside their lines or by lack of attention to detail. Mark my words, I have known Henry Ford for years, and I am a good friend of his, but every outside enterprise he goes into will be a failure. His success is in the Ford car, which he knows in every detail. His railroad is a failure, his Mussel Shoals [power dam] will be a failure, and he admits that his pig iron is now costing him more than if he bought it.

George Westinghouse lived and slept with the airbrake, but when it came to other things, he could not give them his attention in detail. Had he devoted himself the same way to the Westinghouse Electric [Westinghouse lost control of the company that bears his name], he would have made the same success, but a man cannot follow the details of many things.

Remember the last half of that sentence, " . . . a man cannot follow the details of many things." For a business to succeed, someone must be immersed in the intricate details of its day-to-day operation. To prevail in a business, you must master its fundamentals. This takes years to accomplish. To jump into a new venture and not practice the intense level of involvement necessary to make it an eventual success is foolhardy and can prove terribly expensive. You are limited to how many separate businesses you can master in a lifetime. Men and women of great accomplishment most often succeed at only one.

It takes at least five years to master a business. Then it must be watched closely and any expansion monitored carefully. The switch to a completely fresh endeavor needs attention and time. You may not be able to accommodate such demands. David Ogilvy stated flatly, "You have to resist the temptation to diversify into other kinds of business. Those of our competitors who did not resist this temptation lost their shirts. We stuck to our knitting."

The only sensible way I have found to diversify into unfamiliar ventures is through linking up with exceptional people who either are, or you hope they will become, masters of their particular enterprise. These people have apparent talent. You sense or see evidence that they are honest, clever, hardworking, and have every intention of winning. More than anything, they always get the job done. These people are rare, and you must sift through untold deals and personalities to ferret them out. The ability to pick the right people is a definite skill. This talent is honed and refined by observing and dealing with the many characters that come center-stage into your entrepreneurial drama.

When you enter into business deals with people who can make things happen on their own, you are initiating a sideline venture. You watch the evolution of the enterprise primarily from a seat in the audience or along the sidelines. You will always have some input into these deals but primarily your role will be to finance them. New ventures need money. Funding the right person can pile up additional wealth for you, making your overall financial picture far sounder.

Cyrus H. K. Curtis, founder of the Curtis Publishing Company, said, "Find the right man and leave him alone."

How do you refine the ability to pick the right people? Primarily through experience. Perhaps you will have to be burned by losers. You run into these characters in large numbers from the moment you start up. As you nurse your venture along, you may team up with, hire, or start another deal with someone. This exposure to various personalities hones your ability to pick future winners.

Back in my early days, when the gold and silver business was foundering, a visitor brought us news of a breakthrough solar heater that was creating widespread interest. A licensee for the device had set one up in a suburb, and people were flooding in to see it.

My partner, Bernie, and I drove across town to observe the solar heating unit and meet the licensee. Within a few days we had his confidence and were making tentative plans to set up his marketing organization. The unit had impressed us, and the claims for its performance were stupendous. Unlike most alternate energy sources, this one seemed to make economic sense.

The inventor, who lived in another state, was setting up a number of licensees. Our local licensee hoped to steal a march on everyone else and was pushing for national distribution. We had the WATS line and we liked each other's looks. We cut a deal.

Bernie and I immersed ourselves in solar lore. We improvised and pushed ahead with a national franchise package. People began to fly in to eyeball the program. At the time, we were running critically low on money. Our precious metals business was hurting. An infinitesimal number of gold and silver orders trickled in. The solar device began to look like our savior.

Things looked bright. A number of franchise sales were in the hopper. The unit was further researched and investigated by these prospective dealers. Slowly, evidence began to emerge that conflicted with the claims the inventor made for the device.

Bernie and I researched even more fervently and uncovered a question mark about these claims. Eventually, the deal began to disintegrate. The performance claims were frivolous. We hadn't realized we were involved in a fraud. Fortunately, the deal slowly lost momentum and over the months died of neglect.

The inventor of the solar device had advanced what seemed to be powerful and irrefutable facts about the performance of his heater. He bamboozled us and many others. Such a personality crops up in every business career. These people are particularly dangerous because they differ markedly from the normal con artists in that they believe their own lies. The average uncomplicated crook knows when he's stepping over the limits of the law. This kind of personality, however, fails to see errors and untruths in its delusions and fabrications. These people can make you believe almost anything because they believe it themselves. The bigger some of these deals are, the more preposterous they seem.

A finder once called Bernie and me to come look at a revolutionary smelting process that turned out gold. He was raising several hundred thousand dollars, and if we could bring them investors, we would get a lucrative fee to be paid in cash and stock. We called in mining and dredging professional Buzz Potter, an entrepreneur who had once run a gold separation firm with us in the Black Hills of South Dakota.

We went to a plush hotel room to meet the inventor, his lieutenants, and his finders. They tossed out a rough gold bar on the bed and then another they claimed was platinum. The inventor's credentials were impeccable: graduate of a big name university, military officer, advanced degree—he sounded good.

His process boggled the mind. He claimed to be able to mine a graphitic schist and refine it into gold. After a lengthy dissertation by him on the chemistry of transmuting rocks into gold, I was starting to nod my head up and down with understanding. Normally gullible for any new deal, I was coming his way.

Afterward, Buzz doubled us up in laughter as we rode down the elevator. He roasted the scam with a derisive assortment of colorful, earthy comments. After listening to a few moments of his unique cynicism, Bernie and I were soon scoffing wisely at the deal, too.

It was a good way to handle far-out schemes presented by

charlatans. Sit a seasoned authority down in front of them and have at it. Despite the flagrantly unscrupulous nature of gold alchemy, the inventor seemed to believe it. He was sincere and articulate, bright and convincing. His lieutenants and finders saw their personal fortune already made. Nevertheless, it was a fraud presented in a believable, forthright manner. A big contractor was rumored to have ultimately sunk hundreds of thousands of dollars into the process.

I dwell on at length this type of personality because it is surprisingly common and can be terribly costly. You're never too old, or too smart, to get conned one more time. Beware the zealot who carries in his briefcase the billion-dollar breakthrough. Avoid the simple systems that run contrary to physical law. Watch closely the dreamer whose promises don't convert into action. I have been embarrassed and fooled by them all. Nevertheless, to this day in their minds they are still right and I am the one who was wrong.

I initially went into the oil drilling business because a gentleman convinced me he could find oil with a lead weight dangling from a cord. When the weight began to rotate vigorously, oil was supposedly directly below. I drilled three dusters before giving up on that daydream.

Then I placed an aggressive person whom I sensed would be a winner in charge of my oil company. He knew little about oil, but I was willing to back his learning process. This gamble now appears to be paying off. Good deals are most often the result of outstanding people who can master and manage a business.

Why, however, would I stick millions into a venture that I knew nothing about, such as oil drilling? For one thing, I thought I had the right people to run it. More important, however, was the tax consideration. Once I made a lot of money, I fiercely resisted passing it on to the government. Rather than give them half, I invested in oil. This offered almost a total write-off. If we were successful, it would pay back our investment and more, spread over a number of years. It was a way to defer income.

Royal Little, Textron founder, disagrees with this tactic: "If you are a business executive in a growth company forget about cattle, oil wells, and other tax-saving investments. Put your capital in your own company and leave it there. If you and your associates do a good job you'll be far better off in the long run than if you had diverted time and money to a venture in which you would be an absentee owner." In other words, pay your taxes rather than put your money far afield from what you know.

Someone else doesn't have to come up to you with a proposal for a new venture. You can think up an idea yourself and find solid people to run it. You need to find a rare individual with a winning combination of traits to spark success in this kind of diversification, preferably but not necessarily with a background in it. Certain people have an intangible something that compels superb performance. This is the one mandatory ingredient to ultimate profits in a new venture. You can always count on these people to get the job done. They don't need much help, they just go ahead and do it. They have high energy levels and high ambitions. They learn fast. You can readily tell they are inevitably going to be successful. Those are the people you want in charge of your divisions and your diversifications.

Once you find this kind of exceptional individual and latch on to a new product, it may work out that there isn't the opportunity you once thought. Then you need to unfurl a unique selling proposition or a marketing gap. (*Market gaps* and *marketing gaps* are different opportunities. The latter simply means a new marketing twist that gets far better results than the old method. It is a way to redeploy skills and assets.)

When my mutual fund was structured, we needed something unique. There were hundreds of funds we might have to compete with. Without something to crow about, we were doomed before we started. We set up the fund with a commission load that was less than the normal amount charged by similar funds. This innovative low-load gave us a unique selling proposition.

Once we had established a money management company, we needed to find a way to get clients. We were up against big banks, large management firms, and entrenched relationships. We probed the market for a year to find a niche. Finally, we found a class of prospective clients who had been essentially neglected. Then we filled the marketing gap. We sent professionals out to see these prospects. We made them feel important when nobody else did.

A marketing gap is a better way of selling, advertising, or marketing, either with an underutilized product or to an overlooked audience. It is a fresh marketing strategy. For example, a product that doesn't sell through the mail may sell through telemarketing. Marketing gaps imply a bold new strategy to induce sales.

Once you have begun to succeed in your venture and word gets around, a fair sprinkling of deals are going to be shown to you. You may be asked to invest in, make a loan to, or actually operate and control these companies. They may be start-ups, ventures with problems, or firms where an owner wishes to retire.

When you are assessing new ventures, remember that the future potential will be grossly exaggerated. The promoter or entrepreneur has a tendency to see huge profits rolling in almost at once. The venture probably has far less potential than the founder anticipates and, even if it does have outstanding merit, the realization of this windfall remains years downstream.

If you are looking for quick help from a diversification, it must come from a concept associated with your present business. As we have pointed out, raw start-ups generally take at least five years to make much money, and they cost about ten times the initial budget.

When you hear about these deals, always probe for contradictions. If you hear a different fact at the end of a conversation than what was presented initially, you have a red flag. Question these contradictions vigorously. Fibs mean a character weakness, and they are a good way of picking out a deal that should be avoided.

I once jumped into the varnish and ink business in exactly the way an entrepreneur should not diversify. I was called to a morning meeting with the owners of a small plant in my hometown. They were going broke; my business was doing well. I asked them if they had a market gap. They claimed they had. They made some glamorous projections about the future. Inside of an hour, we shook hands and I was the new owner of a varnish company. One year and $500,000 later, I became the former owner of a varnish company.

I knew absolutely nothing about the business. I had acted in haste. I did no background checks on the principals. I questioned none of the firm's customers or competitors. I talked to none of the employees. I had been totally gullible.

More than anything I wanted a business in my old hometown. I followed whim rather than reason. I failed to base my decision on any bottom-line considerations. I wanted to be a big shot for the locals—my ego won out over my logic.

I have thrown my money away on gold dredging schemes, squandered it on oil field doodlebuggers, paid too much for swampland, and bought franchises that never got off the ground —but the varnish and ink venture was the stupidest thing that I had ever done.

There was stiff competition, questionable management, disgruntled employees, not much business, no market gap, and a host of other disquieting problems. A week or two of questioning and probing would easily have uncovered that this business would never work. Even my corporate counsel shrieked at me that it was foolish.

In addition I've made plenty of other mistakes that you don't want to emulate. Early in our evolution as an investment company, I spied a gorgeous color brochure promoting a monthly investment plan for precious metals. I invested heavily in duplicating the concept. It never sold. It's not a bad idea to move into a business where the pioneer is doing well. Don't do what I did, however, and copy a business idea that has yet to prove itself. If you're going to copy something, make sure you're imitating a winner.

Along that line, Leo Baekeland, inventor of Bakelite and the founder of Bakelite Corporation, advised: "Never be a pioneer; it does not pay. Let the other man do the pioneering and then after he has shown what can be done, do it bigger and more quickly; but let the other man take the time and risk to show you how to do it." Leo Baekeland was that rare inventor who possessed a sound business head. He invented a host of products and sold out to Union Carbide for a fortune.

Before learning enough facts about a particular diversification, I've gone ahead and made long-term contractual commitments. When the deal would fail, I still had obligations. Never contract to any unknown person or project for a long period when you've still got lots to learn about it. Keep contracts and agreements on a very short-term basis. When you are in the dark about the future, avoid signing anything that doesn't have a short expiration or an escape clause.

Another point I have learned the hard way is timing. You have to enter a business when the market is appropriate. We once held a heavily advertised precious gem auction. It was a lavish affair with a gala champagne party held on the eve of the event. NBC cameras from "The Today Show" along with newspaper and television reporters widely publicized the hoopla, and a big crowd turned out. But the auction fizzled. Seldom has an event so heavily promoted bombed so badly.

Our timing was wretched. We held an event to sell highly valuable items in the face of a recession. Inflation was waning and commodity prices were softening. Cash was king. We tried to move upstream in heavy current and lost many hundreds of thousands of dollars.

Avoid pushing off your venture in a severely shrinking market. Don't fight economic trends. Most business products and services fluctuate through cycles. Determine some idea of where your diversification is positioned within the ongoing business and economic shifts. Don't buck the major trend.

Many people push into a new business long after the market gap is filled and the field is crowded. This is another example of bad timing. Products can be faddish. When a business peaks, newcomers are still entering the market. Even while inventory levels are bloated, start-ups are trying to get going. Your diversification should be positioned to take advantage of upcoming trends and growth in consumer interest. The best timing of all is to be first or second.

Many fresh developments and new products are better presented to large companies for consideration. A new invention, for example, can be accepted by a large company in exchange for a royalty. Many business novices feel that large companies are poised to steal their ideas and inventions. This fear is greatly exaggerated. You often have no other choice but to show your ideas to these companies. For example, if you have a device that relates to automobiles you can hardly start your own car company.

Since so many new products and gimmicks will be aimed at gaining the blessing of large corporations, a sound procedure should be followed in making a presentation to them.

A company like General Motors, for example, gets over 6,000 new product ideas and improvement suggestions each year. They have a "new devices" department that supervises this inflow of mail and responds to it. You have very little chance of making headway with a huge multinational concern. The people who read your letter most likely don't even understand what you're suggesting. The typical procedure is to give a brief once-over to your idea and send you a standard letter of rejection.

Look at it from their standpoint. Thousands of letters roll in, many from screwball inventors with useless ideas. Some of them are likely to hate GM after they've been turned down. Some convince their friends the big company is trying to steal their billion-dollar concept. There is always the chance the motor company will be sued by a crackpot. Worse, all sorts of false rumors are fostered about big companies cheating some poor inventor out of a priceless idea.

Your attorney should whip up a brief nondisclosure statement to be signed by the persons or companies to whom you show a new concept. However, it may be difficult to get the giants to sign. The best protection is a patent application. Then you can be far more secure in presenting the new item.

When my company financed development of the Cob Camshaft, we had to devise a method to get Chrysler, Ford, and General Motors to look at the device. We called rather than wrote. They were indifferent. We followed up with a bombardment of letters, a telex to the president of each company, plus many more phone calls. The new devices departments told us that in time they would consider our invention. We were frustrated by the slow pace of their examination. "Sometimes it takes months before we answer," they said.

The trick here is to maintain a constant bombardment of intelligent missives. We continued our unrelenting tactics. Finally one company thought it might at least take a look if we brought the device to Detroit. We employed a strategy that always seemed to work with the Big Three. We told the other two of the third company's interest. Immediately they perked up, wanting to see it too. In all our dealing in Detroit, what worked best was playing one company against the other.

I have found that large companies behave much like individuals. They have similar behavior patterns. In dealing with a large company, you should look at them as though they were somewhat like a single, oversized person. The people you deal with are the parts of a unit, but in total the corporation responds to stimuli much as an individual does. That's natural enough, because companies are made up of people. Use the same tactics with a big firm that you use in all successful human relations and you may see progress.

After visiting Detroit and showing our invention, we soon got a letter from General Motors telling us they were not interested. Ford and Chrysler wanted to see more. Months later we headed back with an improved device. We called GM again, and they told us that as long as we were in town to see the others we could come by. Within a few months, General Motors sent us another letter rejecting the device.

We went back again with a second-generation device for Chrysler and Ford to test. GM said to come by again. Suddenly, with Ford stalled and Chrysler doing advanced testing, GM came alive. They ordered several of our cams and began testing in several divisions.

These big companies need plenty of massaging. You can't give up at the first rejection. They have a built-in system to turn you down. They are prejudiced against outside inventions. They assume nobody knows as much about their products as they do. They see all kinds of crazies. They can be sued, accused, criticized, and denounced for an innocent procedure. They all exhibit the "NIH syndrome" (not invented here), which means they tend not to like something they didn't develop themselves. Furthermore, if you have anything good, workers within the company will invariably be working on something vaguely related. They will be threatened or envious and do their best to torpedo your device.

The larger the company, the more likely it will be immovable. Most big organizations are inefficient bureaucracies that resist change. Product breakthroughs are neither visualized nor nurtured. These companies are wedded to the status quo, and their members seem far more interested in protecting their patch of turf than appreciating or comprehending what you are up to.

Another type of large company you may need to deal with is the national retailing giant. Today the bulk of the retail business passes through a few major chains. This represents an enormous change over the past few decades. Unless you can get your product into these big companies, you will have open to you only smaller outlets, specialty shops, or forms of direct selling.

We were able to place our Fotoshow plastic storage device with one major national chain quite rapidly. We placed a number of full-page ads in a newspaper in the city where this company had its home office. It was impressed enough to pick up our device. The unit sold well, so we placed it in all of their stores. A powerful marketing strategy with newspaper and television in the hometown of a major chain may get their attention.

Unless you're a large, well-established firm with successful products, you'll have a difficult task breaking into the big-time distribution system. If you can get the first one, then the others will possibly follow. It's a tough task and a lot of buyers will spurn you. Over time you can wear them down, but don't expect overnight market penetration. Only a dedicated entrepreneur with singleness of vision and relentless concentration and persistence can get this task done.

One of the worst traps in retailing is known as "guaranteed sales." You place your product with a company for a short period of time and if it doesn't sell, they send it back to you. What you get back is a bunch of damaged, mishandled goods, unexpected inventory, and a monumental freight bill. This is a horrible way to do business.

The gem industry frequently operates on a basis equally as bad. Goods are placed on consignment. If they don't sell, the wholesaler gets them back. Whatever business you may be in, don't consign goods. You should either sell your goods or hold on to them. Consignment deals are foolhardy, work out poorly, and are the quintessence of bad business.

Whatever your product, there are national manufacturers' representatives who sell similar goods and will sell yours. They get a small commission and may want to add your product to their current line. You should talk to a number of these reps for no other reason than to pick their brains. They have a fund of marketing and distribution insights. Self-interest insists they be wedded first and foremost to their hot products. They like goods that move. New products always face stiff market resistance, and reps are not the best pioneers. Many talk a good game, but results are something else. If you are manufacturing, you probably need reps if you can't afford your own salespeople. If you are a middleman or a marketing company, a rep tends to duplicate what you are supposed to be doing.

You should always be trying to improvise some new marketing strategy, some new way of approaching customers, or some additional service breakthrough. Anything you can do that goes beyond present systems and methods and helps your customer will work to your benefit. That's what it's all about.

One of the poorest diversifications directs you into providing goods or services for the government. Government agencies don't have needs and requirements based on bottom-line decisions. Corporations judge results by profit or loss. Governments have no similar beacons. Therefore, political considerations, cost cutting, or bureaucratic whim can terminate your relationship. Don't do 100 percent of your business with the government because an all-too-common cancellation or cutoff can ruin you.

Run your diversifications with the same insistence on perfection you have in your mainstream profit centers. Preach the gospel of innovation and service to your project managers. You must check the financial data for these operations and secure the most important facts.

Harold Geneen explains how important "facts" were to him as he managed over two hundred companies. "I had to rely upon hundreds and hundreds of different reports, full of 'facts,' and the decisions I had to make were crucial. That is why I cross-examined the men who brought me those 'facts.' I did not have the time to do the counting myself." Overseeing your diversification means getting the facts.

Have these managers present operating budgets each year and insist they write down long-range goals and plans. Appoint someone in your company who also understands these reports to make sure that you get them in an understandable and timely fashion for review.

When someone brings you a sound business idea that appears to fill a market gap, that person must meet certain criteria before you go ahead with any affiliation. If I see someone aged thirty-five to forty-five with prior experience in a similar venture and a record of getting things done and solving problems quickly, I may have a winner. Add in some past adversity that toughened and seasoned him or her, and I can get enthusiastic.

I like to set up a lucrative commission and incentive arrangement that guarantees the entrepreneur will get rich if the venture prospers. Remember, however, there is always a tendency to overestimate people in the early stages. To reiterate, commitments and contracts should be short-term and allow you some escape if you've made a bad choice.

The ideal diversification would be totally recession-proof and impervious to the business cycle. Such a company probably doesn't exist. Next best would be a venture that offset the cyclical nature of your main business. When it is weak, the diversification is strong and vice versa. A large computer company purchased a finance company several years ago. When interest rates were high and computer sales sluggish, the credit company did well. It seemed a shrewd mix.

A good diversification should add enough muscle to your operation so that you can have a bad year in one part of your company and not perish. That's the purpose of spreading out. Perhaps the shoemaker should stick to the last, but if everybody starts to wear moccasins, he had better have something else to do.

As John Willard Marriott pointed out, "There's a lot to be said for diversification. Don't put all your eggs in one basket they say. There's wisdom in that. If business slumps in one division, there are other divisions to carry it through. All businesses fluctuate. Diversification takes care of it."

It will help your diversification if you take time to visualize and formulate what kind of company you are and what you hope to be. If you see yourself as a broad-based organization in your field, it speeds your evolution. You must define what you are. My firm perceives itself as a financial services company, not simply a gold and silver dealer.

Henry Kaiser, the great diversifier, may have overstated this approach somewhat when he said, "I'm a builder, and if you call yourself a builder you ought to be able to build anything." He founded over a hundred companies, and his ventures were as diverse as resorts, steel, aluminum, shipbuilding, and many kinds of construction. In the 1940s he turned out almost one-third of the ships needed for the war effort. He founded Kaiser Aluminum and the Kaiser Auto Company. The latter flopped and cost him $100 million. That kind of loss is the inevitable consequence of unbridled diversification. Unless the diversification fits into present markets and technologies or is led by a truly exceptional individual, it can turn into an expensive trap. Not only must a diversification "fit," it must feel right. You and your staff should be as proud of your diversifications as you are of your basic business.

Peter Drucker suggests that a company ask itself, " 'What is the least diversification this business needs to accomplish its mission, obtain its objectives, and continue to be viable and prosperous?' Also ask the question, 'What is the most diversification we can manage, the most complexity this business can bear?' The optimum will lie, as a rule, between the two extremes."

Remember, the greater the opportunity, the fewer are those who see it. The more popular and watered down it becomes, the greater the number that is attracted to take action. Finally, most rush in when the opportunity has passed and is really no more than a trap. Investment and business opportunities run similar courses. By the time new start-ups in a particular field are flooding into the marketplace, you can figure the bust is imminent.

In the early 1970s, when I started my financial company, silver and gold were the snake oil of the investment business. Back then, hard-money luminaries and best-selling authors Harry Browne and Jerome Smith formulated startling economic predictions. They laid out a sobering economic scenario for the upcoming decade. Their views on the rise of inflation and the decline of the dollar were scorned by mainstream economists, investment company intelligentsia, and the financial establishment. Nevertheless, the startling accuracy of their forecasts reverberated through the 1970s. The decade closed out in the throes of inflationary panic.

These men and others proved once again that so much of what we accept without question often turns out to be false. "Almost everything is bull——," a cynic once proclaimed to me. It won't hurt you to share at least a portion of that sentiment.

In the beginning I took my dynamic formula on the future of silver to the most prominent investors who would see me. My energy and enthusiasm for this irrefutably ripe opportunity were boundless. I passed out books, lectured with fervor, and called prospects incessantly. Nevertheless, I bombed. I could barely eke out a living. My prognostications on the likelihood of severe inflation and a dramatic price rise in silver registered with the persuasiveness of some dreary religious doomsdayer.

Many people were quick to point out the fallacy of my views. In fact, many of the free-market economic principles that had fostered my opinions were terribly out of favor. The reigning dogma flew in the face of my efforts. You have the greatest opportunity when the mainstream of public thought rejects your ideas and concepts.

The entrepreneur should apply this yardstick of doubt not only to "most human notions," but particularly to popular assumptions about what will or won't work in a business opportunity. Encourage contrary thinking. Position yourself in disagreement with popular beliefs and mythologies. Investment lore is filled with tales of those isolated few who went contrary to the herd and enjoyed huge success. An entrepreneur needs to doubt the present methodology and be suspicious of the current gospel.

It is the entrenched interests that scorn innovation most. The bureaucracy, the financial establishment, and the old business order resist change because their self-interest can be damaged by fresh ideas. They will be the first to sneer, just as they did at Ford. You represent competition. You threaten the status quo. They will hate you and will pull strings to stop you. But they are ripe for the taking. They can be gutted and beaten, in much the same way that Currier Holman demolished the meatpackers.

One person can do a lot—keep that in mind. Repeat it to yourself again and again. One person can do a lot. There is nothing in the world that can stand in the way of someone who is possessed with belief, desire, and perseverance. No organization, business monolith, or institution can withstand one lone, relentless person on a long and difficult journey.

SUMMARY

The best type of diversification moves you into areas that add to the services or products your business currently sells. Unrelated ventures can be costly and unworkable.

You cannot follow many businesses with the thoroughness

and dedication needed to make them successful. It takes five years to make most new companies successful.

One sensible diversification comes through linking up with an outstanding entrepreneurial individual. You invest in him or her.

When looking at new ventures, you must always be alert to dishonest promotions.

Not only are there market gaps, but also marketing gaps. These gaps allow you to redeploy a product and, with new promotions, capture a new market slice.

Be realistic in your projections of profit potential on a new venture.

Don't expect quick help from diversifications; they invariably take far longer to deliver than anyone anticipates.

Avoid long-term contractual commitments; leave a way out on a new venture or relationship.

Some products lend themselves to licensing deals with large companies. You must tackle these big companies with perseverance. They move slowly.

The perfect diversification will make profits when the parent company slumps. The two companies cancel out the negative effects of the business cycle.

10.
What to Do
When Business
Begins to Decline

The only irreparable mistake in business is to run out of cash. Almost any other mistake in business can be remedied in one way or another. But when you run out of cash, they take you out of the game.

—HAROLD GENEEN

All companies, including yours, will see periods of severe financial difficulty. Sales will plummet and losses will mount. This is even more predictable today with our highly cyclical economy. Start-ups are bound to experience sharp retractions. These are periods of great anxiety and personal suffering. They are also times that soften and temper unattractive human traits and build personal strength and character.

Distasteful personality trappings that sometimes flourish in the nouveau-riche entrepreneur are rapidly exterminated by sharp adversity. The personality that successfully negotiates severe setbacks and emerges with enterprise intact is a far more attractive individual. If you are going to be a first-rate entrepreneur, the path to the highest levels of human achievement will treat you to some very nasty but worthwhile experiences.

The worst thing about the decline of your enterprise is that it usually comes right after a period of dramatic growth and fat profits. While you are rich and careless, sleek and cocky, the bottom begins to rot away.

At the peak of my company's span of gigantic growth, I was totally confident. I chartered a Lear jet and, with entourage in tow, streaked off to San Francisco. We stopped in Salt Lake City for more champagne. I rented the best hotel suite on the bay. We shopped and dined extravagantly. We toured the vineyards of the Napa in a limousine, sipping Schramsberg. An earthquake tremor sent us out to our waiting jet. Soon we were hurtling past the lips of the Grand Canyon and then on to Vail. The world was, indeed, my oyster.

The month of that idyllic sojourn turned out to be the beginning of another journey too. Starting then, my company would lose money for eighteen consecutive months. It was the first red ink I had known in years. It caught me off guard. I was about to learn a heartbreaking lesson: how to retreat.

The bitter period of decline comes suddenly and sweeps all before it. There is no blunting it, no turning it back. You seem powerless to stem the decline, and events appear out of control. Bad news begets more bad news. In a few short months, your infallible judgment and remarkably astute decisions are replaced with blunders and bad luck. The gods have deserted you —even turned against you.

These bleak times generally mirror the business cycle. Recessions inevitably lead to a slump in your business. We know that during these periods the numbers of bankruptcies soar. But as business writer Thomas P. Murphy points out, "Most business failures do not stem from bad times. They come from poor management, and bad times just precipitate the crisis."

Murphy heads a venture-capital firm and writes a regular column in *Forbes* magazine. He writes about IBM founder, Thomas Watson, Sr.,

> While the rest of the world was wringing its hands or sitting on them, Tom Watson was forceful, confident and

moving ahead. But prosperity unsettled him. He was uneasy with it. Like a good ship's engineer, he could detect those faint sounds of trouble others found easy to ignore.

Why this curious fear of good times in business? It was only after I had been through a whole economic cycle in the venture business that I realized why Tom Watson was unsettled by good times. They really are the times when we sow the seeds of our own later destruction. Recessions are blamed for failures, but in fact they are simply harvest times for the crops of seeds so lightheartedly sown in better days.

What are these seeds of failure Murphy warns about? There is a tendency to overhire during boom times. You may quickly add an extra layer of management, an extra layer of fat. Keep your employees stretched to the maximum. Try to resist the various managers' requests for more help.

At the top you tend to use more outside consultants, become more generous with office supplies, buy the big computer, become wasteful with postage, pass out fat wage hikes, become sloppy on cost control, print extras that you ultimately waste, overadvertise, and indulge in scores of other minor wasteful procedures.

You should periodically hold meetings with your management staff to explore cost-cutting measures. When business really booms you are likely to be sloppy with expenditures. You will be amazed at how much you can slice away as your managers propose a surprising number of ways to reduce overhead. Make this slashing and cutting of expenses a high priority for your company. Eliminate waste. Build a reputation as a fearsome cutter.

One simple way to keep abreast of your employees' ideas on cost-cutting measures is to have a suggestion box. Each idea you adopt should earn the employee a handsome reward. We give a five-ounce bar of silver for each suggestion adopted. A suggestion box may sound old-fashioned, but what better way to improve your operation than to have your employees at every level search for ways to make your company run smoother and be more cost-efficient?

However, don't expect to put out a suggestion box and have

it run itself. A suggestion box must be managed. Each suggestion must be considered by the responsible department head and, if rejected, the reason conveyed to the employee who made the proposal. When in doubt about a suggestion, give the reward anyway. Put a competent person in charge of the suggestion box. A poorly run program will cause you more problems than it's worth.

Too much prosperity makes many companies lax in service and quality. If your company loses customers for this reason, your lack of attention to detail will eventually kill your business. Your employees might adopt these loose procedures also and some may even become rude or indifferent to good customers. If you are to stay at the top you must be ever-watchful of slipshod patterns.

Stanely Marcus describes the onset of this ailment at one of his favorite restaurants:

> The subtleties of fine-food preparation and service suffer from bigness and the absence of the all-seeing eye of the proprietor. Trader Vic's was one of the great American restaurants when it had a single location in Oakland, and it even survived the installation of a San Francisco branch. Then Vic Bergerson, the founder, succumbed to the lure of establishing Trader Vic's restaurants in hotels all over the country.
>
> Vic had created a unique menu of foods and drinks with recipes of reputed Polynesian origin and with a stage-setting South Seas decor. Despite the fact that Vic had never been west of San Francisco, his research was so good that everything came off with apparent authenticity, at least to the eyes and tastes of most of his customers who hadn't visited Pago Pago themselves.
>
> One night I dined at the Trader Vic's restaurant in the Plaza Hotel in New York where I ordered my favorite Trader Vic dish, Indonesian lamb, which is served with a generous portion of viscous peanut-butter sauce blended, I've always suspected, with soy and mustard. On this particular evening, there was only a small, firm ball of the peanut butter, tightly packed from a number-four ice-cream scooper and placed in a small pleated-paper cup. The con-

sistency was stiff and the extra ingredients had been skimped on. It was obvious an efficiency expert had reduced both the size of the portion and the ingredients in its recipe.

Trader was probably one of the first restaurateurs to introduce the Japanese oshibori, the steamed towelettes, to wipe both fingers and lips. Our waiter brought them, after removing our plates, and said, "Hot towels." They were damp and cool. I complained, but the waiter had done his job by announcing that they were hot. Whether they were hot or cold was a matter of no concern to him or the captain who stood nearby.

Trader Vic's was noted for pioneering the sale of good American wines in California, but in New York there was no wine list, and wine by the glass was available only under duress. The final indignity to Vic's great restaurant tradition was when the waiter placed the water pitcher on the head of one of the large wooden Tikis, a decorative element in Vic's carefully conceived design scheme. Out of respect to Vic, and the god the Tiki represented, I asked the captain to remove it, but a few minutes later the waiter replaced it and the captain made no protest. The staff, doubtlessly, had been trained according to carefully planned service manuals, but unfortunately Vic had not foreseen that a waiter might use the head of a Tiki as a service station. This gaucherie may have gone unobserved by most of the diners; many who saw it probably paid no attention, but any institution catering to customers who want the best and are willing to pay the price for it must be concerned with its ability to satisfy the minority. They are the ones who know the difference; they are the ones that the majority will follow.

You must not let down during the good times. You must not succumb to weakness in these luxuriant peaks. Thomas Murphy asks, "What is the difference between taking advantage of prosperity and being beguiled by it?

"One sign, I think—it is a broad one—is taking on projects that have to succeed or they will take the company down with them. This is the kind of project some businessmen are tempted to undertake when things are booming and they are feeling especially macho. There is rarely justification for reacting like

a poker player turned compulsive gambler and pushing everything into the center of the table."

Another question is What are you doing with your cash? Periods
of high profits are important times to build valuable surpluses
and repair your balance sheet. If you launch too many expan-
sions and diversifications, you are going to run down your capital base.

While it is certainly tempting to spend money on new ventures and expend profits rather than give them to the IRS, you
can go much too far. Better to pay half in taxes and keep the rest
to build a cash surplus.

When my company soared, I jumped into several new and
costly ventures to avoid a heavy tax load. Drilling for oil may
have temporarily reduced taxes, but when the wells came up
dry, it also reduced profits and my supply of cash. I was to suffer
far more for these diversifications than would have been necessary had I held on to more capital.

It may be that a better time to be aggressive is during leaner
periods. Thomas Murphy believes this and chronicles Tom
Watson's advice, " 'Just as booms are a time for caution, so are
recessions a time for boldness.' Watson knew this well. During
the depths of the depression, Watson, unwilling to lay people
off, kept turning out punch-card machines for which there was
no visible market. Then came the New Deal and Social Security,
and IBM made a great step forward when other companies were
pulling in their horns.

"The time to be bold is when nearly everyone else is timid.
But when nearly everyone else is bold, a little timidity is an
excellent thing to have."

Another source of business decline can come from competition.
Once you have your company established, you must be diligent
in watching the moves of your competitors. Subscribe to and
examine all your industry's publications and periodicals. Scruti-
nize the other people's advertising and promotions. Keep
abreast of your industry—watch the new players and the old-
line companies closely.

When you keep tabs on the others you will pick up new
ideas that benefit you. Copy any innovation that appears worthwhile. Occasionally you can take someone else's breakthrough

and improve on it. You certainly don't want to be left behind by a competitor's new idea. To capitalize on ideas that don't originate from within your company, you must keep an open mind. Sometimes your leadership in an industry will blind you to a superior idea. You might belittle an idea that doesn't come from you. A good leader will turn the competition's attacks into advantages by picking up on a good idea and bettering its execution.

One of the most frustrating types of competition comes from former employees who absorb the details of your business while on your payroll and leave to start a competing firm. They often take corporate secrets, customer lists, sources of supply, and other trade information that is terribly advantageous to them.

There is no value in hating these homegrown competitors. You must overlook their betrayal. Often they will attack you by attempting to steal customers or they will resort to verbal abuse. There is only one way to deal with these upstarts. Bury them. Leave them behind in a cloud of competitive zeal. A vigorous counterattack makes your company dominant. Outsell them, outperform them, outservice them, outmarket them, and outsmart them.

Look for chinks or weaknesses in their quality and service. Attack there. Bore in through your advertising on these soft spots. Point out these flaws to the marketplace. Hit them again and again with advertising salvos that reveal where they are inferior. If they show any dishonesty, you can wipe them out with it.

The last thing you can allow to happen is to have an upstart competitor make serious inroads into your market share. The value of new competitors will be to spur you on. If they are former employees, that will drive you all the more. Don't worry too much about these newcomers; use them to invigorate you, spur you on, and ensure success and dominance.

Another safeguard against bankruptcy and disaster comes through the control of your ego. The riches that come with a successful enterprise may spoil you. If you develop an arrogant and rude personality from a glut of money, you are more likely to be totally defeated by the inevitable comeuppance.

Henry Ford claimed, "Money doesn't change men, it

merely unmasks them. If a man is naturally selfish, or arrogant, or greedy, the money brings it out; that's all."

Occasionally we see young people in their twenties or early thirties make tremendous fortunes. If their behavior becomes intolerable, you can be sure they will lose their wealth. So often these nouveaux riches are cocky and arrogant. That is why most young people who make a lot of money lose it. They abandon whatever sound perspective they once had.

Money is easier to make than it is to keep. It takes experience and adroit management to hold on to money. Most successful people really blossom around the age of forty. By that time they have the magical blend of experience, toughness, and controlled energy that enables them to prevail. They are also more likely to have a degree of humility and good sense as well as the financial perspectives that allow them to hang on to their wealth.

A measure of their maturity can be seen in the unchanged nature of their personality. They maintain a semblance of modesty and do not become flamboyant or showy. One of the greatest compliments I ever received came from my friend Ron Schara, outdoor editor of the *Minneapolis Star and Tribune.* "I knew you when you were poor," he said, "and now that you're rich, you haven't changed very much." He added that I was still an SOB, but the compliment was clear.

If you are going to weather the nasty bouts of adversity ahead, it behooves you to remain humble. Edmund Burke said, "No man had ever a point of pride that was not injurious to him." In business this pride and ego lead you to decisions based on what makes you look important, rather than what is the best financial decision. When you begin to believe you are great, you are on the eve of making a fool out of yourself. Humility is a critical personality trait that will allow you to get past your setbacks and slumps. If you have no humility, you will get it fast, and a bankruptcy is one infallible instructor.

Some people can't handle any kind of financial success. I once knew a young man who set up a mobile-home dealership. He arranged financing from a local businessman. There was a need in the community and he was soon racking up some good profits. Then he went crazy. He bought a big car and towed a huge boat and trailer behind. He took off with a pocket full of cash, flitting from one resort to another, spending lavishly. At one stop he fell in love. He ignored the business. Next, he milked the company of its working capital. Customers were neglected, service was nil, and sales ended. He just kept spending. Within a few months, everything was lost.

If you are going to continue to flourish after experiencing your first round of success, you must hang on to some of your money. An overblown ego seems to go hand in hand with financial extravagance. If you display these traits, you are going to lose everything. You are going back to zero. You will be humiliated, wiped out, and scorned. Whenever you see some upstart wheeler-dealer throwing money around and acting like a mogul, you know that failure is imminent.

The key to getting through a financial debacle lies with how well you can cut. The first time you experience a major decline you have a tendency to resist slashing overhead. Cutting means letting people go. That hurts. You have a sense of loyalty toward your employees, sympathy with their circumstances, and pride in your organization. It hurts you terribly to dismantle your joy —the company you built.

A well-known economist wrote in a newsweekly that a company can expect no loyalty if it cuts employees every time business recedes. I believed that. Therefore, I let many people linger too long who should have been trimmed. As I edged toward disaster, someone suggested it would be foolhardy to keep a hefty payroll and go under because of it. Far better to turn people out, keep only a few jobs and leave the company intact. The economist was wrong. The best policy is to cut when necessary. Overall corporate survival insists on it.

People are expensive. Not just because of their paychecks —they have benefits, use telephones, need supplies, and require space. More than anything, they spend money. Employees are the center of your overhead. When you turn from black ink to red, you should immediately begin to cut them.

When your business has shot straight up for many months, it is a good policy to use a lot of temporaries. When the decline begins, they are easier to let go. The psychological damage is far less severe for them and for you.

Each month of your decline you must comb through the ranks of your employees and weed out the expendable. There's no point in stalling. Inevitably you will be forced to come to this painful conclusion. You should adopt this policy now, make a mental note of it, and don't hesitate to cut when adversity strikes.

My company's decline lasted eighteen months. Business volume fell 90 percent. From 250 proud employees, we withered away until 60 were left. I hated every day of it. The primary spur to my cuts was the terror of losing everything. Each month, volume declined precipitously. From $500 million in sales, we dropped to $50 million. Few companies could have survived. We cut expenses but never could get under our monthly revenues because they fell so fast. There is no greater anxiety, no more immobilizing fear. Over the months, the fits of terror, humiliation, and sorrow seem endless. Only some sort of special help can get you through.

The bank turned its back on me, after having promised to warn me if it became uncomfortable with my credit line. No such luck. It called in our inventory loan and posted guards while counting the coins and bullion. While the employees looked on, a contingent of bank mercenaries locked our doors. The humiliation was almost unbearable. Of course, everything they were counting was there.

The manager of my company's large wholesale division made a deal with the same bank, who agreed to finance him. He went out the door with half my company. Many employees whom I counted on walked out with him.

Business volume took another vicious tumble. We were locked into certain expenses, such as rent and equipment payments. All our diversification attempts were flops or were taking far longer than planned. Some of them required more money. We rescheduled some payments, but the future seemed bleak. We kept on losing a staggering monthly sum.

One day my secretary confided to me that meetings of my officers and managers were being held secretly. They had invited in some of the directors and sounded an alarm. Their aim was to oust me. A contingent of lawyers met with me and suggested I step down. I told them to go to hell.

Although the senior managers and directors attacked me, they could not overcome my controlling interest. We battled through two stormy directors meetings with a tremendous amount of misinformation, finger pointing, and bitterness.

Then, a special directors and shareholders meeting was called. One of the directors brought an outside attorney. We clashed. I threw him out. By this time, certain directors were in my camp. Opponents battled but the meeting calmed down, and I finally won a vote of confidence.

Three vice-presidents and one department head resigned, and my controller went to work for a competitor. The worst was over. For days I lapsed into momentary flashes of fear. The final four months of the year-and-a-half slide had brought crisis after crisis. With each round of pain and anxiety, I would assure myself it could get no worse. I had passed the test. But within weeks another fearful experience would erupt, worse than the last.

Finally, the markets bottomed out and volume spruced up. The many thousands of satisfied customers we had developed began to buy again. My critics had forgotten about those loyal customers. They saved us. At last we turned the corner. My judgments and arguments proved reasonably accurate for the next six months, and the directors and shareholders voted me a year-end bonus.

I would have received no such vindication, however, had I not had the control. I would have been ejected from the company I had built, loved, nurtured. Heed my warning: never relinquish control.

When my officers and managers resigned, we were relieved of a huge chunk of overhead. Shockingly, their loss made absolutely no difference to our operation. Our business shrinkage had apparently left most of them with nothing to do but plot. We never missed them.

My high-priced managers left in a period of crisis. The proper strategy is to cut some of these expensive senior managers loose at an earlier date. You will have the most loyalty to these employees, but when their job requirements diminish, you simply don't need them. They must be terminated expeditiously, as they are your major overhead.

If your company starts to slip into losses, you may want to implement a stringent "need-to-know" philosophy. Many companies follow a policy of letting employees become aware only of what they need to know. In other words, you may be wise to keep your financial plight between yourself and a few managers. I have found, however, that keeping a secret in a company is next to impossible. Everyone seems to know what everyone else makes, and any inequity is widely broadcast. But it does make sense to try to keep the gory financial details on a need-to-know basis.

One of the many accusations hurled at me suggested that the company could not meet future financial commitments, payments, and contracts with its present level of income. On the face of it, that was true. However, you will find that these obligations can be rescheduled or that partial payments can be made on them. Nearly everybody will bend with you. I was amazed at the ease with which I could renegotiate and extend these matters. Don't think you are doomed because of this payment predicament.

You can work your way through the maze of financial problems you face. Don't ever fear them so much that you give up. They are far worse in your mind than they are in reality. You can deal with them. The nasty events and experiences in life that torment you come unexpectedly. The things you worry about seldom, if ever, happen.

When business circumstances become desperate, certain people are tempted to do something dishonest. You can't give in to any such temptation. This is the worst possible tactic, since you avoid meeting your problems head-on. This is the one option open to you that will cinch your failure. By cheating or stealing, you avoid bravery and skill. Thus, you will be upended. That is another immutable law of enterprise.

One of the nice things about the pain you experience in business struggles is that inevitably, if you persevere, it will go away. In time you even forget how sharp and debilitating it was. As I survey the landscape of three separate business traumas, I can't sort out which one was worse. I suspect that the first two prepared me for the third. How else can I explain my staying power when those around me crumbled and quit? After you have weathered these acrid bouts of adversity, you set the stage for dramatic financial gains and business resurgence. As Harvey Firestone noted, "A business is not a business until it has been hardened by fire and water."

When things go bad, they pile up, one on top of another. At the most inopportune time there will be a strike, freaky weather, canceled orders, or a lost shipment to make matters worse. Just after Henry Ford bought out the last of his stockholders in 1919 and borrowed a huge sum of money from the bank, everything went awry. At the time, demand for cars was great and Ford Motor Company was then making half of all automobiles produced. In late summer three national strikes in the steel, coal, and railroad industries ruined production. Instead of selling a million cars as planned, the company sold three-quarters of that amount. As production slumped, the Federal Reserve jacked up the discount rate by the single greatest leap in history. Installment sales withered. On Christmas Eve of 1920 Ford was forced to shut down for the first time since it was founded. Ford's huge note was due at the bank within four months. To make matters worse, the country was slipping into a nasty recession.

Business adversity seems inevitably to follow the same pattern. All sorts of unexpected devils jump up. Here was Henry Ford, one of the richest and most famous personages of his time, hanging on to the ropes. No one but an entrepreneur who has experienced similar straits can comprehend the intensity of suffering that accompanies these traumatic events. Ford must have agonized. The loss of all he had built and become must have been a terrifying thought.

At this juncture in the evolution of all companies, a tremendous chorus of criticism resounds through the boardrooms, plants, and hallways. Entrepreneurs are quickly roasted if business falters. At this moment in your company history, you had better have control. Without it, as so many entrepreneurs have found out, you are going to be removed from your duties. All companies hit snags and, if you don't have a majority interest, you can be sure that at least a few of your trusted advisers, friends, employees, directors, and shareholders are going to arrange for your early retirement. It can get vicious.

I believe people instinctively turn on a leader who appears to have slipped badly. Certainly in prehistory, when food and survival might hinge on the leader's direction, a failing chief could very well be pushed over a ledge. How else to explain the dethroning of so many once-vaunted leaders, the lack of loyalty, and the loss of confidence?

Certainly Henry Ford would have been challenged by his shareholders had they still owned their stock in 1921. By then, however, he owned every single share of the Ford Motor Company. A month after closing, Henry Ford was ready to start up again. His biographer Carol Gelderman writes in her fascinating portrayal, *Ford*, "On February 1 he called his workers back, produced ninety thousand Model T's in six weeks, and shipped them to his dealers. Although the country suffered from a severe recession, Ford insisted that his dealers accept cars allotted to them or lose their franchises. Every dealer had to pay cash on delivery. By April, Ford was able to pay off his debts; his dealers and their smalltown bankers had bailed him out of trouble."

It was a brilliant strategy. Over the years, Ford had enabled the dealers to prosper handsomely. He called in his markers. The dealers paid up and thereby paved the way to a sound future for themselves and Ford.

SUMMARY

A decline usually begins when a company reaches the peak of its prosperity.

Bad management becomes magnified by a business recession. When profits are large, unnecessary expenses build up. Always try to cut costs in good times or bad.

Don't get into too many business projects. Better to pay taxes than to start up losers.

Learn to thrive on competition. Don't allow competitors to cause your decline. Imitate their successful ideas.

When you are in a serious decline, you must cut staff. People are the chief source of overhead.

In a business decline, critics will thrash you. The reason you maintain control is for times like this.

If you have financial problems, you need to cut senior managers. You can work your way through tight spots by restructuring payment, making vendors be flexible.

11.
What to Consider Before You Decide to Step Down

It will be a great mistake for a community to shoot the millionaires, for they are the bees that make the most honey, and contribute most to the hive after they have gorged themselves full.

—ANDREW CARNEGIE

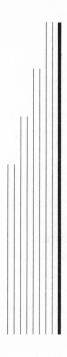

Once they become comfortable and secure, many entrepreneurs lose their innovative edge. Some decide to sell out. They lose their taste for the struggle and turn away from their ventures. If you can put away enough money to assure your security and comfort for the balance of your life, who can blame you for quitting? Especially if you are tired of the struggle. And if you become bored with it, why not do something else?

The demanding realities of the entrepreneurial challenge require constant attention. Alfred Sloan sums it up marvelously:

> Growth and progress are related, for there is no resting place for an enterprise in a competitive economy. Obsta-

cles, conflicts, new problems in various shapes, and new horizons arise to stir the imagination and continue the progress of industry. Success, however, may bring self-satisfaction. In that event, the urge for competitive survival, the strongest of all economic incentives, is dulled. The spirit of venture is lost in the inertia of the mind against change. When such influences develop, growth may be arrested or a decline may set in, caused by the failure to recognize advancing technology or altered consumer needs, or perhaps by competition that is more virile and aggressive. The perpetuation of an unusual success or the maintenance of an unusually high standard of leadership in any industry is sometimes more difficult than the attainment of that success or leadership in the first place. This is the greatest challenge to be met by the leader of an industry.

You are probably better off selling at least a portion of your business interest than trying to manage it halfheartedly. Remember this fundamental rule: The further you remove yourself from your business, the more lax and vulnerable to competition it will become.

I wouldn't rush into a decision to give up your business, however. It takes a wide array of diversified assets to offset the ravages of inflation and other economic shocks. Nothing spins off money like a proprietary enterprise. There is no finer asset.

Henry Ford commented, "Up to the age of forty, a man is in training—every man is. He is assembling the tools with which to work. When the tools are at hand, they can be put to their real uses. Should he quit then, he would quit a failure. Should he sell out and retire, he would be the sorriest failure of all."

George Eastman said, "The man who thinks he has done all that he can do has stopped thinking. He is what might be called 'up and out.' Excepting that he has more money, his case really is not very different from that of the man who is *down* and out.'"

One issue you must face as you approach a decision to sell out, merge, or go public is the effect this new direction will have on the company you have built.

Stanley Marcus points out the liabilities of turning your enterprise over to large companies and professional managers:

The absorption of small businesses into large, publicly held companies has also resulted in the replacement of "proprietor ownership" by "professional managers," men who have been educated to run anything from a bottling plant to a shoe factory, from a department-store basement to a bookstore chain. They know the principles of good management and capital enhancement without having any specialized knowledge of an industry. They do well in high-volume operations, which make the best use of their skills; but the qualitative aspects of a fine business suffer under this type of direction—for quality comes about as the result of the experience of an expert who has an intimate understanding of the thousand details involved in its achievement. There is an old Spanish proverb which expresses this idea succinctly: *"El ojo del amo engorda el caballo,"* or "The eye of the owner fattens the horse." It's difficult for the professional manager to develop the eye of an owner, for he doesn't have the horse.

There may be examples of professional managers who actually founded fine-quality businesses, but if there are, I am unaware of them. Essentially, they are caretakers and accumulators, capable of expanding established companies and improving their operating statements and P/E [price/earnings] ratios, of adding by acquisition. Nowhere is quality more closely related to owner-management than in the restaurant business. In the month of March, a few years back, I was dining for the first time at LeLavandou, a restaurant on East Sixty-first Street in New York, and ordered melon for dessert. I remember the month, for it occurred to me that anyone ordering melon in March had no right to complain if it wasn't good. The patron walked through the dining room attired in his chef's hat and apron, speaking to the guests he knew and smiling at those he didn't. My melon arrived, and though nice in appearance, it was hard. I was able to dig out one spoonful and I quit. When the waiter came back to clear the table, I made no complaint, for, after all, it was March. In a few minutes the waiter returned with another slice of melon and said, "The chef thinks this might please you better." The owner-chef, seeing the piece of melon minus one spoonful, found out what was wrong, and on his own volition replaced it. That's a quality peculiar to proprietorship.

If you have built a big and successful business, no one needs to tell you that maintaining service and quality is even more difficult in a large organization. Stanley Marcus comments on the dangers of bigness and the consequences of going public with your large company.

Bigness in itself is a destructive influence on high-quality operations, because it not only diminishes the personal involvement of top management in many vital areas but brings with it other distractions that are an even greater threat. Bigger businesses entail bigger problems in finance, labor relations, building programs, employee training, executive development. The ultimate solution often leads in the direction of public ownership, either through the marketing of capital stock or merger. The moment an entrepreneur of fine quality takes in one outside partner or three thousand stockholders, the quality of his business can be affected, for the shareholders invest for three reasons only: security, dividends, and growth. They are notoriously unsentimental about their investments; they are not interested in the architectural style of the factories or the cleanliness of the lavatories—they want increased dividends and higher market prices, and they are perfectly willing for the operating standards of the business to be bent in favor of their own priorities. No longer is the entrepreneur the complete master of his business; to meet the demands of his stockholders, he starts making compromises with his traditional quality. His new status as a publicly held company may force him to become more efficient, which is one of the pluses of having outside stockholders, but when he starts to depreciate the quality of his product by the elimination of two of the ten coats of lacquer on a chair or the pinking of the seams of a dress, or by the substitution of plastic for freshwater-pearl buttons on a sportshirt, he defaults in his position as a quality-maker.

When Al Lindner, fishing editor and star of his own television show on angling, sold out his tackle company to a large corporation, it wasn't long before he realized he had made a mistake. Quality suffered. He had been asked to stay on at a good salary to help promote the company. All he was required to do was fish. One day he piled up a batch of newly imported tackle in the front yard of the company and set it on fire. This unique method of resigning emphasized his distaste for the new owner's lack of quality. Within a few years the money-losing company was sold again to new owners who reinstated Al's quality concerns and made the company profitable again.

Can a company maintain its commitment to quality and service after its founder or driving force has left the scene? In many cases, the answer is yes. Stanley Marcus recounts his admiration for C. R. Smith, the guiding force of American Airlines for thirty-five years, and their discussion of the preservation of excellence:

> He [Smith] recognized that after safety, courtesy and better service were the ingredients to build his airline into a position of national pre-eminence. He was not content simply to write directives on the subject, but he rode the line from coast to coast to preach the gospel, becoming personally acquainted with crew members, ground personnel, and ticket sellers. He observed that a certain percentage of passengers had problems of some sort at the ticket counters, and instead of letting them fume to the point that they were "going to write a letter to the president," he defused them by stationing a special passenger-service agent in front of the counter to give the irate passengers an opportunity to pour forth their wrath. He understood that once the problems were solved, the travelers relaxed and continued their journeys in a state of pleasure rather than in one of indignation, thereby eliminating subsequent word-of-mouth denunciations of American.
>
> (I watched this problem-solving technique and applied it to Neiman-Marcus whenever we had customers lined up waiting for some particular kind of service, such as the giftwrapping department immediately prior to Christmas. It paid off for us equally well.)
>
> He recognized the fact, ignored by so many business

leaders, that each employee of American was more interested in his own future than in the company's, so he established programs designed to improve the capabilities of
each individual. He insisted on giving not only pilots the
best training possible but mechanics as well, for, he said,
"There's nothing a pilot can do if the plane falls apart in
midair." He built the first stewardess-training school to
teach not only the intricacies of cabin service, but to incul-
cate a standard of courtesy and graciousness that has never
been met or surpassed by any airline. He wanted his stew-
ardesses to come off their trips with the feeling of satisfaction of a job well done.

Not only in the school but on his frequent flights, he
would tell the flight attendants that they were the best and
most important representatives of the company. "I won't
order you to be courteous," he would say, "but I want to
prove that it is good for you. If you are rough with passengers, it's bad for them, for the company, and for you! It
doesn't take more time to be courteous than discourteous,
and both the recipient and giver of service and courtesy
benefit by having a happier day."

C. R. and I developed a healthy mutual respect and
whenever we met, on a plane or in my office, we usually got
around to the problems of maintaining the kind of service
we both thought was of such great importance to our re-
spective businesses. The last time I saw him, I posed the
query as to whether standards of quality and service could
survive their founders and, if so, for how long. Could the
insistence on the best over a long period act as a semiperma-
nent inoculation for a business? "Sure," he replied, "if you
give it booster shots."

If the employees have for so long been accustomed to
providing good service that this has become an ingrained
habit, a high standard of service will continue for some time
after change of management, even if that management
proves to be inept. In some organizations, a high standard
of service is difficult to eradicate on any immediate basis.
On the other hand, a reputation for poor service is hard to
overcome. The airline business provides two opposite examples.

In the early days of commercial aviation, when business to Florida was highly profitable, before the yet, which popularized island hopping, Rickenbacker and Eastern had a monopoly on the New York–Florida business. It was so easy to sell space to Florida that Eastern began to believe it was doing the customer a favor to take a reservation. Eastern was then one of the most prosperous of the airlines.

For a long time the service on Eastern was so poor that "I hate Eastern" clubs were formed by disgruntled passengers. In varying degrees, the reputation of Eastern for poor service has endured for more than twenty-five years. Subsequent managements have tried to improve the Eastern image, though that has always proved to be difficult. Today, after many years, the image is brightening, due to the leadership of Frank Borman, but it did take a long time.

American, on the other hand, has been able to retain a substantial part of its reputation for good service. In many cases, the employees retained their own concept of good service and provided it, because they had been accustomed to rendering it for a long time. It is comforting to realize that good principles, soundly embedded, are not quickly erased.

Perhaps the pithiest tribute to C. R. was one that appeared in *Forbes:* "Cyrus Rowlett Smith made American Airlines the standard of the domestic industry by treating his passengers like royalty and his employees (with whom he sometimes shot crap) like partners. Under Smith's successor, American became just another airline."

I think that C. R. and I would both disagree with the last sentence of the comment, because there are people at American who still remember the lessons he instilled, sometimes with choice profanity, and they are transmitting them to another generation of employees.

Despite your concern for what happens to your company, your overriding consideration must be for your own welfare. You must pin down your financial security.

Once you sell out there is no guarantee that you will be financially secure forever. A dear old gentleman I once knew owned a superb reinsurance agency. Year after year through the 1940s and 1950s, he took down a salary of over $100,000. That was a huge paycheck in those days. (One of the keys to building riches lies in consistently drawing a large annual wage.) Finally, in his mid-sixties, he decided to sell out.

With the chunk of cash from the sale of his agency, he bought a resort hotel on Collins Avenue in North Miami Beach. He picked up some racehorses. He invested heavily in gas wells in Kentucky. He lived well and spent his money to maintain a handsome life-style. Eventually his investments—the wells, the hotel, the horses—drained away his precious capital. Before long he lost everything. This proud and highly respected business leader was tapped. A few years ago I gave him $3,000 to get his teeth fixed. If there was ever a law that you needed to focus on, it is the one that says, "It is harder to keep money than it is to make it." You don't want to part with your enterprise until you have an infallible financial plan and enough assets to see you through your retirement.

Once a certain level of wealth and security is reached, the entrepreneur may need some other motivation to keep going. Rather than sell out, it may be sensible to take up a worthwhile cause and direct a segment of your ongoing profits toward that end. If you are cranked up over a charitable endeavor, it may renew your desire to stay at the helm and make money.

I use my assets to buy wetlands. I own several thousand acres of these beautiful ponds and marshes. These tranquil areas are fertile havens for wildlife. I have a fervent desire to preserve them, so much so that it drives me to enlarge my business. More profits mean more assets can be diverted into saving wetlands.

There is no end to the worthy causes and charities to bankroll. If you can focus on one that is particularly close to your heart, it may give you added incentive. This is one way to continue the aggressive growth of your corporation.

A less attractive option is one Thomas Edison used. I believe one of the reasons he accomplished so much in his life was that he never piled up a huge fortune. He lost vast sums on various projects. Constantly in search of money-making ideas, he made many false starts and always spent the money he made with abandon. This inability to score in the way Ford or Carnegie did spurred him on to project after project. The denial of his financial goals gave energy to his creations.

Once you reach a certain level of wealth you need to do something worthwhile with your money. You can use only so much. Emerson warned, "Beware of too much good staying in your hands. It will fast corrupt and worm worms. Pay it away quickly in some sort."

One of the worst things you can do is pile up a huge sum to be handed over to your children and grandchildren upon your demise. This kind of legacy will weaken your heirs. When you relieve people of the need to make their own way, to struggle for their bread, you take too much away from them. People need hurdles in order to grow. They should have financial tribulation or they become weak.

"Sweet are the uses of adversity," wrote Shakespeare. Most of us would agree that struggle makes us stronger. The physician grinds through years of difficult hurdles before emerging into a respected profession. All who climb to the upper levels of human achievement endure profound hardships.

We learn most from our bitterest experiences. Life often seems to be a series of painful events for us to overcome. Consequently we grow. No one escapes these circumstances. One by one we come to our faith in our own painful ways.

Perhaps the most significant of all human struggles is economic. From ancient times, men and women have tenaciously overcome obstacles to feed, clothe, and shelter themselves and ultimately to acquire goods and services. This pursuit built America. To the extent that each person struggled and endured so did they prosper, grow, and become wise. Hardship begat skill and ability.

Conversely, those who are relieved of these economic struggles miss out on this toughening process. They do not benefit from the adversity that accompanies making one's own way.

Thomas Mellon, the original source of the Mellon fortune, commented a century ago that "The normal condition of man is hard work, self-denial, acquisition and accumulation; and as soon as his descendants are freed from the necessity of such exertion they begin to degenerate sooner or later in both body and mind." It seems far better to bring children up with an entrepreneurial leaning. We aim our children toward higher education and the professions. Why not raise them to believe that someday they might run their own businesses?

My one-time partner, Bernie, crystallized the matter in one of his most pungent statements, "There is no greater difference among us than between those who inherit great wealth and those who must earn it."

A. P. Giannini, founder of the Bank of America, commented, "Of what use would great wealth be to me? My wants are simple. I could spend no more than my income. Leave it to my children? The last wish in my heart would be to handicap them with great riches and steal away their fund of individual initiative. Any man should think a long time before he bars his children from the opportunity of creative effort or the fashioning and determination of their own lives and happiness."

Giannini could have piled up a huge fortune. He could have easily been one of the richest men in America. From the beginning of his banking innovations that fostered Bank of America and Transamerica Corporation, he turned money away.

His innovative operating philosophy made him a business and banking legend. "If a business is worth having, it is worth going after," said Giannini upon the opening of his first bank. He set out to drum up business through advertising. The solicitation of depositors was a sharp break from tradition, and the competition vilified him (a sure sign he was hurting them). "How can people know what a bank will do for them unless they're told?" he rebutted.

As director of San Francisco Savings and Loan, Giannini had become frustrated by his fellow directors' refusal to make loans to anyone but old-line institutions. Consequently, he raised $150,000 to start "a clean bank run for the little fellow."

Right from the start, his approach was radical and innovative. His bank made loans to small businessmen and merchants, an astonishing departure from the norm. He lent to anyone with security of almost any sort, no matter what his race, creed, or background. He started the children's savings programs in the schools. He established a special department for women. He was the founder of branch banking in the United States. He sold bank shares to his customers on easy terms and shared his profits with his employees. A popular slogan in those days stated, "Make a friend of your banker." Giannini taught his officers to "make a friend of the customer."

In the terrible San Francisco earthquake and fire of 1906, this towering entrepreneur witnessed his bank about to go up in flames, transported the bank's assets in cash, gold, and silver to a safe place, placed his desk on the waterfront dock, and conducted business with his panic-stricken customers while the city in front of him burned.

His business operated primarily to make others profit, rather than himself. He limited his personal wealth to $500,000. In 1927 he spurned a $1.5 million bonus (the equivalent of about fifteen million dollars today) from the bank's directors. "I don't need it and won't accept it," he said. The money eventually went to set up a foundation to help farmers. Late in life, when he noticed he had almost a million dollars, he immediately gave half of it away. "Hell," he said, "why should a man pile up a lot of god-damned money for somebody else to spend after he's gone?"

Through the business history of our country, most of the entrepreneurs who piled up the big money did their best to give it away. These so-called robber barons directed their profits and earnings to the public good on a strictly voluntary basis. Andrew Carnegie directed his vast fortune toward building libraries and public places, many of which still bear his name. He hired a special task force to help him spend his fortune. He had earned so much, it had trouble making a dent in it.

Ray Kroc asked, "What are you going to do with money? I eat one steak at a time and I buy my clothes off the rack—can't stand custom-made clothes. All money represents to me is pride of accomplishment."

If you persist long and hard enough, you will have more money than you can ever use. Why not embrace A. P. Giannini's philosophy? Give it away. Far better to do good with your money while you live than have others direct its use after you're dead. Perhaps Charles Schwab had the right idea. "I spent mine," he said.

When John MacArthur died he left a billion dollars to a foundation. With that money, he could have saved the whales or spawned a bevy of entrepreneurs in far-flung, impoverished nations. He could have preserved a host of beautiful wild places or nurtured initiative among the budding entrepreneurs of some impoverished nation. The causes and tasks are legion. Money, for its own sake, has little merit. It is what you do with it that shows your class.

The wealth you accrue may be invested with others in their start-up ventures. James Duke, founder of Duke University and American Tobacco, said, "Reservoirs of wealth in the hands of individuals are just as necessary as in the hands of banks and insurance and trust companies, because individuals can take risks and undertake enterprises which such institutions cannot."

A great entrepreneurial growth company allows the key employees to participate in a measure of the bounty. That may be one way to disseminate your worth. Andrew Carnegie made millionaires of well over a hundred employees. Some of these men started as unskilled workers and reached the highest levels of compensation.

Once you have built a well-entrenched company, you may be tempted to secure your position by flirting with the government. Many companies suggest legislation that would kill competition. They are eager to protect themselves and, if necessary, will resort to such shabby tactics.

A few years ago, when airlines faced deregulation, many of them argued against it. Those that gave the worst service cried the loudest. Those that did their best to discourage lower fares and competition were the same companies most guilty of bad service and gross inconsideration toward their customers.

I have suggested that you always be on the lookout for bad service. Many domestic airlines are good places to study inferior treatment. When you fly with good airlines, you may study service at its best: great food, marvelous service, and true concern for the customer. No wonder certain competitors wish to ban them from their routes.

From the standpoint of the entrepreneur, competition should be welcomed; it keeps you sharp. The continuous struggle with rivals makes for a more efficient company. The major beneficiary of competition is the consumer. If you believe that the interests of consumers should be served, you have no right to squelch competitors by encouraging restrictive legislation. There are few more loathsome corporate examples than management trumpeting free enterprise while slinking off to Washington to thwart competition. Unfortunately, this is widespread policy.

Many of these entrenched monoliths are fearful of change and innovation. They dislike the entrepreneurial challenge. Once stripped of the legislation that protects them, they would be forced to service their customers far more effectively or perish. Companies granted franchises and monopoly from the government are generally mediocre without competition to spur them on.

Usually, it is the government bureaucracy tied up with labor interests and corporate institutions that resists innovation and human advancement. Entrepreneurs assault this established order. While corporate lackeys court the state to promote their special interests, entrepreneurs stand valiantly alone confronting these bloated conspirators.

No man or woman worthy of the title of entrepreneur runs to the state to curry favor. No brave man or woman sucks up to the government for subsidies, loans, and handouts. Have enough pride to turn away from the seamy temptation of something for nothing. You have no moral right to the earnings of others. You have no ethical basis for which to stifle your competitors with legislation.

Take nothing from the government. Give them nothing more than the essentials required by the law. The state is not your ally or friend, but the architect of intrusion into the free markets which foster entrepreneurs. Left to their own ends and linked with their entrenched corporate and labor minions, they will eliminate you if they can.

Large companies and government agencies are bureaucracies. If you ever have to deal with large corporations you will note their indifference, unresponsiveness, and inflexibility. They are terribly frustrating people to deal with. Only when you locate that rare take-charge type of individual in these companies can you make any progress with them. For the most part, they are inept. Big companies are locked into an operational mode that makes little allowance for change or rapid response to markets. They lack innovation and strong personalities. A smaller, entrepreneurial company should be able to compete with these dinosaurs. You have seen what Japanese entrepreneurs have done. Many of these Oriental companies were built from ashes into positions of market dominance since the end of World War II. They learned how to do things better than the rigid and oversatisfied competition.

Another problem for entrepreneurs today is the ongoing promotion of hostility toward business. Entertainment and the media color entrepreneurs as greed-ridden crooks or bumbling Babbitts.

Professor Henry Nash Smith of the University of California commented, "Serious novelists of our day have not even

attempted to consider the possibly heroic traits and accomplishments of the businessman. Virtually all of them create protago-
nists who are antiheroes—outcasts, pariahs, etc. The search for
a capitalist hero has thus led to no viable results and there is
little indication that it will be more successful in the future."

Criticism of free markets emanates from press and pulpit,
professors and politicians. This erroneous attack against the
source of human comforts and prosperity works to impair and
seriously harm the interests of entrepreneurs. Without free markets you are little more than a serf forced to comply with the
whims of the state.

Recognize your enemies. These foes of enterprise will
abolish you if given the chance. (Cut off their lifeblood. Never
advance a dime for a cause or an institution that promotes
antienterprise drivel.) Some business buffoons support these
purveyors of distortion and hostility toward enterprise. They
sharpen the blade for their own beheading.

There are numerous organizations that teach the merits of
free enterprise that need your financial support. These groups
advance sound economic principles and attempt to educate our
citizenry on the value of the market economy and the role of the
entrepreneur. They are deserving of your contribution. As E. F.
Hutton noted, "If business is going to continue to sell through
the decades, it must also promote an understanding of what
made those products possible, what is necessary to a free market,
and what our free market means to the individual liberty of each
of us."

The battle to gain the public's support for free enterprise
must be a ceaseless struggle. As Bernard Daley would say, "It
is one mind at a time." Each entrepreneur must proselytize and
argue for the system of wealth creation. Leonard Read, the
free-market philosopher, instructed us that persuasion could
come only through positive statements and gentle discussion
rather than arguments and criticism. He advocated listening,
questioning, and instructing rather than dogmatic certitude. He
argued that through self-improvement and the personal study of
economics and liberty, each individual would become a wellspring of influence leading others to realize that economic freedom and human liberty are part of the same equation.

One of the more common attacks on the market system pinpoints the pursuit of self-interest as the essential evil of free enterprise. Business writer E. A. Butler comments,

> Unless a man has a firm grasp on these first principles of ethics, he is liable to view legitimate self-seeking in the business world as some kind of betrayal of a vague ideal, that all men should be simple-minded brothers, somehow loving each other in a great international be-in. Fortunately, the great thinkers, from Aristotle on, who have constructed viable ethical systems, have recognized that self-interest is the primary force in human behavior. Those who preach vague universal love and brainless benevolence are in fact usually among the most hustling self-seekers, in their own mealy-mouthed way. It is appalling that the proponents of such an essentially moronic philosophy of life could manage to brainwash even one intelligent businessman.

A free-market economy is in harmony with man's acquisitive nature. Self-interest must be directed into new products and services that benefit consumers before profits arise. The claim that free enterprise promotes greed misses the mark. Service to others is the exact opposite of greed.

Also remember that the current emphasis on corporate social responsibility can easily be overdone. The finest thing any company can do is to serve its customers so well that it is rewarded with a profit. By serving others in a dedicated fashion it becomes difficult to violate areas of social responsibility. This attention to priorities will keep a company from deluding itself about its motives and its role.

Albert Lasker, founder of Lord & Thomas, the best ad agency of its day, said, "I don't know of any advertiser whom I have served through the years who went into an advertising campaign primarily because he felt impelled to render a social service. On this I want to be candid and emphatic. His fundamental thought was that he make a profit."

Making big money brings special problems. Your actions can quickly generate far more than normal hostility among your fellow citizens. You must be exceedingly careful to avoid any brushes with the law. Society loves to make examples out of the wealthy. You may even get an extra measure of justice.

Unfavorable attention in the media may have a negative effect on your venture. Watch your step. Keep out of binds. Think ahead. For example, I always try to avoid residences and parties where I suspect the possibility of drugs.

Some entrepreneurs wind up with immense hostilities being directed toward them in their lifetime. John MacArthur made a game of infuriating his Palm Beach neighbors. John D. Rockefeller remains vilified to this day. Henry Ford tarnished his once heroic image. Some of this is unnecessary.

MacArthur seems to have reacted to criticism by purposely aggravating the situation. As a wealthy entrepreneur, you are going to be talked about and watched closely for any attempts to push your weight around. The criticisms leveled at you are the reward of any rich person who comes into the limelight. People are going to say some horrible and inaccurate things about you. These can be the same folks who fawn over you in person. So what? That's no reason to isolate yourself or to become withdrawn as some rich men and women do. Keep your common touch, mingle with people, and forgive them for the canards directed your way. You are the living example of the success available within the enterprise system. You should be perceived as a positive reinforcement for the system that allowed you to rise.

Remembered only as a bad example of a businessman, John D. Rockefeller brought low-priced lamp oil to the householder. His business practices were greatly faulted. In the last century, competitive business warfare was the rule, and he waged it better than his competition. We maintain a harsh memory of Rockefeller by applying a contemporary yardstick. But today's rules are different.

When one of my salesmen leaves my employ and takes the clients I gave him to service, it enrages me. I trained him, taught him the business, lifted him from a low-paying job, and here he is starting up against me. Not only that, he stole my customer list for which he had signed an employment agreement promising not to. A hundred years ago when such a competitor popped up, you could squeeze his suppliers, pressure his financiers, buy up what he needed, and shut him out of the market. Not so today. Nowadays you overlook and forget these insults. Your business practices must adhere to more noble guidelines.

Remember that there are many who would love to smear you and overlook the sum of your efforts by discovering some lapse or oversight on your part.

As your accomplishments grow you will be the subject of various newspaper and magazine articles. Some of them will be positive. Infrequently you will be treated to a negative broadside. This type of article can cause you significant pain and make you feel miserable for a while. Too often the reporter's political prejudices and envy color the tone of the article. Some writers are more interested in negatives and gossip than in anything positive.

My company has been the subject of numerous articles in the national and local press. Not one has ever uncovered the essential ingredients that make my company great. They are more interested in what they can ferret out from a disgruntled former employee or a bitter competitor whom we are handily whipping.

Nobody likes to be treated badly by magazine writers or by the press, but if you are successful enough you are going to get kicked in the teeth. The good you do will be forgotten. You will be accused of selfish ulterior motives; the reputation and image you spend years building may be destroyed in a day. Success will bring you enemies, and you will be attacked by those you helped. Do it all anyway and avoid hating. You must love people and understand them.

Henry Ford became the most famous and revered personality of his time, but by age sixty, he was growing bitter over adverse publicity. An unfortunate trial he instigated in 1915 held him up to public ridicule. Attempts to kick off a political career backfired. Ford was an excellent entrepreneur up to the middle of the 1920s. Then he faltered. Tremendous wealth often seems to foster an opinionated personality. Ford grew blinders to the marketplace, which now demanded variety and luxury in automobiles. He saw the stinging political rebuke and ongoing press criticism as a measure of public ingratitude. He had done so much for so many. He became stubborn and willful and began to vent ill-advised personal prejudices. The louder the wail of criticism, the more Ford aggravated the critics. His offhand, autocratic management of Ford led to the loss of its dominance and leadership in the industry.

I suspect that wealth brings on a state of intolerance in many people. The accumulation of a vast fortune may create a sense of superiority and impatience with others. Shipping magnate Aristotle Onassis was said to have become so angered by an hourlong wait in a physician's office that he went into a violent rage and consequently became ill enough to be hospitalized.

If any one thing might be pointed out as leading to the decline of the Ford Motor Company in the late 1920s, it was Henry Ford's inflexibility. This may well have stemmed from his intolerance—a vice that must be paid for.

In some ways Ford's behavior pattern ran similar to that of John MacArthur. MacArthur was frequently criticized. "Lots of people got uppity about the way I operated during the depression. . . . Sure I did things that look bad now. But they were common practice then." His sensitivity to the integrity issue spilled out when he explained the constant battles with his Florida neighbors: "Like everybody else, they thought I had to be crooked." He purposely violated the zoning laws to aggravate them.

This arbitrary, stubborn, and spiteful behavior may be a defense against the perpetual doses of criticism both these men were subjected to. As I have pointed out, the richer you are the greater the chance of negative media attention. The purveyors of this ongoing antibusiness bias revel in opportunities to scald some highly visible and successful mogul. The history of your entrepreneurial accomplishment is not going to lose its luster permanently because of these sideline critics. But the best way to blunt their effect is always to remain thoughtful and prudent in your response to hostility and criticism.

Remember that an improper statement or an inept quote in the press can brand you with a lifelong label. You must be careful to avoid offending certain viewpoints and social norms. It does not pay to criticize, curse, brag, or offer too many opinions to the press.

Many people who become experts in a given field lose perspective. Great accomplishment in one arena seems to give them a soapbox for opinions on a wide diversity of other subjects. In this opinionated mode they are guilty of grievous presumption. You can know only a tiny fraction of anything. How can you postulate about matters you've hardly cracked a book on? Some entrepreneurs with fortunes made see themselves in the role of social commentator. No one cares about your opinion. Let your actions do your talking. Suppress your opinions on topics outside your immediate range of skills. Remember the counsel of Delco founder Charles Kettering, "We are ignorant insofar as we think we are wise, and we are wise insofar as we know we are ignorant."

As you add zeros to the sum of your wealth, you will be wise to accept this great financial tribute with humility and spend it beneficially.

In this book I have brought you from the beginning to the end of the entrepreneurial drama and conveyed the formula practiced by all who reach high levels of achievement. I have given you the concrete steps and procedures that will carry you to the top in your venture.

If you follow my instructions to the letter, if you read and study the books recommended in the Appendix and get on intimate terms with Napoleon Hill's philosophy of success, then you will inevitably become rich. You have the opportunity to acquire a level of wealth few individuals on earth have ever controlled. You who do so will be the Fords, the Edisons, the Sloans, and the Firestones of the future.

In terms of progress and the expectations of humankind, you are the benevolent future—the heroic entrepreneur. Strive mightily, but ethically; serve and have faith.

SUMMARY

Sell out when you lose interest. Half-hearted management will damage your company.

Be sure you have enough money before you sell out. It takes a lot of money to live comfortably.

If you go public, your company's service and quality may suffer.

Rather than sell, you might find a charitable endeavor that

motivates you to continue making money. Most big business winners have used their money for the good of all citizens.

Be on guard to keep your reputation sound. Don't be too sensitive to negative articles in the press. Support the free enterprise system and give no financial support to those who don't. Don't try to isolate your company from legitimate competition by pulling political strings. Don't aggravate the public. Stay humble and don't voice too many opinions.

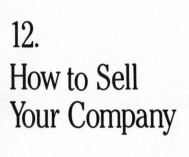

12.
How to Sell
Your Company

Everything I had was in the company and if it fell, I would fall too.

—HARVEY FIRESTONE
Founder, Firestone Tire & Rubber Co.

If and when you make the decision to sell your business, you will no doubt already have a solid relationship with an attorney and an accountant. You will need their best work to conclude a deal favorable to you.

No matter how much money you sell out for, the primary requirement on your part should be to get as much money as possible up front. Buyers welch on many business sales. In some cases, they find they can't pay and in others they refuse to pay. Consequently, long drawn-out terms and time payments can be disastrous for the seller.

When we sold our water business in Florida, we were fortunate enough to procure an excellent business attorney. He worked for weeks structuring a complex agreement. We berated him about the time he spent on our contract and complained about the bill, but later we thanked him.

After a down payment, we were to get the balance in quarterly payments over a two-year period. Immediately after the buyers took control, they began to complain. Things weren't as rosy as they had pictured. They found out that running a business properly demanded time and effort. Since they were lousy managers, they lost a few good accounts. When the first quarterly payment came due, we got wind of their grievances. They delayed the payment, but we finally got the money after a number of phone calls.

As the following payments came due, we learned the value of our attorney's efforts. Our contract was scrutinized at the buyers' law firm. They could find no escape clauses or loopholes. Our lawyer had made sure the contract carried no warranties or guarantees on our part. We had clear-cut remedies if they didn't pay. They had given us notes due from them, and we also managed to get personal guarantees. They desperately searched for a way out but found none. When the later payments were delayed, our attorney hounded them until they came through.

We were lucky. One of my business associates sold a division of his precious metals company to a refinery which made a small down payment and refused to cough up a penny of the million-dollar balance. Much to the seller's chagrin, he was forced to litigate, a process that takes two to three years. When you are counting on an important payment, such a delay can be disastrous. By the time your case reaches the court, the buyer may not be around.

My company purchased an unproven product from a foreign corporation. We paid $2,000,000 over time with $200,000 down. The seller made extensive warranties that the tooling for this product worked flawlessly. Unfortunately, the tooling never did work. As the large payments became more onerous, I asked for more liberal billing terms. After a few years, the seller tired of my revised payment schedule and sued. Fortunately, the contract spells out enough tooling guarantees so that our side of the issue has merit. In this case, as the buyer, we welcomed a lengthy lawsuit.

My friend Conrad Schmidt was one of the earliest entrepreneurs to enter the alcohol treatment business. After building a substantial enterprise, he decided to sell for a healthy sum. When I asked him about the terms, he chuckled and explained that he got almost all the money up front. That's the clever way to do it—get paid the full amount of the sale and pay the taxes at the capital-gain rate. You have a big chunk of money and no residual worries.

Taxes are another crucial area that bears significant scrutiny by lawyers and accountants. You want to structure your sale to pay the lowest possible tax rate. An insurance agent I know sold his agency to a larger competitor. The purchase agreement included a paragraph stating that he would not compete. The buyers valued that clause as a significant part of the purchase price. In other words, they paid a little for the agency and a lot for the noncompete clause, allowing them to deduct from taxes part of the purchase price. The poor buyers, however, had to pay tax on the proceeds at the highest rate. Rather than rely on first-class legal and accounting advice, they had plunged ahead on their own and been duped.

It would be pointless for me to give you specific tax advice here. Many books exist already on various tax strategies. Furthermore, you need to rely on experts face to face when you are executing a momentous decision such as the sale of your enterprise. You need to talk through these matters with lawyer and accountant until you clearly understand every nuance of the sale. Naturally you should always read these important contracts yourself and think them through.

The greater the financial worth of your buyers, the better off you are. You should check them out thoroughly. Even large companies with supposedly plentiful assets need scrutinizing. Most companies aren't nearly as well off as most people think. You need to get extensive credit checks and background reports on the principals. Things are seldom as they appear, so dig deep. Never trust appearance. Look for a clinker. In most cases, you will find a reason to go slowly.

The previous descriptions have been of private sales to individuals or companies. If your company becomes large enough, one of the best ways to liquidate your interest is through a public sale. Generally companies go public during their infancy to raise capital for growth. They tend to go to the public again and again for layers of financing. This, of course, may leave the entrepreneur naked when problems arise and a majority interest lies elsewhere. Takeovers, potential shareholder suits, dissenting directors, and numerous other irritants may exasperate the founder. Those are the rules of that marketplace, however, and if you are going to play you may have to pay.

For the established company, the public route can be the best way to gain immediate liquidity for the founder and to attract a maximum price. If your company makes a decent profit, shows steady expansion or at least a good potential for growth, and if the balance sheet seems free of clutter, then sell out to the public.

Always strive for the most prestigious underwriter your company warrants. Spend time with a number of brokerage firms before you pick one. These companies will acquaint you with the intricacies of this financial step.

You can sell off your entire interest or a portion of it. In the latter instance, you can ease out of the balance when you need cash, when tax considerations warrant selling, or when the price of the stock climbs.

Going public can also liquefy any stock holdings you might have gifted to your heirs. Furthermore, if you should die suddenly, your heirs face far fewer inheritance tax problems with a liquid security that can be sold to pay taxes. They are much better off with 10 percent of a public company than the same amount of a private firm.

Going public helps resolve concerns over finding a good manager to run and perpetuate the company, which may be a major consideration for some founders. Usually public companies single out the most capable candidate for the presidency. They generally have more hiring options than private companies where heirs may have a say in the management choices.

If you prefer staying private so that family members can run your company when you retire, perhaps you can structure a buyout of your shares from profits or dividends. Many companies have flourished under the tutelage of their founders' children or in-laws. More have not. This ticklish decision should be predicated on the relatives' experience, work habits, and desire for the job.

If you want to bring children or grandchildren into your

business, don't ruin them with easy money. As hardships strengthen your heirs, so does the opposite weaken them.

I once did extensive business with a family who had inherited millions of dollars of stock in a New York Stock Exchange company founded by their father. They were snobs, unchallenged by any need to work or to save or even manage money. Spoiled and self-indulgent, they wasted their fortune. Now they are locked into permanent poverty, untrained for any kind of work, but maintaining the old superiority over those who are.

For those corporate proprietors who would like to go public but don't feel they have the pizzazz or the financial clout to secure a fair price through an underwriting, other options may be available. My friend Buzz Potter runs a sizable dredging company. Part of his business deals with mineral recovery and land reclamation. Both would be considered the high-tech end of a rather bland business.

He took over a *shell corporation* (an idle company with no liabilities) that ten years before had traded publicly. As the company had no liabilities, it could easily be revived for trading. Then he exchanged the dredging divisions of his old company for the majority of the stock in the shell company. Consequently, he has a brand-new, publicly traded corporation with a clean balance sheet. If the new dredging concepts earn what he expects, he will have neatly liquefied his private holdings and he may gradually retire at his leisure.

A final word of advice on the sale of your company relates to the possibility of a sale after your sudden death. You should have a will that clearly stipulates who gets what. You should also take a close look at who will be advising your heirs. These people—attorneys, accountants, directors, friends, relatives—may actively pursue their own self-interest and influence the management or sale of your company.

When my partner and friend Bernie Daley passed away, his budding company attracted interest. I was approached to buy the company and began to structure a deal that would be fair to his family. A few advisers preferred other buyers who might subsequently employ their services. The sale bogged down until the key manager informed the board and the advisers that he would resign if anyone other than my company bought the business. The other suitors backed off, and we closed the sale.

An attorney once told me, "You can't control events after you are deceased, so it's pointless to try." While still alive, however, you can arrange through a will to divide your assets fairly. Imbue your heirs with responsibility and prudence and choose advisers who will look out for your family's best interests.

SUMMARY

When you sell your company, get most of the money up front. Many buyers try to find excuses not to pay. Make sure your contract is airtight.

Weigh all tax matters before you close the deal. Check out the buyer carefully.

If your company merits it, sell out by going public. You have more selling options and more liquidity.

Some companies go public through the acquisition of a shell corporation.

In case your company must be sold after your death, make sure your advisers will look out for your heirs.

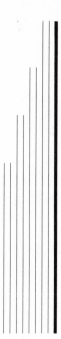

Appendix

My friend and former business partner Jay Anderson was prone to say that the mind must be used and exercised if it is to grow and strengthen. "The more you use your mind, the more it will improve your ability to think," he would say. I doubted his thesis, but as we both reached higher levels of business success, the scope of our mental abilities seemed to be expanding as well, although we had both been barely able to escape high school.

Thomas Edison said, "The brain can be developed just the same as the muscles can be developed, if one will only take the pains to train the mind to think," and, "The brain that isn't used rusts. The brain that is used responds. The brain is exactly like any other part of the body: it can be strengthened by proper exercise, by proper use. Put your arm in a sling and keep it there for a considerable length of time, and, when you take it out, you find that you can't use it. In the same way, the brain that isn't used suffers atrophy."

Books strengthen the mind. I have chosen reading over formal education as a personal means to provide a cultural backdrop to entrepreneuring. Every crumb of knowledge you gain, whether it be an obscure historical fact or philosophical musing, will contribute in some small fashion to your ultimate business success. Books are instructors on virtually all subjects. They have hastened my career and can most assuredly complement yours.

Because one book has helped me more than any single volume, I would recommend it first to any potential entrepreneur. How this volume came to be written makes an interesting entrepreneurial story in itself.

One day in 1908, the richest man in the world invited a young man into his office and offered him the greater part of his vast fortune. It was not cash, however, that he offered. He proposed to instruct the young man on the manner and method in which to accumulate such a fortune for himself.

He explained that great success, fortune, and fame could be enjoyed by anyone willing to follow a specific formula. In fact, he vowed that no one could achieve great success without practicing this formula.

The wealthy man was no less than the legendary steel magnate Andrew Carnegie. In 1901, the respected Carnegie had packaged his interests into one company and sold his shares to the public. The result was the formation of U.S. Steel and a $390 million windfall to Carnegie.

The younger man was Napoleon Hill, a writer and college student. His interview with Carnegie extended far beyond the allotted time. Carnegie explained the rudiments of his philosophy, formed from his experience as the world's most successful entrepreneur. He proposed that Hill take his ideas and reinforce them with the thoughts and experiences of hundreds of other successful entrepreneurs, each of whom Hill was to interview extensively. Eventually, the young man was to write a book on the results.

Carnegie offered little or no financial inducement. He promised only to open doors for Hill's interviews. The whole process was to take twenty or more years. To understand his success formula, Carnegie knew that Hill must share the experiences that all successful entrepreneurs have known. He must learn the philosophy by succeeding himself. Hill chose to accept the challenge.

Over the next two decades, he went about the arduous task of analyzing hundreds of successful men. Among these were Thomas Edison, Henry Ford, James J. Hill, Harvey Firestone, Luther Burbank, and Clarence Darrow. From this experience, he was able to articulate the success formula used by those who gained great wealth and achievement.

Through the 1930s and 1940s, Hill published a number of books. All were big sellers. The greatest of these volumes, *Think and Grow Rich*, ensured Hill's success and gave him financial independence. Through two decades of struggle Hill had also learned the lessons of lasting accomplishment.

Napoleon Hill was the first person to formulate a success philosophy that offered concrete guidelines to entrepreneurs and others seeking noteworthy achievements.

Since Hill's initial formula was articulated, various authors have published a host of other success and self-help books. Their contributions notwithstanding, the greatest of these books remains Hill's.

Original ideas, services, and products are generally copied and imitated. Sometimes we forget to contrast the remarkable difference between what went into an original and the far easier task facing an imitator.

Hill fathered the self-help, motivation, and success industry. The dimension of his thought and the power of his writing entitle him to noteworthy credit.

Napoleon Hill wrote about, learned from, and existed alongside a group of entrepreneurs who dramatically advanced civilization. Their towering accomplishments are prodigious enough to designate their era a golden age. Not since the time of Pericles has such a brief span of years proved so fruitful to mankind.

Napoleon Hill distilled the elements of human progress and added powerful truths to our stock of wisdom. His words are immortal, his message timeless.

Napoleon Hill discovered from his interviews a simple truth that is not only the core premise of self-help and motivation, but an acknowledged fact in the science of human behavior. Human beings are what they think they are. Our self-image guides our conduct. You can be only what you think you can be.

The next step for Hill was to formulate methods that alter, in a positive way, the dominating thoughts people hold in their minds. For the entrepreneur, this means the establishment of an idea, plan, or purpose to be arrived at by concentrating on your desires. The first step is to know exactly what you want—a step that ninety-eight out of a hundred people never bother to articulate beyond an occasional daydream.

If you want something badly enough and you enhance that desire by holding it in your mind in a variety of ways outlined by Hill, you will "cloak that desire in the physical equivalent." If desire becomes great enough, it will subtly change your perception of what you can do, and it will motivate you to proceed toward your goal. "Everything man creates or acquires begins in the form of desire."

Your thoughts control your actions, according to Hill. Therefore, you must learn to direct your thoughts in a positive and productive way. Hill postulated in *Think and Grow Rich* that it is no more difficult to aim high in life and achieve prosperity than it is to accept and live with poverty and misery.

He stressed that most people never do more than scratch the surface of their potential. To convince his readers, he penned these words: "Somewhere in your make-up there lies *sleeping,* the seed of achievement which, if aroused and put into action, would carry you to heights, such as you may never have hoped to attain."

Hill explains the knowledge available through the cooperation of others, the famous *Master Mind Principle,* defined as a "coordination of knowledge and effort, in a spirit of harmony, between two or more people." All successful men and women have availed themselves of the advice and cooperation of other people who contribute their own store of knowledge and experience. Beyond that, Hill advances this powerful hypothesis, "No two minds ever come together without, thereby, creating a third, invisible, intangible force which may be likened to a third mind."

Another cornerstone of Hill's formula is the importance of

persistence. He teaches an infallible lesson on how to become persistent and how to overcome failures: "Remember that all who succeed in life get off to a bad start, and pass through many heartbreaking struggles before they 'arrive.' "

He set down one of life's greatest truths, "Every adversity, every failure and every heartache carries with it the Seed of an equivalent or a greater Benefit." To Hill, persistence was to human character "what carbon is to steel." Without it, you are doomed to failure, with it literally nothing can stand in your way.

Napoleon Hill spoke of faith as a state of mind that can be induced through the encouragement of positive emotions and the application of self-suggestion. Faith is a key ingredient and starting point in the accumulation of all riches. He counseled faith in yourself, faith in the future, faith in the infinite.

When I first read Hill's admonition to have faith in the infinite, it disturbed my rationalist soul. I had lifted Bertrand Russell's opinions to the forefront of my self-directed educational inquiry. It was Russell who defined faith as "the belief in something for which there is no evidence."

For all of Russell's skepticism, both he and Hill held many views that were not incompatible. Like Russell, Hill also deplored the so-called faith of religious doctrines that relied on fear to instruct or punish.

The culmination of my understanding of Hill's philosophy came only with my own reliance on the intangible. Gripped with anxiety because of the looming collapse of my ten-year-old empire, I had no choice. There was no saving action to be taken, no concrete steps to be implemented. I had tried them all and they had failed.

There was no other relief from the tremendous pressure, no other escape from the pain, no other way to sleep at night. Faith —in myself, in the future, in the infinite. No fancy doctrines or tortuous dogma, just a simple and firmly held belief that all would be well. And so it was.

Aside from *Think and Grow Rich* Napoleon Hill wrote two other books, which entrepreneurs are advised to read to augment their understanding of his success philosophy. *The Master-Key to Riches* and *Grow Rich! With Peace of Mind* were both published in the 1940s, completing an indispensable trilogy for entrepreneurs and anyone else wishing to explore the rules and requirements of success. Nothing else that I know of can help you get through the difficult times that cause so many hopeful entrepreneurs to give up and quit.

From the first day of your new venture, you will be whipsawed by petty doubts and fears. At times black circumstance will escalate these anxieties into moments of real terror. Then you will want to flee, to recapture the simple security of your past.

When you are on the verge of such a decision, when the money is gone, when your ideas draw brutal rejection, when your credit cards are canceled and the snarling bill collectors sap your will, when the sound of a ringing telephone claws at your guts, when you cannot see the possibility of ever making your deal work—then you must do one thing.

Turn to one of Hill's books and read until the gloom fades. There you will find a spark of strength to bring you through the bleakest moments. You must do this faithfully whenever you begin to fold. Before you quit, before you walk away, before you seek the relief that seems so alluring, you must turn to his pages one more time and read.

If you have read this far, you know that I have offered many ideas to you. You may embrace what you wish. In return, I ask one small favor of you. On the day you make the final decision to return to the old ways, before you end whatever it is that you started, turn to those pages of Hill's that I have advanced so ardently—and read.

Bibliography

WORKS CITED

Books

BUTLER, E. A. *The Big Buck and The New Business Breed.* New York: The Macmillan Company, 1972.

CARNEGIE, ANDREW. *Autobiography of Andrew Carnegie.* Boston and New York: Houghton Mifflin, 1920.

DRUCKER, PETER F. *Adventures of a Bystander.* New York: Harper & Row, 1978.

FIERRO, ROBERT. *The New American Entrepreneur.* New York: William Morrow, 1982.

FORBES, B. C. *Thoughts on the Business of Life.* New York: Forbes, Inc., 1976.

FORD, HENRY, and CROUTHER, SAMUEL. *My Life and Work.* New York: Doubleday, Page, 1925.

GELDERMAN, CAROL. *Henry Ford.* New York: Dial Press, 1981.

GILDER, GEORGE. *The Spirit of Enterprise.* New York: Simon & Schuster, 1984.

HILL, NAPOLEON. *The Law of Success.* Chicago: Success Unlimited, Inc., 1979.

HILTON, CONRAD N. *Be My Guest.* Englewood Cliffs, N.J.: Prentice-Hall, 1957.

KROC, RAY. *Grinding It Out.* New York: Berkeley, 1978.

MARCUS, STANLEY. *Minding the Store.* Boston: Little, Brown, 1974.

———. *Quest for the Best.* New York: The Viking Press, 1979.

McCORMICK, CYRUS. *The Century of the Reaper.* Boston and New York: Houghton Mifflin, 1931.

MILLER, FLOYD. *Statler.* New York: The Statler Foundation, 1968.

MISES, LUDWIG VON. *Human Action.* Chicago: Henry Regnery Company, 1949.

OGILVY, DAVID. *Blood, Brains and Beer.* New York: Atheneum, 1978.

PENNEY, J. C. *Fifty Years with the Golden Rule.* New York: Harper & Bros., 1950.

PETERS, THOMAS J., and WATERMAN, ROBERT M., JR. *In Search of Excellence.* New York: Harper & Row, 1982.

POUND, ARTHUR, and MOORE, SAMUEL TAYLOR. *My Life and Work.* New York: Harper & Bros., 1930.

SHOOK, ROBERT L. *The Entrepreneurs.* New York: Barnes & Noble Books, 1980.

SLOAN, ALFRED P., JR. *My Years with General Motors.* New York: Doubleday & Co., 1964.

Periodicals

Forbes magazine, issues for 1983 and 1984.

System Magazine of Business, issues from 1917 through 1925.

American Magazine, issues from 1920 through 1928.

RECOMMENDED READING

BROWN, SUSAN LOVE, KEATING, KARL, MELLINGER, DAVID, POST, PATREA, SMITH, STUART, and TUDOR, CATRIONA. *The Incredible Bread Machine.* San Diego, Calif.: World Research Inc., 1974. This book can help you forecast and think clearly about politics and economics.

CARNEGIE, DALE. *How to Win Friends and Influence People*, rev. ed. New York: Simon & Schuster, 1981. This all-time best-seller teaches you just what the title promises.

DRUCKER, PETER F. *Management Tasks, Responsibilities, Practices.* New York: Harper & Row, 1973. The guru of management gives lucid and helpful advice that provides a bridge from little to big.

FLESCH, RUDOLF. *How to Write, Speak and Think More Effectively.* New York: Harper & Row, 1946. If you want to improve your copywriting skills, several chapters in this book are the best ever written on the subject.

GENEEN, HAROLD, and MOSCOW, ALVIN. *Managing.* Garden City, N.Y.: Doubleday & Co., 1984. Geneen recounts how he put together and managed over two hundred companies. Helpful if you are planning to diversify.

HANAN, MACK. *Fast-Growth Management.* New York: AMACOM, 1979. Insights on business strategies for fast growth that are working right now for many dominant companies.

HILL, NAPOLEON. *Grow Rich! With Peace of Mind.* New York: Fawcett Crest, 1978. The first and most influential best-seller in the success trilogy.

———. *The Master-Key to Riches.* New York: Fawcett Crest, 1978.

———. *Think and Grow Rich.* New York: Fawcett Crest, 1979.

HOPKINS, CLAUDE G. *My Life in Advertising, Scientific Advertising.* Chicago: Crain Books, Division of Crain Communications, 1966. The premier copywriter of his day teaches us the fundamentals of advertising—a masterpiece worthy of your study.

LASSER, J. K. Tax Institute. *How to Run a Small Business.* New York: McGraw-Hill Book Company, 1982. An excellent primer on the mechanics of enterprise.

LOWRY, ALBERT J. *How to Become Financially Successful by Owning Your Own Business.* New York: Simon & Schuster, 1981. A potpourri of useful business ideas from a self-made real estate expert.

OGILVY, DAVID. *Confessions of an Advertising Man.* New York: Atheneum, 1960. The founder of one of America's leading ad agencies explores the details of his business and provides insights into what it takes to advertise effectively.

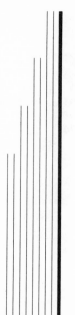

Index